COLERIDGE TO CATCH-22

By the same author

E. M. Forster: The Personal Voice
E. M. Forster: A Passage to India
Coleridge: Critic of Society
Coleridge: On the Constitution of the Church and State (ed.)
Coleridge: Selected Poems (ed.)
Patrick White: Riders in the Chariot
Approaches to the Novel (ed.)
Mainly Modern (ed.)
New Choice (ed.)
Shakespeare: Henry IV, Pt. 1 (ed.)

COLERIDGE TO CATCH-22

Images of Society

JOHN COLMER

Professor of English
University of Adelaide

First edition 1978
Reprinted 1980

Published by
THE MACMILLAN PRESS LTD
London and Basingstoke
Associated companies in Delhi
Dublin Hong Kong Johannesburg Lagos
Melbourne New York Singapore Tokyo

Printed in Great Britain by
REDWOOD BURN LTD
Trowbridge and Esher

British Library Cataloguing in Publication Data

Colmer, John
Coleridge to 'Catch-22'
1. English fiction — 19th century 2. English fiction — 20th century 3. England — Social conditions
4. England in literature
I. Title
823'.009'32 PR830.E/

ISBN 0-333-23301-8

Contents

Preface

This study argues that a radically different attitude towards society developed towards the end of the eighteenth century. It traces the attempts made by nineteenth- and twentieth-century prose writers to criticise society through the various methods of analysis, realistic rendering, persuasion, utopian fantasy, and protest. Occasional reference to the Romantic poets and the poets of the thirties serves to remind the reader that they too were important critics of society, but limitation of space has necessitated that they should be largely ignored in the present work, which combines a detailed analysis of major prose classics often studied in the Universities with briefer accounts of lesser-known works that serve to place the major texts in a wider context. Since no familiarity with the social and intellectual background is taken for granted, relevant details about authors, political events, changing social conditions, and the history of ideas are incorporated into the text.

Three major themes recur throughout the following chapters and give the book its unity. These are the connection between political meaning and literary form, the connection between literary criticism and sociology, and the idea that language is an index of cultural health, an idea that figures prominently in writers as unlike each other as Coleridge, George Orwell, Joseph Heller, and Shirley Hazzard.

The first chapter places the subject of the writer and society in historical perspective and outlines the main argument of the book. The next two chapters contrast the idealist and utilitarian approaches to culture and society, illustrating the continuity of the first from Coleridge to T. S. Eliot and analysing J. S. Mill's failure to effect a synthesis between the two traditions. As a contrast, chapter 4 shows how Thomas Love Peacock exploited the comic spirit to criticise extremes of Romanticism and Utilitarianism in the novel of ideas, a form that was largely his own creation. Chapters 5 and 6 examine the main impulses that prompted Disraeli, Dickens, Mrs Gaskell, George Eliot and Charles Kingsley to criticise society in their novels. Apart from establishing Carlyle's importance in transmitting the idealist attack on mechanism to the Victorian novelists, these chapters offer a detailed account of such Victorian Condition of England novels as Disraeli's *Sybil*, Dickens's *Hard Times*, Mrs Gaskell's *Mary Barton* and *North and South*,

George Eliot's *Felix Holt*, and Kingsley's *Alton Locke*. To continue this section of the book there is a chapter on a group of novels concerned with the crisis of conscience that arises when personal and public morality are in conflict as the result of membership of a secret society. James's *The Princess Casamassima* is taken as a model of the secret society novel that renders its criticism of society through its total imaginative organization. Chapter 8 then focuses on the theme of 'Sex, Family, and the New Woman', through texts as varied in date and manner as Mrs Lynne Linton's *The Girl of the Period* (1860), Mark Rutherford's *Clara Hopgood* (1896). Gissing's *The Odd Women* (1893), Wells's *Ann Veronica* (1909) and Ford Madox Ford's *Some Do Not* (1924).

Chapter 9 bridges the chronological halves of the book by exploring patterns of continuity and change in the social and philosophical background as reflected in a mixed body of works by Butler, Gissing and Edward Carpenter, a neglected prophet who influenced both Forster and Lawrence.

The second half of the book examines the variety of forms that criticism of society has taken in twentieth-century prose fiction. Chapter 10 looks at some of the works of Masterman, Wells, Ford Madox Ford, E. M. Forster, and D. H. Lawrence under the heading of the Modern Condition of England novel. Apart from analysing the connection between social vision and literary form, the chapter links these Edwardian writers with their predecessors through discussion of recurrent themes and images, especially the city, the country house, and escape to the greenwoods. Three closely related chapters examine the popularity of Utopian fantasy and science fiction as vehicles for social criticism in the present century. One of these, chapter 12, takes a close look at some of the works of Rex Warner, George Orwell, and Shirley Hazzard that warn readers of the insidious attractions of power and the ways in which the written word may be manipulated to produce an authoritarian culture. A chapter on protest and anti-war literature shows how such popular novels as Heller's *Catch-22* and Vonnegut's *Slaughterhouse-Five* develop an inclusive and penetrating criticism through an unusual blend of farce, black comedy and tragedy.

The concluding chapter tentatively affirms the continuing role of the writer as a critic of society. It defines the function of literary criticism in elucidating the political meanings of the writer's 'images' of society. And it affirms the role of the reading public in resisting the current erosions of language and humane values.

1 The Writer as Critic of Society

A study of the writer as a critic of society that ends with science-fiction fantasies and anti-war novels such as *A Clockwork Orange*, *Fahrenheit 451*, *Slaughterhouse 5* and *Catch-22* had better acquire what academic respectability it can by starting with the ancient Greeks, with Plato in fact. In Plato's *Republic*, that early blueprint for a benevolent dictatorship and first example of Utopian fantasy, no place can be found for the imaginative writer. In justification Plato gives three reasons. The poet, he argues, deals with reality at two removes. He tells lies about the gods and heroes, a complaint that is not difficult to translate into terms that would be applicable to any modern dictatorship. And he appeals to emotions, when he should appeal to man's noblest faculty, the reason. 'We shall,' says Plato 'bow down before a being with such miraculous powers of giving pleasure; but we shall tell him that we are not allowed to have any such person in our commonwealth; we shall crown him with fillets of wool, anoint his head with myrrh, and conduct him to another country' (*Republic*, Book 10). Regretfully, because Plato is certainly not unaware of the sublime powers possessed by the inspired poet, but firmly and magisterially, this stern moral puritan dismisses the poet from his ideal state. Here, then, in Plato's *Republic*, we have the first memorable statement of the clash between two ideals of order: the inspired order of the artist and the imposed order of the state, an opposition that permeates Romantic and post-Romantic literature. And in exiling the artist from his ideal state, Plato is the first to create for him that very modern role, the Outsider.

Does the poet fare any better in the modern world today? Not if we are to believe the modern novelist Barry Oakley. In his comic novel, *Let's Hear it for Prendergast*, the poet Prendergast is both rejected and repelled by his fellow workers, if not exactly by the state. As he waits in the pub, he complacently boasts to his friend Morley, a failed writer, of the effect his poems will have when he reads them to the workers of Foley Bros Monumental Masons in their lunchtime break.

> 'They'll listen to me,' he says calmly, crossing his legs.
> 'The workers? They'll tear you limb from limb.'
> 'I've got something to tell 'em Morley. About the world. And what

it's doing to them. About the dignity of labour.'
'Can you make the race results rhyme?'
'Always the cynic, never the bride.'
'And here they come, thirsting for culture.'

The workers view the two at the bar with suspicion and contempt; and their attempts to establish themselves as fellow-workers are unsuccessful.

' 'Ere, give us a gander at your hands then.' Prendergast extending his pale palms for their inspection.
'See? White as a fucking lily. Gives you away pal. Worker my arse.'

A little later, after he has read his poetic attack on suburbia, perched on a tombstone, the poet Prendergast finds himself tumbled out of the main gate, glasses broken. Still undismayed, he shouts: 'So my own countrymen won't listen, I'll go to the bloody Europeans! I'll try it out on them.' But his visit to a large lingerie factory employing emigrant labour is even less successful and he runs away, 'pursued by a crowd of gesticulating women, some laughing, others shrieking abuse in their native tongue'. The fate of the writer as a critic of society, whether it be in ancient Greece or in modern Australia, is not, it would seem, a happy one.

The successful critic of society, it may be suggested, is the writer who learns the wisdom of indirection. He is the writer who learns to combine instruction with delight, without in any way compromising his integrity of blunting the force of his social criticism. Some literary forms are especially suited to methods of indirect attack: satire, for example. From the time of the Greeks onwards, satirists have invented a variety of ways to maintain apparent detachment and the indirect approach, while pressing home their attack. The three commonest forms are the beast fable, the imaginary journey, and Utopian fantasy. The beast fable has been used by the Greek dramatist Aristophanes in the *Frogs*, by Chaucer in the *Nun's Priest's Tale*, and by George Orwell in *Animal Farm*. Swift's *Gulliver's Travels* provides a model for the imaginary journey, while the history of literary utopias stretches — to take it no further — from More's sixteenth-century *Utopia*, to Butler's *Erewhon* (1872), Morris's *News From Nowhere* (1891), and Huxley's *Brave New World* (1932). It is essential for the satirist's purpose to shock us into seeing our own familiar world through unfamiliar eyes; some radical change of perspective is therefore absolutely necessary. Each of the three devices, the beast fable, the imaginary journey, and Utopian fantasy achieves this end. Although Utopian fantasy, because it has produced so vast and various a body of fine works, is treated as a separate form in this study, satire and Utopian fantasy are not really separable, since the first is a criticism of the real world in the name of something better and the second an optimistic picture of a world that might be. And when Utopias become anti-Utopias, as they do in *Brave New World* and *Nineteen Eighty-Four*, the distinction between the two forms disappears altogether. In science fiction the three qualities of detachment, indirection and new perspective are carried to their logical extreme. The centre of interest is no longer man, as we know him, nor even this earth. We escape into other worlds. We come to accept other concepts of space and time. But, in the end, only to return to our own world with a new view of its possible fate.

A simple but illuminating grouping of social critics that partly cuts across any classification according to particular literary forms and technical devices is the division into those who seek to render, those who claim to analyse, and those whose main aim is to reform. The writer who adopts the first approach is content to render the state of society with such fidelity to its outward forms or inward spirit that the very truth of his picture makes it assume the status of a powerful critique. Included within this general approach is the whole great tradition of European realism sketched in by Raymond Williams in *The Long Revolution*. But it also includes the artist who purports to cultivate a godlike detachment. This is Flaubert's method. It is Henry James's, too, especially in such novels as *The Bostonians*, which renders the world of public charlatanism and Women's Emancipation in America, *The Princess Casamassima*, which renders the worlds of anarchy and social order in the London of the eighteen-eighties, and *The Awkward Age*, which renders the minutiae of the marriage market in polite society at the turn of the century. It is also the way chosen by Ford Madox Ford, a disciple of both Flaubert and James, in his great novel, *The Good Soldier* (1915). Together with Wells's *Tono Bungay* and Forster's *Howards End*, *The Good Soldier* offers one of the most complete images of the Edwardian Age. But, by contrast with *Tono Bungay*, which adds direct comment and argument to its vivid rendering, *The Good Soldier* renders the deep divisions in Edwardian society and its conflicting codes of behaviour without comment from its author, who uses a dramatised American narrator as a polar contrast and alter ego to the English feudal hero. The novel illustrates particularly well that the method of rendering at its best depends on selection of significant detail, the creation of exactly the right characters, and the setting up of contrasting viewpoints to capture the authentic ambiguity of the historic moment. Yet, for all their suggestive authenticity, such works have little or no short-term effect in changing society. In this respect, it is worth recalling the distinction drawn between short-term and long-term art by the Marxist art critic and novelist, John Berger. The purpose of long-term art, Berger insists, 'is not to iron out the ambiguities, but to contain and define the totality in which they exist. In this way art becomes an aid to increasing self-consciousness instead of an immediate guide to direct action.' Literature itself is a form of action. What we have in those novels of James and Ford Madox Ford that seek to render a small part of the world and make it a microcosm of truth is what David Caute calls 'action by disclosure, — a contribution to a more reflective general consciousness'. By a curious paradox it may be the least politically motivated novelists whose works most commend themselves to us as true images of society.

Of course, the process of rendering depends ultimately on analysis. A writer's synthesis can only be as good as his analysis. But the point is that the analysis is largely intuitive and lies behind the work; it is not a formal part of the rendering. By contrast, the writer who chooses the method of analysis places society beneath a searching scrutiny and then offers his readers an account of how it works or, more often, how it fails to work. He exposes its basic mechanism. And his choice of subjects, characters, and plots is determined by this overriding purpose. A good example of this mode in fiction is Dickens's *Hard Times*, an anatomy of Victorian society in terms of the clash between machinery and imagination, reason and passion. A good example in discursive prose is Matthew Arnold's *Culture and Anarchy*, an anatomy of Victorian society in terms of the clash between machinery and culture (or the pursuit of sweetness and light).

> If culture, then, is a study of perfection, and of harmonious perfection, general perfection, and perfection which consists in becoming something rather than in having something, in an inward condition of the mind and spirit, not in an outward set of circumstances, — it is clear that culture, . . . has a very important function to fulfil for mankind. And this function is particularly important in our modern world, of which the whole civilisation is, to a much greater degree than the civilisation of Greece and Rome, mechanical and external, and tends constantly to become more so. But above all in our own country has culture a weighty part to perform, because here that mechanical character, which civilisation tends to take everywhere, is shown in the most eminent degree. Indeed nearly all the characters of perfection, as culture teaches us to fix them, meet in this country with some powerful tendency which thwarts them and sets them at defiance.[1]

Before passing on to consider the third kind of approach open to the writer as critic of society it is necessary to anticipate an objection. It is clear that many works of social analysis include recommendations for reform, so that in fact the distinction between the last two categories (works that analyse and works that reform) is a narrow one. But it is not an arbitrary one. The writer who is primarily motivated by the desire to bring about reform constructs his work so that it will persuade his readers to make changes in the existing state of society. His mode is that of rhetorical persuasion; to call it propaganda is to introduce emotive overtones and to be unfair to the kind. The characteristic tone is urgent, often strident. Certainly this urgency may be heard in Gissing's angry protest against the debasement of the novelist by the three-decker novel, in *New Grub Street*. But there it is only incidental; it does not permeate the novel, as it does in Upton Sinclair's cumulative descriptions of the horrors of the Chicago meat-trade in *The Jungle*.

In seeking to reform society, the imaginative writer aims to move his readers in one or more ways. He may try to move him so deeply that he undergoes a change of heart; this is Mrs Gaskell's way in her two industrial novels, *Mary Barton* and *North and South*, where she suggests, somewhat improbably, that a change of heart will end the conflict between master and men. Alternatively, the novelist may move his readers to demand new legislation, as Upton Sinclair did with his attack on the conditions of the Chicago stockyards. Or he may move the reader to demand a change of government, as Disraeli did in *Coningsby*, *Sybil* and *Tancred*, a political trilogy that he wrote as part of his programme to overturn the Whig oligarchy, and replace it with a reformed Young Tory Party.

The definitions of the three main categories of works, those that render society, those that analyse it, and those that seek to reform it, are intended only as a rough framework of reference. In fact, we may expect to find a mixture of categories within most works. Yet, the recognition of the dominant mode is often a necessary step towards full understanding.

In addition to examining the interplay of these modes in the works of the major critics of society, the following chapters draw attention to the problem relating to the status and moral responsibility of the writer; his responsibility to himself and to the state; the relevance of his relation to the reading public and his place in society; the connection between economic classes and cultural elites (a question specifically raised by T. S. Eliot's *Notes Towards a Definition of Culture*); the nature of the political imagination; and the role of social prophecy.

Any consideration of the problems and principles relating to freedom of speech and censorship must necessarily be more concerned with the writer and the state than with society at large. For convenience the problems can be grouped under two heads: those that affect the writer and those that affect the state. As a responsible moral agent, responsible to his own conscience for his private motives and to the state for his public actions, Coleridge, for example, finds himself in effect asking the questions:

> Have I a moral obligation to speak the truth as I see it, irrespective of the effect of doing so on myself, other individuals, the state, or society at large?
>
> Have I a moral duty to consider the likely effects of my writing before deciding to publish?
>
> Have I a moral duty to consider into whose hands these writings may fall and therefore to see that the form of publication is appropriate to their intended purpose?

These are questions Coleridge first raised and explored in detail in his essays 'On the Communication of Truth', in *The Friend*. They are sufficient to indicate the recurrent opposition between moral absolutes and prudential considerations.

The problems that face the state are less complex but no less difficult to solve. The state, as a sovereign power, is obliged to act in such a way as to protect its sovereignty. Whether it decides to impose strict political censorship or to allow wide freedom of expression to all shades of political thought, even to dangerous errors, its decision will ultimately be determined by what it considers will best serve society and not destroy its sovereignty. The reference to dangerous errors is worth making at this stage, since most liberal nation states have come to accept, in however modified a form, the position first stated by John Stuart Mill in his famous essay *On Liberty* (1859). There Mill argued that a state should permit the publication of error on the grounds that its publication might act as a powerful incentive to the forces of truth. Totalitarian regimes, on the other hand, have always sought to stamp out error, or what appeared to be error, according to the prevailing ideology. Is man to be left free to choose? Or is he to be compelled to choose the truth? In his *Two Concepts of Liberty*, Sir Isaiah Berlin explores the two intellectual traditions, while Orwell's *Nineteen Eighty-Four* illustrates the forms compulsion may take in the modern world. Coleridge, Mill and Orwell, three of the writers discussed in the main body of the book, spent much of their lives thinking about the problems relating to the communication of truth.

The approach throughout this study is distinctively literary. It is not intended as a contribution to political theory or to nineteenth- and twentieth-century history, but its findings should be of interest to people working in both these areas. Although distinctively literary the work takes account of political questions and problems relating to historical interpretation, and does not overlook the relevance of non-literary writings. For example, it would seem to be essential for any real understanding of Mrs Gaskell to compare her picture of Manchester and the trade union movement in the eighteen-forties with Engels' detailed account in the *Condition of the Working Class in England*, and to compare both with Samuel Bamford's superb autobiography, *Passages in the Life of a Radical*, a retrospective account of Bamford's life in Manchester, among the early unionists.

Then, again, it would be obviously naive to discuss nineteenth- and twentieth-century critiques of industrialism without reference to Marxist theory, and theories derived from Marx about the nature and causes of alienation. In this context, Fritz Pappenheim's *The Alienation of Modern Man* is brilliantly illuminating. To illustrate the essence of alienation, he takes Goya's drawing of a starving Spanish woman who steals a gold tooth from a man on the gallows. As she stretches out one hand to satisfy her economic need, she holds a cloth to her face with the other, so that by not seeing her own action her basic humanity is not outraged by her inhuman deed. This, we must agree, is a most telling image of the way modern man is alienated from his true nature by economic need. In the same book, Pappenheim expounds the vital distinction drawn by the German writer Tönnies between *Gemeinschaft* and *Gesellschaft*. The first, *Gemeinschaft*, is the community that comes into being naturally and not as the result of conscious or external design, one that is essentially rural in foundation, homogeneous in beliefs, values and ways of life. The second, *Gesellschaft*, is the social unity that is the product of contractual obligation, a legal unity that one enters to secure ends that one could not secure if one stood alone, but which can become oppressive and the instrument of alienation. In contradistinction with the rural *Gemeinschaft*, the *Gesellschaft* is urban based, essentially heterogeneous; its relations ignore or cut across family, regional, and folk ties.

While the intellectual origins of this Marxist-developed distinction may be found in the rival organicist and utilitarian theories of the state exemplified by Coleridge and Mill, the traces of the opposition are to be found everywhere in the fiction of the nineteenth and twentieth century. Many of the writers considered in this book look back to an organic society (*Gemeinschaft*) and contrast it unfavourably with the mechanical society (*Gesellschaft*) that causes personal alienation. Mrs Gaskell, for example, evokes a nostalgic image of the organic society in *Mary Barton* through the folk memories of Annie Wilson; the notion of an organic society figures prominently in William Morris, where it becomes 'Merrie England', medieval and united; it lingers on in H. G. Wells's picture of Bladesover in *Tono Bungay* and D. H. Lawrence's descriptions of working-class life. As we shall see later, the distinction between the two kinds of order (both in some sense myths) too easily turns into feudal nostalgia, a refusal to acknowledge that the processes of industrialisation are irreversible. On this subject Marx is ambivalent, Morris evasive, especially in *News from Nowhere*.

Clearly, then, my literary approach must give full weight to sociological concepts, but it must always be remembered, as both

Raymond Williams and Richard Hoggart have reminded us, that literary texts are not the same as historical facts or documents. They can therefore never be treated as such without confusion and loss. The reader requires special qualities of imagination and literary tact to be able to bring to life, to interpret, and to evaluate the meaning and relevance of, say, Disraeli's *Sybil*. Its truth or otherwise is not to be settled by reference to Government Blue Books, from which so many of the details were taken. The general principle that guides the approach is the one defined by Leavis as 'the principle that literature will yield to the sociologist, or anyone else, what it has to give only if it is apprehended *as literature*' ('Sociology and Literature', *The Common Pursuit*). And here, as I see it, is the special contribution that the discipline of literary criticism may make to historical and political studies. It must go on insisting that literature must be read as literature and not as something else — not as documentary evidence for the sociologist or political theorist. The meaning of a poem or a novel is something more than its paraphrasable content, a fact consistently stressed by Lucien Goldmann in a late essay on sociology and literature in the *International Social Science Journal* (vol. xix, no. 4, 1967). The significance of any character, incident or piece of dialogue depends on its exact place in an imaginative whole. In their treatment of passages out of context, historians and sociologists are often little better than our moral censors, who object to four-letter words irrespective of context or precise function.

The study of literature is grounded in the concrete and the particular. It teaches us to be wary of abstractions and to resist the hypnotic appeal of isms. In the novel, ideas only become of interest when they are fully embodied in a human context of some complexity. The relevance of this to a study of the writer as critic of society may be seen from two quotations, the first from Leavis and the second from Coleridge. 'You can't contemplate the nature of literature,' Leavis writes in *The Common Pursuit* (p. 185) 'without acquiring some inhibition in respect of that antithesis, "the individual and society", and losing any innocent freedom you may have enjoyed in handling it; without, that is, acquiring some inhibiting apprehensions of the subtleties that lie behind the antithesis.' The quotation from Coleridge is briefer. 'The poet is not only the man made to solve the riddle of the universe, but he is also the man who feels where it is *not* to be solved.' Literary study involves a restraining discipline in subtlety of response and a sceptical awareness of human limitations, even the limitations of great writers.

Major writers from the time of the Greeks to today have often incorporated some critical elements in their writings. In most ages, the favourite targets for ridicule or attack have been politicians, poets, pedants, women and the church. But this critical element has frequently been incidental; and no-one, I imagine, would think of writing a book called 'Donne: Critic of Society' because Donne happened to express a critical attitude towards women in some of his poems or because he wrote a handful of formal satires. Of all the early writers, perhaps only Dante, Langland, Chaucer and Swift developed a vision of life that was sufficiently critical and socially comprehensive to justify the title 'Critic of Society'. Indeed, Langland is our first great social prophet. Allowing for these four exceptional cases, I should like to suggest that, until the Romantics, the moral and social consciousness of English writers expressed itself in attacks on particular follies and vices or particular characters or character-types and that the writer had little conception of something called 'society' of which he was a part, but of which he was highly critical and from which he felt alienated in many respects. Pope seems to move towards such a view in *The Dunciad*, when the satire upon Grub Street develops into a nightmare vision of a society returning to anarchy and moral chaos.

> Lo! thy dread Empire, CHAOS! is restor'd;
> Light dies before thy uncreating word:
> Thy hand, great Anarch! lets the curtain fall;
> And Universal Darkness buries All.
>
> (Book IV, ll. 653–6)

This vision makes an interesting comparison with Gissing's vision of moral and literary decay as the result of literature becoming a commodity, the 'Literary Machine' of Marian's imagining in the British Museum, 'hapless flies caught in a huge web, its nucleus the great circle of the Catalogue', or Milvain's image of the three-volume novel system as 'a triple-headed monster, sucking the blood of the English novelist'. Interesting as the connection between Pope's and Gissing's insight into the causes of literary decay may be, it remains true that for all Pope's extensive grasp of moral anarchy, most of the pre-Romantic writers who wrote on social issues were concerned either with what Karl Popper has called 'piecemeal social engineering' or with the general exposure of folly and castigation of vice, not with the analysis of society as a whole. Their ideal of man was based on a static, unchanging model inherited from classical times, and whatever large-scale criticisms they developed were made with reference to a community of moral values that belonged to the whole European cultural tradition and not to the values of a national society at a particular historic moment.

About the time of the Romantics, it may be argued, there developed a new form of political and historical consciousness. No doubt it developed partly in response to the challenge of democratic theories of government in Revolutionary France, partly in response to the effect of the industrial revolution on the older, semi-feudal class structure, partly in response to the growing spirit of nationalism throughout Europe, partly in response to the decay of the church and the rise of the secular state in the nineteenth century. One of the major changes in consciousness relates to an imaginative understanding of the past and its continued life in the present; another to a recognition of the large-scale forces at work reshaping culture and society; and yet another to the growth of an organic view of the connection between man and society. In England, as John Stuart Mill recognised, it was the poet Coleridge more than any other man who developed a philosophy of history and sociology capable of interpreting the nineteenth century. For this reason, if for no other, a whole chapter is devoted to Coleridge's ideas on culture and society and the influence of this idealist tradition on such later thinkers as Matthew Arnold and T. S. Eliot. After a brief but necessary discussion of the Utilitarian approach to culture and society and Mill's failure to achieve a synthesis between the Idealist and Utilitarian traditions, succeeding chapters trace this distinctly modern form of political consciousness that stems from Coleridge. The chapters on the nineteenth- and twentieth-century novelists are concerned not only with the originality of what they have to say about society but even more with how they say it, since it is in the special tone, texture and vocabulary of their writing that we are able to detect what is characteristic — and characteristically *human* — in their social criticism.

In this respect, John Holloway's *Victorian Sage* is especially valuable. In the first chapter on the message and methods of the Victorian Sage, Holloway draws attention to three characteristic features of the writing of Carlyle, Disraeli, George Eliot and Matthew Arnold. Firstly, 'the acquiring of wisdom is somehow an opening of the eyes, making us see in our experience what we failed to see before', obviously a fictional inheritance from Wordsworth's and Coleridge's attempts in the *Lyrical Ballads* to remove the 'film of familiarity' from everyday objects; secondly, 'that when these writers' outlooks are reduced to summary they lose their essential life and interest', which is true of many writers, but especially true of those for whom figurative language is the organ not the decoration of thought; thirdly, 'that they quicken the reader to a new capacity for experience'. And the novelist 'is every bit as well equipped as the discursive essayist to mediate a view of life'. The main method of most of the writers considered in my later chapters, whether they are novelists or essayists, is not to produce a logical sequence of arguments but to make their visions incarnate through metaphor and symbol. It follows therefore that our response both as ordinary readers and as critics must take full account of the figurative language, of its functions and effects. Attending carefully to these, we will find that many of the same figures tend to recur in writer after writer, and that certain contrasting figures are frequently presented in pairs. For example, both in Dickens's *Hard Times* and Arnold's *Culture and Anarchy*, metaphors of mechanism are frequently contrasted with metaphors of natural movement and life. Because the main object of attack for most nineteenth- and twentieth-century critics of society have been the forces of mechanism that dehumanise and degrade men, this particular figurative contrast is the commonest. We find it first in Coleridge, then in Carlyle, from whom it passes into Dickens and Mrs Gaskell.

The concrete image or metaphor is only one of the means by which these writers avoid empty abstraction and easy generalisation. It is only one of the ways of grounding their critical and prophetic visions in reality. Another way, if they are novelists, is by creating characters fully representative of the clash of class and opinion, for example George Eliot's strongly contrasted figures of Felix Holt, the idealist working-class radical, and Harold Transome, the upper-class radical, who turns to this persuasion as an act of political opportunism. Such characters become typical representatives of the deep currents of social change in the nineteenth century. It is in this sense that both Lukács and Goldmann insist that characters should be 'typical' and not in the sense that they should be conventional stereotypes. Yet another way in which the nineteenth-century novelists body forth their criticism of society is by creating highly dramatic — often melodramatic — scenes. Obvious examples of scenes that render the tension and violence of political conflict are the burning of Mowbray Castle in Disraeli's *Sybil*, the Treby Riot in George Eliot's *Felix Holt*, the trial scene in Mrs Gaskell's *Mary Barton*, and the workers' attack on the Thornton factory in her other industrial novel, *North and South*. It is in connection with such explosive scenes and the working out of the political implications of the plot that one of our chief critical problems is likely to arise: the difficulty of sorting out the design of the artist, the observations of the moralist and the conditioned reflexes of the social conformist. To what extent is it true that the middle-class nineteenth century novelists ultimately evade or distort the main political issues by resolving them through the expedience of a highly artificial plot? Answers to this question vary.

Stephen Gill, for example, is critical of Mrs Gaskell's decision to centre the plot of *Mary Barton* on the murder of the factory owner's son, Carson, by the working-man, John Barton. Most perceptively he draws attention to the fact that the novelist's warm natural sympathies for the sufferings of the factory workers and her inherited class prejudices are in conflict. He remarks that

> Mrs Gaskell is wavering between what she has seen and felt to be the case, and what her middle-class upbringing has taught her is the case. As an imaginative artist she is literally seeing more than she can finally declare in her role as mediator between the classes. Sympathy, observation, imagination is at war with all of the inherited, half-considered attitudes by which one class regulated its conduct to another.[2]

The comment is made by someone capable of standing within the tradition in which Mrs Gaskell lived and wrote, and of standing outside it and viewing it dispassionately in the light of greater historical understanding of working-class leaders and working-class movements in the nineteenth century. We now see rather more clearly than the Victorian reading public saw that the dramatic focus on the murder of a factory owner's son by a trade unionist was largely the means by which a Victorian novelist expressed the simple equation: unionism equals violence. But such murders did happen. Engels, in his *Condition of the Working Class in England*, provides a close parallel to Mrs Gaskell's central incident.

> In 1831, at a time of serious labour unrest, young Mr [Thomas] Ashton, [the son of] a manufacturer of Hyde, near Manchester, was shot dead one evening while walking across some fields. No trace of the murderer was ever discovered. There is no doubt that this deed was committed by the workers and inspired by vengeance.

There is no doubt therefore that such incidents as the murder of young Carson occurred in real life. What we object to, in *Mary Barton*, is the failure to realise the full human implications of such outbreaks of violence. We also object to the simple Christian solution provided to the conflict between masters and men. The reconciliation scene between old Mr Carson and John Barton is deeply moving, but finally unconvincing. And, death — that trusty servant of the novelist in distress — conveniently despatches John Barton.

> 'God be merciful to us sinners. — — Forgive us our trespasses as we forgive them that trespass against us.'
>
> And when the words were said, John Barton lay a corpse in Mr Carson's arms.
>
> So ended the tragedy of a poor man's life.

Mary Barton, like many other Victorian novels that develop a powerful criticism of society, raises in an acute form the problem of what our canons of judgment should be. Are the criteria to be primarily aesthetic? Or are they to be primarily moral and political? In the case of a novel like James's *The Princess Casamassima* or Conrad's *The Secret Agent*, are we chiefly concerned with deciding whether each is a satisfactory aesthetic whole? Or are we evaluating each according to the novelist's political insight; in particular, his insight into the effects of secret societies on the moral life of the individual and the state? Can a 'bad' novel give a 'good' criticism of society? And, vice versa, can a 'good' novel give a 'bad' criticism of society? And, 'bad' in what sense? Bad, because the ideology is invalid or because, although the ideology is perfectly valid, the novel fails as a piece of rhetorical persuasion?

There are further complications. Are we justified in applying the same criteria to all imaginative critiques of society, irrespective of their particular literary form. Is Arnold's *Culture and Anarchy* to be judged by the same critical standards as Disraeli's novel *Sybil*? Both offer an analysis of English society in terms of its class structure and cultural elites; in Arnold, the division is into the Barbarians, Philistines and Populace, while in Disraeli it is a more radical division into the 'Two Nations', the 'Rich and the Poor'. Both writers depend for much of their peculiar power on literary artistry, unlike Engels in the *Condition of the Working-Class* or Marx in the *Communist Manifesto* or *Das Kapital*. And what standards are we to apply to Utopian fantasies, such as *Brave New World*? Surely not the same as to realistic fiction, with its rounded characters and probable plots, its action set so carefully in a known and densely realised social context. In all Utopian fiction there is a deliberate simplification of character, plot and setting in order to highlight the issues and throw the main emphasis on the play of ideas; and the same is true of Peacock's *Nightmare Abbey* and *Crotchet Castle*, both light-hearted and comic in tone, but the latter, certainly, developing a more damaging and more profound criticism of nineteenth-century utilitarianism than Mill's two celebrated essays on Bentham and Coleridge.

Two problems that recur frequently in the ensuing chapters are first, the relevance of Marxist theory and sociological thought to the judgment of the literary texts, and second the relevance of the present Counter-Culture to an examination of a vast and varied body of social criticism that is almost entirely based on a respect for reason and the written word, both of which the prophets of the Counter-Culture have sought to discredit.

Marxist theory, whatever our ideological attitude to it may be, must inevitably sharpen our understanding of the conflict between classes and the interplay between ideas and economic forces. Inevitably, it must make us more aware that the values embodied in the nineteenth-century novel and endorsed by the novelist are, at least in part, the values of an economically privileged class, intent on maintaining its position and defending itself from attack. But it is one thing to use Marxist analysis in this way and quite another to use it to condemn the early nineteenth-century novelists for not understanding the revolutionary role of the working classes. Engels wrote to a minor English novelist, Margaret Harkness, the author of *City Girl*, and complained that in it

> the working class appears as a passive mass, incapable of helping itself. All attempts to raise it out of its natural poverty come from

> outside, from above. . . . The revolutionary response of the members of the working class to oppression that surrounds them, their convulsive attempts — semi-conscious or conscious — to attain their rights as human beings, belong to history and may therefore lay claim to a place in the domain of realism.

Engels might have brought the same criticism against most of the nineteenth-century novelists. But does the weakness of this type of novel arise from the failure of the novelist to grasp the revolutionary role of the working class, a role that it has yet to assume in most countries of the world? Or, rather, does it not arise from the middle-class author's somewhat limited knowledge of the details of working-class life, so that the conditions of daily labour and the elusive ethos with which he has no first-hand experience are not presented with that imaginative inwardness that is a novelist's greatest single strength as a critic of society. Forster's intermittent weakness in creating Leonard Bast in *Howards End* is primarily a weakness of imaginative inwardness, not of political ideology, yet the conception as a whole adds up to an inspired guess at a way of life and mode of consciousness alien to the author's. Such a guess was beyond George Eliot, as we see from her attempt to make conscientious documentation an adequate substitute for imaginative inwardness in her portrait of the working-class radical, Felix Holt. The problem is more complex than I have suggested here, and there is certainly a closer connection between political ideology and imaginative inwardness than it is possible to explore at this stage in the argument. But, from the start, we need to be cautious in condemning the earlier novelists for not having an insight into the revolutionary role of the working-class. Such a vision belongs to a post-Marxist, not a pre-Marxist, era, though we must always recognise the writer's prophetic role in foreshadowing the future (a role celebrated by Shelley), and also his role in preparing for later forms of consciousness, new visions of man and society. Of the full import of his work he may be only dimly aware and its inner meaning may differ markedly from his conscious intentions. Hence Lucien Goldmann's insistence on our not 'attaching special importance, in the comprehension of the work, to the conscious intentions of individuals and, in the case of literary works, to the conscious intentions of their authors' ('*International Social Science Journal*, vol. xix, no. 4, 1967, p. 496).

It is one thing to see that the unconscious may be wiser than the conscious in the mind of the creator, but it is quite another to discredit reason and to devalue traditional literary values. Two of the main planks in the platform of the so-called Counter-Culture are the attack upon the Word and belief in the revolutionary power of liberated sex. George Steiner has drawn attention to the significance of the first, not only in *The Language of Silence*, but in the later *In Bluebeard's Castle: Some*

Notes Towards the Re-definition of Culture. He sees that respect for the rational order of discourse is the direct reflection of a culture that attributes supreme importance to reason. The value system is embodied in the very words we use and their place in a grammatical schema. Steiner writes:

> An explicit grammar is an acceptance of order. . . . The counter-culture is perfectly aware of where to begin the job of demolition. The violent illiteracies of the graffiti, the clenched silence of the adolescent, the nonsense-cries from the stage-happening, are resolutely strategic. The insurgent and the freak-out have broken off discourse with a cultural system which they despise as a cruel, antiquated fraud. (*In Bluebeard's Castle*, pp. 88–9)

The older cultural system that Steiner refers to is, in fact, the system of values partly created and certainly kept alive by such writers as Coleridge, Arnold, Carlyle, Dickens and D. H. Lawrence. Of course, creative writers have not invented this system themselves. It is their cultural inheritance. What they have done is to take their critical stand in the midst of the system. From this vantage point they have subjected the whole European liberal tradition to a searching scrutiny, using for this purpose an unique combination of rational analysis and imaginative intuition. They have worked *through* the Word, most of them believing, as Coleridge did, that words are both an expression of and an index to the health or disease of national culture. If one wished to change the structure of society, Coleridge argued, one must purify the structure of language, by analysing political hypocrisy and cant, a view very similar to Orwell's in his essay on 'Politics and the English Language'. In all the writers discussed in the later chapters of this book there is a constant preoccupation with language, as the most powerful organ of truth, but also as the instrument by which the enemies of truth can impose their will on the people. In Huxley's scientific utopia, *Brave New World*, literature is reduced to 'emotional engineering'; and in *Nineteen Eighty-Four*, Orwell invents a new language 'Newspeak' and a new form of logical thought 'double think', on the model of war-time perversions of language, to illustrate the means by which totalitarian regimes brainwash society. The best answer to the spokesmen for the Counter-Culture is that the culture that is based on the Word has its own critics, critics who see both the strengths and the weaknesses of the liberal tradition. They see more clearly than the fashionable prophets of the Counter-Culture that abdication from the word, from a primarily verbal culture that demands patience and invites dissent, is the first step towards totalitarianism and slavery. And yet it would be foolish not to recognise the truth of McLuhan's claim that the electronic revolution has necessarily produced a new tension between traditional culture based on the word and the new non-verbal cultures. Out of this tension the new art and the new society must be born.

The second main plank of the Counter-Culture, the belief in the revolutionary power of liberated sex, important and powerful as it is, may perhaps assume a different perspective at the end of this study. What we shall notice in the writers under consideration is a growing recognition of the tendency in a machine-dominated culture to repress and control the free play of sex and loving emotions. In a number of the earlier writers there are interesting anticipations of Marcuse's ideas in *Eros and Civilisation*, but none of them goes as far as Reich in suggesting that sexual liberation is a universal panacea. As we should expect, in the Victorian novel any overt reference to sex as sex is distinctly muted, but the modern reader sees clearly enough that in *Hard Times* it is not only the creative powers of love and imagination that are stunted and repressed by an education in machinery and facts; so, too, are the free play of instincts and sexual passions. In Mrs Gaskell's *North and South*, the presentation of the strained and tortuous relations between Margaret Hale and the factory owner, Mr Thornton, has much of Lawrence's insight into the conflict between the will to power and the instinct for sexual fulfilment. In many ways, *North and South* forms an interesting anticipation of *Women in Love*. It is not only in the novels that criticise an industrial society for destroying a more natural order of life that the importance of sexual fulfilment is recognised. It occupies a vital place in the growing number of works dealing with the theme of the New Woman. Gissing's sombre and impressive novel *The Odd Women*, for instance, draws special attention to the disproportion between the number of single men and women in Victorian society and gives a comprehensive picture of the multiple distortions of personality that society imposes on its surplus women. At about the same time, Edward Carpenter, an utopian socialist and early protester against the pollution of the environment, was advocating free expression of sex, including homosexuality, as part of a critique of modern industrial civilisation. Both Huxley and Orwell saw the creative and revolutionary force of sex in their Utopias. It is sex that threatens the whole overturning of the planned regime and which must therefore be made subservient to the system. The slogan 'make love, not war' has a much longer and more distinguished history than modern champions realise.

Undoubtedly, the writers who scare us most are not those who picture our alienation in a realistically drawn social world, but people like Zamyatin, Huxley, and Orwell, who show us how easily our dreams of social heaven may be translated into living hells. Zamyatin's *We*, Huxley's *Brave New World* and Orwell's *Nineteen Eighty-Four* are, as David Caute has suggested, the authentic political allegories of our age (*The Illusion*, 1972, p. 261). They have, too, a remarkable recurrence of theme. All reveal 'an obsessive fear of the eradication of all human individuality'; all express a fear of 'political manipulation of the sexual impulses' (by means of state licence in Zamyatin and Huxley and by repression in Orwell); and all express horror at the absolute abandonment of love, at the destruction of the family, at the supremacy of the state, and at the distortion of history in the interest of the ruling power. But is it true, as Caute claims, that 'these pessimistic documents outstrip in political and literary authenticity almost all the socialist forward looking novels of the age'? And if so, what does this imply about the writer's role as a critic of society? Does it imply that he can only be effective as a prophet of doom? Such a conclusion would not only be too pessimistic but would ignore the fact that some of our greatest writers have managed to write major works of art that were also major works of social criticism. And they have done so either by virtue of their controlled satiric vision, or by their skill in rendering, or by their incisive analysis, or by their powerful advocacy of reform. Just how, will emerge in the following chapters.

2 The Idealist Vision

The word culture, as Raymond Williams has pointed out, in *The Long Revolution* (p. 41), may be used in the sense of culture as an ideal, a state or process of human perfection; it may be used in the sense of culture as a body of intellectual and artistic works; and it may be used, as the sociologists and anthropologists use it, to describe a particular way of life, including institutions and ordinary behaviour as well as literature and art. Clearly the third of these is the product of a radically different approach to society, an approach that purports to be scientific and free from value judgments and which has its origin in the Benthamite Utilitarian tradition examined in the following chapter. It is important to keep these three senses of culture in mind in reading the works of Coleridge, Matthew Arnold and T. S. Eliot; and, as will emerge more clearly later, one of Eliot's great weaknesses in *The Idea of a Christian Society* and *Notes Towards Definition of Culture* is his tendency to confuse these distinct senses at the very moment he claims to be distinguishing between them.

The two great pioneers in offering a criticism of society as an analysis of its state of culture are Coleridge and Matthew Arnold. The main impetus behind Coleridge's analysis is his passionate conviction that the state of society is a direct reflection of the prevailing philosophy of the age. A materialistic philosophy creates a materialistic society. The only way of seeing that men are not treated as mere things and that society is not regarded as an intricate mechanism, is to re-educate the governing classes in a philosophy of ideas. Only an education in ideas can give men a sense of the ultimate end for which the state and society exist. The main impetus behind Arnold's analysis of society, in *Culture and Anarchy*, is his passionate desire to convert the English middle classes to the pursuit of sweetness and light, that is to the way of culture, a way that involves holding in a just balance the moral and spiritual elements, or, as Arnold calls them, Hebraism (the moral) and Hellenism (the spiritual). Ultimately, Coleridge's writings spring from a dissatisfaction with the rulers, Arnold's from disgust with the middle classes, especially middle-class nonconformists, among whom his time as a school inspector was spent.

In spite of these differences both Coleridge and Arnold use the same basic approach. They see mind in control of matter, ideas shaping and controlling the whole of life. This is one great tradition of cultural analysis, and Coleridge is its founder. The opposite and rival tradition sees the matter in control of mind, ideas as the automatic product of the material environment. In offering reform, the Coleridgean says, 'you must change your whole philosophy of life'. The rival tradition says 'you must change the physical and economic environment'. But, if we are mere products of our environment, by what power can we rise superior to it and change it?

The main elements of Coleridge's theory of culture and society may be found in three works. These are *The Statesman's Manual* (1816), *A Lay Sermon Addressed to the Higher and Middle Class on the Existing Distresses and Discontents* (1817), (both reprinted in R. J. White's *Political Tracts*), and *On the Constitution of the Church and State* (1830). All are rather forbidding in structure and tone. It is easy to make fun of them, since they so obviously contain Coleridge's main weaknesses as well as his typical strengths. Hazlitt, in his characteristically malicious and unprincipled manner, wrote several anonymous reviews of *The Statesman's Manual*, the first before he had even read the work. In his review in *The Edinburgh*, he speaks of the author of *The Statesman's Manual* 'drawing a metaphysical bandage off his eyes' and 'talking in his sleep'. This is simply offensive without being amusing. It lacks the sustained and penetrating humour of Peacock's parody of Coleridge in *Nightmare Abbey* or the wit of Byron's couplet on Coleridge in *Don Juan*

> Explaining metaphysics to the nation
> I wish he would explain his Explanation

More patient, though not necessarily more sympathetic readers, like John Stuart Mill in the nineteenth century, and Raymond Williams in our own, have found in the *Lay Sermons* and *Church and State* the most comprehensive and profound analysis of nineteenth-century culture and society.

The first thing to stress, because this has usually been missed, is that for all his emphasis on the influence of ideas on a society, Coleridge is acutely aware of the part played by economic causes. In fact, he wrote his two *Lay Sermons* to examine the economic crisis that followed the end of the Napoleonic Wars. And one of the most original sections is his analysis of the periodic booms and crashes that afflict the economy — what we have now come to call the trade cycle. De Quincey said Coleridge knew nothing about economics. John Stuart Mill said that on such topics he wrote like 'an arrant driveller'. But these partisan views can no longer be accepted in the light of modern research. Coleridge's criticism of the theories of Ricardo and Malthus shows remarkable understanding of economic theory, and Hazlitt simply parroted Coleridge's views in his criticism of Malthus in *The Spirit of the Age*. Anticipating later thinkers, Coleridge recognised that a religion that habitually took for granted all truths necessarily leaves the understanding vacant and at leisure for a thorough insight into present and temporal interests, in other words for success in business. In developing this insight into the relationship between religion and the rise of capitalism, he foreshadowed the historian R. H. Tawney's approach by a hundred years. And where Arnold mainly expressed distaste for the limitations and self-righteousness of non-conformity, Coleridge analysed the connection between non-conformity and capitalism. In many ways, Coleridge anticipated some of the essentials of twentieth-century Keynesian thought, especially in his attempt to form a synthesis between the humanities and economics, an aspect that has been fully explored by W. F. Kennedy, in *Humanist versus Economist*.[1] In view of all this, it may be said that Coleridge's analysis of culture and society is altogether more broadly based than Arnold's. It recognises the importance of economic as well as spiritual and ideological forces, and it takes account of the subtle interplay and reaction between these forces.

John Stuart Mill, in his essays on Bentham and Coleridge, said that Coleridge was one of the first men to show the need for a philosophy of history and a philosophy of society. Coleridge's analysis of contemporary England was carried out in the light of these two philosophies. It was also determined by his theory of the constitution. An appreciation of its main elements helps us to understand the nature of his cultural analysis.

In a most interesting way Coleridge foreshadows our modern ideal of an open dynamic society, a point firmly made by D. L. Munby in *The Idea of a Secular Society*.[2] In his account of what he calls the idea of the constitution, Coleridge explains that it consists of two forces: the forces of permanence and the forces of progression, both of which, however, depend on a third force, a civilising force that he calls the National Church, or Clerisy. Both terms rather obscure the essential modernity of his conception of this third force, but his account of it in *Church and State* will clarify its nature and function. In chapter 5 of *Church and State*, he suggests that in most states a certain portion of the national wealth is inalienably set aside for the National Church or for whatever body takes upon itself the responsibility of maintaining and continuing the spiritual and cultural life of the nation. His account does not claim to be minutely historical, but is intended to explain the ultimate end for which such an order exists.

> [This national wealth], therefore, was reserved for the support and maintenance of a permanent class or order, with the following duties. A certain smaller number were to remain at the fountain heads of the

> humanities, in cultivating and enlarging the knowledge already possessed, and in watching over the interests of physical and moral science; being, likewise, the instructors of such as constituted, or were to constitute, the remaining more numerous classes of the order. This latter and far more numerous body were to be distributed throughout the country, so as not to leave even the smallest integral part or division without a resident guide, guardian, and instructor; the objects and final intention of the whole order being these — to preserve the stores, to guard the treasures, of past civilization, and thus to bind the present to the past; to perfect and add to the same, and thus to connect the present with the future; but especially to diffuse through the whole community, and to every native entitled to its laws and rights, that quantity and quality of knowledge which was indispensable both for the understanding of those rights, and for the performance of the duties correspondent. . . . The object of the two former estates of the realm, which conjointly form the State, was to reconcile the interests of permanence with that of progression — law with liberty. The object of . . . the third remaining estate of the realm, was to secure and improve that civilization, without which the nation could be neither permanent nor progressive. (Everyman ed., p. 34)

It is important to remember that when Coleridge wrote this there was no national scheme of education, there was no national endowment of the arts, and no-one had previously outlined a theory of the constitution that contained within it the essential features of the modern State, nor had anyone before given to learning, science, culture and the arts such a crucial role in the life of the State.

Much that is most original and seminal in Coleridge's criticism of society springs from his idea of this third order in the State. Where nineteenth-century *laissez-faire* theory minimised the positive ends of government, Coleridge stressed them. His definition of two of these positive ends immediately reveals his concern with the cultural health of the individual, with personal fulfilment and the balanced development of the whole man. He writes, in chapter 8 of *Church and State*

> The one [positive] end is, to secure to the subjects of the realm generally, the hope, the chance, of bettering their own or their children's condition. . . . The other is, to develop, in every native of the country, those faculties, and to provide for every native that knowledge and those attainments, which are necessary to qualify him for a member of the State, the free subject of a civilized realm.

With this enlightened ideal of the positive ends of the State as a guiding principle, Coleridge criticises everything in his society that tends to thwart these ends, everything that tends to dehumanise and degrade. Thus, he attacks the use of child labour in the cotton mills. On a broader front, he holds the mechanical philosophy of the age responsible for treating the men and women who worked in industry as mere things and not persons in their own right, in violation of the 'sacred principle', derived from Kant, that 'a person can never become a thing, nor be treated as such without wrong'. A passage in *A Lay Sermon* (1817), a work written to diagnose the radical causes of social and economic distresses that followed the end of the Napoleonic Wars, illustrates Coleridge's typical combination of compassionate humanity and incisive analysis.

> . . . Thus, instead of the position that all things find, it would be less equivocal and far more descriptive of the fact to say that things are always finding their level: which might be taken as the paraphrase or ironical definition of a storm. . . . But persons are not things — but man does not find his level. Neither in body nor in soul does the man find his level! After a hard and calamitous season, during which the thousand wheels of some vast manufactory had remained silent as a frozen waterfall, be it that plenty has returned and that trade has once more become brisk and stirring: go, ask the overseer, and question the parish doctor, whether the workman's health and temperance with the staid and respectful manners best taught by the inward dignity of conscious self-support, have found their level again? Alas! I have more than once seen a group of children in Dorsetshire, during the heat of the dog-days, each with its little shoulders up to its ears, and its chest pinched inward — the very habit and fixtures, as it were, that had been impressed on their frames by the former ill-fed, ill-clothed, and unfuelled winters. But as with the body, so or still worse with the mind. Nor is the effect confined to the labouring classes, whom by an ominous but too appropriate a change in our phraseology we are now accustomed to call the labouring poor. I cannot persuade myself that the frequency of failures with all the disgraceful secrets of fraud and folly, of unprincipled vanity in expending and desperate speculation in retrieving, can be familiarized to the thoughts and experience of men, as matters of daily occurrence, without serious injury to the moral sense: more especially in times when bankruptcies spread like a fever, at once contagious and epidemic; swift too as the travel of an earthquake, that with one and the same chain of shocks opens the ruinous chasm in cities that have an ocean between them! – in times when the fate flies swifter than the fear, and yet the report that follows the flash has a ruin of its own, and arrives but to multiply the blow! – when princely capitals are often but the telegraphs of distant calamity: and still worse, when no man's treasure is safe who

> has adopted the ordinary means of safety, neither the high nor the humble; when the lord's rents and the farmer's store, entrusted perhaps but as yesterday, are asked after at closed doors! – but worst of all, in its moral influences as well as in the cruelty of suffering, when the old labourer's savings, the precious robberies of self-denial from every day's comfort; when the orphan's funds, the widow's livelihood, the fond confiding sister's humble fortune, are found among the victims to the remorseless mania of dishonest speculation, or to the desperate cowardice of embarrassment, and the drunken stupor of a usurious selfishness that for a few months' respite dares incur a debt of guilt and infamy, for which the grave itself can plead no statute of limitation. Name to me any revolution recorded in history that was not followed by a depravation of the national morals. The Roman character during the Triumvirate, and under Tiberius, the reign of Charles the Second, and Paris at the present moment, are obvious instances. What is the main cause? The sense of insecurity. On what ground, then, dare we hope that, with the same accompaniment, commercial revolutions should not produce the same effect in proportion to the extent of their sphere?[3]

The approach of the Victorian novelists who portrayed and attacked the effects of a mechanical philosophy and industrialism on society was very similar to Coleridge's. His influence on Disraeli was direct, but in the case of Dickens and Mrs Gaskell it was mediated through Carlyle, to whom both formally acknowledge their debts.

Coleridge criticised the nineteenth-century educational system for being too mechanical, too utilitarian, too concerned with serving a machine state. In doing so, he drew the distinction between education and instruction, a distinction that was to be taken up a century later by T. S. Eliot. Education educes, it draws out latent powers and develops the whole man: instruction pours in factual knowledge. Another distinction, that between civilisation and cultivation, has also proved influential. By the word civilisation, Coleridge means the material riches of a society; by cultivation, he means the immaterial riches. The same distinction lies behind *Civilization: Its Cause and Cure* (1889), a work written by Edward Carpenter,[4] a late-Victorian social prophet who was a curate under F. D. Maurice, one of Coleridge's most persuasive disciples. Through Carpenter's Utopian socialism, some of Coleridge's most seminal ideas germinated in the novels of D. H. Lawrence and E. M. Forster. Undoubtedly, the two most valuable and influential elements in Coleridge's criticism of society were his ideal of a harmonious development of all the human faculties for the individual (transmuted in Carpenter and subsequently in Lawrence and others into ideals of 'wholeness' and 'health'); and, secondly, the idea that the cultural health of a society was an accurate index to the state of the nation as a whole. And allied to the second idea was a recognition of the importance of language, both as an index of cultural health and as a means of maintaining, transmitting and adding to a nation's cultural heritage. Both Dickens and Mrs Gaskell follow Coleridge in exploring the insidious implication of the use of 'hands' for the men and women who worked in the factories.

When we turn from Coleridge to Arnold, we notice immediately that it is the ideal of harmonious individual development that inspires Arnold's major work of social criticism, *Culture and Anarchy*. In Arnold's Preface, the idea recurs again and again. He defines culture as being, 'a pursuit of our total perfection'; a few pages later, he defines 'true human perfection', as 'a harmonious perfection, developing all sides of our humanity'; and as 'a general perfection, developing all parts of society'; on the same page, he says that the Nonconformists need to add sweetness and light and 'develop their full humanity more perfectly'; on the following page, he repeats that what they need is 'a more full and harmonious development of their humanity'; a little later, we have the phrase 'full perfection of our humanity', followed by the phrase 'culture and harmonious perfection'; and then 'culture, and the harmonious perfection of our whole being, and what we call totality'. And so it continues.

Does this obvious debt to Coleridge mean that Arnold's idea of culture is the same as Coleridge's? Does it mean that his analysis of England in 1869 is the same as Coleridge's in 1829. The answer to both questions would seem to be, no. Coleridge's idea of culture and society takes much greater notice of the interplay of economic and humanistic forces. Secondly, Coleridge is much more concerned than Arnold is with criticising specific abuses in the light of his general theory. Arnold, for all his well-directed irony and suave satire, touches on few particular social abuses. For all his quotations from speeches and newspapers, his discussion tends to be more abstract than Coleridge's. At his best, as I have suggested elsewhere, Coleridge combines the roles of poet, novelist, and sociologist.[5]

Raymond Williams claims that it is a common error to believe that Arnold recommends 'a merely selfish personal cultivation'. To refute this error, he quotes a passage from the early part of *Culture and Anarchy* that enforces the obligation on the individual 'to carry others along with him in his march towards perfection'. Williams is right to point to this passage. He could also point to passages in the last sections but, personally, I seem to discover a marked emphasis at least on cultivation for the private individual, and a conspicuous neglect of some of the broader issues, relating to the total culture of a society and the relationship between this and the economic and political philosophy of the age.

Like Eliot after him, but unlike his predecessor Coleridge, Matthew Arnold sees society as a closed society divided into three main classes.

Coleridge's vision, on the other hand, was of a dynamic society, in which there was a healthy tension between the three main estates or forces (permanence, progression, clerisy) and opportunities for movement from class to class. Arnold's division of the nation into the aristocratic class, the middle class, and the working class, and his invention of the terms Barbarians, Philistines and Populace to correspond with these classes and to epitomise the weakness of each, contributes to the polemical force of *Culture and Anarchy*. But the distinctions are hardly very sophisticated tools of sociological analysis. The chief defect of the aristocracy, the Barbarians, is that their culture is purely external; of the middle class, the Philistines, that they worship machinery and material success, and make an exclusive virtue of the principle of 'doing what one likes'; of the working class or Populace, a lack of human sympathy and absence of either internal or external culture. It is Arnold's main thesis that a society that worships material success and regards as sacred the principle of doing as one likes is well on the way to anarchy. Doing what one likes leads to cultural fragmentation, self opinionatedness, and parochialism.

Arnold's solution is twofold. Firstly, the pursuit of culture, of sweetness and light, in all three classes. Secondly, a strong government that would take active steps to develop the best selves of its citizens. Thus, culture becomes a cohesive force in society. As I shall show later in the chapter on Mill's essays on Coleridge and Bentham, Coleridge alone gave a satisfactory account of the cohesive forces that bind men together in society. This John Stuart Mill recognised and singled out for special praise. Arnold's account is too abstract, too academic, too lacking in any real insight into individual and social psychology. As an educational administrator he was used to drawing up blueprints for the ideal boy, the ideal school; but the critic of society needs to know how real men behave in specific cases in an actual society. Perhaps the worst preparation for becoming a great critic of society is to be a teacher of any kind.

It is a simple and natural transition from Coleridge's *On the Constitution of the Church and State, According to the Idea of Each*, and Matthew Arnold's *Culture and Anarchy*, to T. S. Eliot's two brief works, *The Idea of a Christian Society* (1939) and *Notes Towards the Definition of Culture*, since both, in conception and in key terminology, owe much to those earlier critiques of culture and society. Eliot formally acknowledges his debt and frequently refers to Coleridge and Arnold in developing his own arguments.

In approaching Eliot's two works on culture and society, it is useful to see their connection not only with the work of his predecessors but also with the poet's other writings. His best-known early essay, 'Tradition and the Individual Talent' (1919), which argues that each work is not only related to the tradition but actually modifies the whole order of works in that tradition, clearly foreshadows his later preoccupation with the themes of cultural continuity and order. His formal declaration, in the Preface to the collection of essays *For Lancelot Andrewes* (1928), that he was a Royalist, high Anglican and conservative, indicated clearly enough the kind of order he soon came to value, and his plays, especially *Murder in the Cathedral*, reveal his concern with the preservation of a specifically Christian culture. In the late 1920s and early 1930s, Eliot took an active interest in the Catholic Action Française and in the Social Credit movement in England. He also wrote numerous essays on social and political issues for *The Criterion*, which he himself edited. Although his literary and political journalism takes up the main issues of the day, it remains uncommitted to any party or policy. By weaving fine distinctions that are not always clear to the reader, Eliot remained aloof and detached while insisting that 'the function of political theory is not to form a working party, but to permeate society and consequently all parties'. His faith in Christianity and in the permeating force of a cultural elite led him to become a member of a group known as the 'Moot' that held several weekend conferences each year between April 1938 and July 1945.[6] Among its members were the Catholic writer, Christopher Dawson, the refugee Jewish sociologist, Karl Mannheim, and the writer John Middleton Murry. It also included the founder of the *Christian Newsletter*, J. H. Oldham, and several distinguished academics and theologians. On the basis of his early membership of this and similar groups and starting from a personal interpretation of what Coleridge meant by the 'clerisy', Eliot came to work out his idea of the 'Community of Christians' or Christian elite. A paper that he prepared for discussion at the Moot Meeting of December 1944, called 'On the Place and Function of the Clerisy', provides interesting evidence that, at this stage, he did not link the idea of an elite as closely with a privileged economic class as he did a year later in the published work *Notes Towards the Definition of Culture*. Since Eliot is something of an old possum among political cats, it is often necessary to relate the argument of his two cultural tracts to much else in his life and writings before deciding whether he is making important distinctions or being characteristically evasive.

Raymond Williams begins his chapter on Eliot, in *Culture and Society: 1780—1950*, by saying 'We can say of Eliot what Mill said of Coleridge, that an "enlightened Radical or Liberal" ought to rejoice over such a conservative.' The grounds for such rejoicing seem dubious, to say the least. In most of the crucial areas Eliot is either muddle-headed or evasive. The general direction of his arguments in fact leads towards an authoritarian view of culture and society, distinguishable from Fascism, it is true, but so inextricably bound up with the protection of economic privilege and the existing class-structure that it can have little appeal to anyone with a developed sense of an open, dynamic society. Moreover, his ponderous handling of Coleridgean ideas and distinctions destroys what was originally seminal and creative.

In *The Idea of a Christian Society* (1939), Eliot borrows the word 'idea' from Coleridge to mean the ultimate end or aim; he borrows the distinction between 'education' and 'instruction'; and he borrows, but confuses, Coleridge's three-fold distinction between the Universal Church with Christ at its head, the Church of England, and the National Church or Clerisy. Eliot's distinction is between the Church, the Christian Community, and the Community of Christians. Not much comes from this muddle-headed re-interpretation of Coleridge. He does, however, use the idea of a Christian Society as an effective means of demonstrating just how far England in the nineteen-thirties had deviated from any recognisable scale of Christian values. Gross materialism, the abuse of natural resources, the treatment of the individual as an anonymous economic unit, the selfish pursuit of profit, the absence of humane industrial legislation — all these features of society were utterly contrary to the Christian ideal. According to Eliot, 'the choice before us is between the formation of a new Christian culture, and the acceptance of a pagan one'. One sentence in his outline of the 'idea' of a Christian Society illustrates clearly Elliot's sardonic paternalism: 'It would be a society in which the natural end of man — virtue and well-being in community — is acknowledged for all, and the supernatural end — beatitude — for those who have eyes to see it.'

The more interesting of Eliot's two works for us today is undoubtedly *Notes towards the Definition of Culture*, although its title embodies Eliot's characteristic evasiveness. It is not 'Notes on Culture' nor 'A Definition of Culture', but *Notes Towards the Definition of Culture*. Could anything be more cautious and evasive? The special interest for us today lies in Eliot's discussion of the relation between regional culture and metropolitan culture and, secondly, his discussion of the relation between classes and elites. In examining the first, he stresses that the health of a nation's culture in part depends on the strength and diversity of regional culture. A dynamic interaction between the two should be the ideal. In this context, one might notice that many public cultural organisations in Britain deliberately foster regional dialects and cultural tradition. The BBC does, for example. Some of the comparative thinness of many colonial cultures may indeed arise from the absence of such strong distinctive regional traditions and the corresponding absence of any fostering of those that do exist.

T. S. Eliot's discussion of elites is far less satisfactory than his discussion of regional culture, but his views are at least interesting enough to be taken seriously by later writers of text-books on Elites and Elitism, for example by Bottomore; and Eliot can be given the credit for being one of the first English writers to see the significance of Elitism. As the notes reveal, he was taking up ideas he had found in Karl Mannheim, one of the most active members of 'the Moot'. Because high culture demands exceptional sensitivity and some specialist education in one or more of the arts, it is likely to depend on an elitist group. Popular culture, because its appeal is broader and because it makes few demands on specialised knowledge or expertise, obviously does not depend upon elites in the same way. The points Eliot makes in relation to 'high culture' are perfectly valid, given his terms. But what is radically unsatisfactory is his complacent assumption that there is a close and necessary connection between the cultural elites and the class system. He assumes that the first, the cultural elite, justifies the second. Terry Eagleton notes, in his essay 'Eliot and a Common Culture',

> By placing culture above politics, in the timeless values of a small personal group, or below politics, in the unconscious rhythms of an instinctive way of life [clearly represented in the 'folk' regional traditions] Eliot evades a number of crucial questions. On the one front, politics is attacked as a set of formulations falsely abstracted from a whole texture of life; on another, it is criticized as part of a shallow, unreflective quality of that life, from the standpoint of a finely conscious *élite*. (*Eliot in Perspective*, ed. G. Martin, p. 291)

But Eagleton is finally forced to admit that 'it is part of the strength of Eliot's conception of culture that he refuses to confine it to an elite; culture is ideally *a whole way of life*, lived commonly and variously by a whole people'. If this is Eliot's great strength, his great weakness as an analyst of English culture is his ingrained, unexamined, extreme right-wing authoritarian political views. A similar right-wing arrogance and contempt for the English working classes also vitiates much that Lawrence and Yeats have to say about modern cultures and society.

In considering writers as critics of society we need to consider not only the intrinsic value of what they say, but also how they say it, and its effect on others. Viewing Coleridge, Arnold and Eliot from this viewpoint, it is evident that what Coleridge says is intrinsically more important and that the texture of his writing more clearly embodies that harmonious perfection that characterises his ideal of culture. But Arnold's rhetorical skill had more practical effect and Eliot makes fewer demands on his readers; he deals in high-minded platitudes and is consequently frequently prescribed reading in that institutional anomaly, a University Department of Education. But the sensibility reflected in *Culture and Anarchy* and in *Notes Towards the Definition of Cultures* falls far short of any ideal of cultural perfection. Arnold's suave complacency and sardonic mockery reflect a limited range of human sympathy, and Eliot's arid abstractions and colourless prose reflect a sensibility cut off from the richness and diversity of the culture he claims to value and champion.

In this chapter I have traced only one tradition, the tradition represented by Coleridge, Arnold and Eliot. This is the idealist tradition that measures the wealth of a country according to the richness and diversity of its cultural life and not by the size of the gross national product. But there is another tradition, the Utilitarian tradition, the tradition of Bentham, John Stuart Mill, and most modern economists and sociologists. For them the health and wealth of a country must be measured by material riches and the growth and development of legislative and institutional life. It is with this tradition that I shall be concerned in the next chapter in my discussion of Mill's essays on Coleridge and Bentham.

3 The Utilitarian Approach

When John Stuart Mill lay dying in Avignon in May 1873, his last words to his step-daughter and faithful companion, Helen Taylor, were: 'You know that I have done my work.' They were the words of a man who had dedicated his whole life to the service of freedom and truth, a radical and agnostic who had shocked Victorian public opinion by his uncompromising intellectual honesty. He was a champion of individual liberty, whether it was liberty of conscience for the intellectual or liberty for the prostitute to refuse compulsory medical examination. When, three years before his death, he gave evidence before the Royal Commission on the Contagious Diseases Bill, a Bill that compelled prostitutes but not their customers to be medically examined, he shocked his questioner, Sir John Packington, by exposing the Victorian dual system of morality. 'It seems to me', said Mill, 'that if the object is to protect those who are not unchaste, the way to do this is to bring motive to bear on the man not the woman.' Earlier, he saw the logical implications of Malthus's arguments that restraint could prevent the population explosion. When he was only seventeen, he was arrested for distributing pamphlets advocating birth control. The magistrate, like Sir John Packington, indeed like most men in Victorian society, preferred to restrict logic to the schools. Even today there are countries in the world that resist the implications of Mill's remorseless logic, not only in the sphere of sexual morality, but in the spheres of religion and politics as well.

When Mill spoke of his work as having been done, he was looking back on over fifty years of authorship and public duty. Born in 1806, his initiation into authorship came early. His irascible father James Mill, who found it difficult to control his impatience, tested him in Latin and Greek as he compiled his great *History of India* at the same table. The boy helped his father with the proofs, and in retrospect, in his *Autobiography*, spoke of his father's *History of India* as contributing largely to his education. His initiation into the world of public duty came a little later, at the age of seventeen, when his father obtained a clerkship for him at India House in 1823. In the same year, the younger Mill founded the Utilitarian Society, a society that met at Bentham's house every fortnight. Mill claimed to have originated the word 'utilitarian' which he took, he says, from John Galt's novel, *The Annals of the Poor.* But, actually, Bentham had suggested the term 'utilitarian' in preference to Benthamism, in a letter to Dumont, as early as 1802. When the meetings at Bentham's house came to an end two years later, a dozen of Mill's friends met twice a week on their way to their offices to discuss politics, economics and philosophy. The practice at these gatherings of never abandoning a question until all points had been settled formed Mill's initiation into habits of rigorous intellectual analysis. At this time he was also the leading figure in the London Debating Society, where he met many young Coleridgeans, including John Sterling (a brilliant young man, friend of Carlyle), and F. D. Maurice, the founder of Christian Socialism. By the passing of the first Reform Bill in 1832, Mill had already established a reputation as a political journalist, notably for his 'Spirit of the Age' essays in *The Examiner* in 1831; and, though debarred from sitting in Parliament himself, he collaborated with the Philosophical Radicals to ensure that the Reform Bill passed, though he was always more critical of this measure than his father. He thought that the existing machinery of Government was too outworn to be patched up by such measures.

For the student of philosophy, Mill is the author of *A System of Logic*, first published in 1843. It was his great achievement, Karl Britton remarks, 'to have found logic deductive and to have left it both inductive and deductive' (*John Stuart Mill*, p. 147). For the student of politics, Mill is the author of *The Principles of Political Economy* (1848), the essay *On Liberty* (1859), *Representative Government* (1861), and the *Subjection of Women* (1861). For the student of literature, he is the author of the essays on Bentham and Coleridge and of an *Autobiography* (1873), which is a searching analysis of his intellectual and emotional development, comparable in interest if not in imaginative depth with Edmund Gosse's *Father and Son* (1907) and Butler's *The Way of All Flesh* (1903). All three record the clash of temperament and the ideological conflict between different generations in the nineteenth century. They thus constitute invaluable informal critiques of the age.

Somewhat extravagant claims have been made for Mill's essays on Bentham and Coleridge. It is therefore necessary to distinguish between their special interest for students of literature and their importance in Mill's work as a whole. No student of literature can afford to ignore them, but Mill's status as a logician or philosopher hardly depends upon them at all. Like most modern philosophers, his chief preoccupation was with technical problems and not with constructing an all-embracing vision, theory, or system of life.

With some justification Dr Leavis has complained that no-one told him to read Mill's essays on Bentham and Coleridge when he was an undergraduate at Cambridge. He would no doubt be better served in many universities today. In the Introduction to his edition of the essays, first published in 1949, he claims that the essays are key works around which a student may organise his knowledge of the nineteenth century.[1] With this judgment I agree. And I share Leavis's exasperation with university syllabuses and teaching methods that reduce what should be a study of literature and life at the deepest level to an examination of form and style, an approach that largely ignores intellectual content, the play of ideas, the sociological and political implications of literary works. However, when Dr Leavis comes to trace the main movement of mind in the nineteenth century, he undoubtedly exaggerates the importance of Mill's two essays. He seems to forget that Mill was not only the liberal modifier of Utilitarianism, but also the prototype of that Utilitarianism that Dickens satirised in Mr Gradgrind, in *Hard Times*. And Mill referred to Dickens angrily and contemptuously as 'that creature', on account of his treatment of female social reformers in *Bleak House*. Leavis does not fully recognise that Mill's greatest contribution to nineteenth-century thought came mainly from his other works, and not from these essays. This contribution was three-fold. Firstly, it lay in his strenuous call to truth; secondly, in his passion for intellectual freedom; and thirdly, his belief in the clerisy, or a nationally endowed class to maintain and enrich the cultural life of the nation, a belief that he derived from Coleridge. The call to truth is reflected in most of the great novels of the nineteenth and twentieth century, while the basic conflict between truthfulness and self-deception, between personal integrity and complex social forces, soon become paramount in fiction. This may be seen in Flaubert, in George Eliot pre-eminently, in Henry James, Hardy, Butler, Conrad and Lawrence. For the most part, this is an indirect influence, but in the case of Hardy it is very direct: Sue Bridehead spouts pure Mill in *Jude the Obscure*. The passion for intellectual freedom inspired much of the subsequent opposition to censorship and to the encroachment of social legislation on free thought. But of these three great contributions to modern thought, only Mill's ideas about the clerisy are fully reflected in the essays. For example, on p. 148 of Leavis's edition of the essays, Mill specifically honours Coleridge 'for having vindicated against Bentham and Adam Smith and the whole eighteenth century, the principle of an endowed class, for the cultivation of learning, and for diffusing its results among the community'. Today, we are the heirs of that tradition, whether we are teachers or students. We are the clerisy. And our special task is to assert the intrinsic value of immaterial ends in a materialistic society, to scrutinise contemporary culture in the light of the great nineteenth-century tradition of cultural analysis.

Mill's connections with Bentham and Coleridge were not equally close. He knew Coleridge only through his writings and through friendship with his disciples: John Sterling and F. D. Maurice, together with other members of the London Debating Society, many of whom had been deeply influenced by Coleridge's religious and political ideas. Mill's knowledge of Bentham, on the other hand was direct, intimate and of long duration. Bentham found a house for the Mills, near his own in London, where they lived for over twenty years, and invited them to spend their summer holidays with him at his country house, Ford Abbey in Somerset. Between the ages of nine and twelve, Mill was plunged into the strenuous but stimulating intellectual life at Ford Abbey, where Bentham was visited by men like Francis Place, the radical London tailor, and by other disciples. John Stuart Mill's first major literary task was to translate one of Bentham's works from French into English (thus giving some point to Hazlitt's joke in *The Spirit of the Age* that 'his works have been translated into French — they ought to be translated into English'). This work, *The Rationale of Judicial Evidence*, no longer satisfied Bentham. After it had appeared in French, he had made two different revisions. The task of his nineteen-year-old disciple was to collate all three versions and produce a lucid English text. He succeeded triumphantly, but modestly refrained from adding his name to the title page, until persuaded to do so by the delighted author. A little earlier, Mill had become thoroughly indoctrinated with Benthamism when his father had put in his hands Dumont's edition of Bentham's *Traité de Législation*. As the result of reading this work the principle of utility (Mill writes in the *Autobiography*), 'fell exactly into its place as the keystone which held together the detached and fragmentary component parts of my knowledge and belief'. Nothing that happened in his later intellectual life ever dislodged that keystone. He modified the greatest happiness principle by making happiness only the *indirect* end of life, by stating that 'the only chance' was to treat, 'not happiness, but some end external to it, as the purpose of life' (a very illogical manoeuvre); he found in Wordsworth's poetry 'the very culture of feelings' he was in search of; he saw that Coleridge's understanding of history and his psychology of government were infinitely superior to Bentham's; the Romantics liberated him from his father's arid influence; yet he never altogether abandoned his Benthamist position. In the essay on Coleridge he wrote that the truth 'lies with the school of Locke and of Bentham' (p. 114).

Bentham was felt as a compelling presence, physical as well as intellectual, even after his death in 1832. As soon as he was dead, an old sheet was thrown over his body, which was then transported to the Webb School of Anatomy in a piano-dealer's van. Once the dissection had been completed, Bentham's skeleton was dressed up in his usual clothes, his favourite stick which he called 'Dapple' was placed in a gloved hand, and a head made by Mme Tussaud put in position. In this grisly form, he presided over the weekly dinners of his disciples, until even *they* found his continued presence chilling rather than inspiring. He now rests in the Library of University College London, where he is regularly taken out and given a good pummelling to remove the dust and moths.

The essays on Bentham and Coleridge first appeared in *The London and Westminster Review* in 1838 and 1840 respectively. The *Westminster Review*, a radical journal, was founded in 1823 by Bentham and James Mill, to counter the influence of the *Edinburgh Review* and the *Quarterly*. In 1840 John Stuart Mill wrote to Sterling that he would carry on the revived *Review* to another number simply in order to publish the article on Coleridge, whose works he was re-reading. He asked Sterling for advice and help, which was liberally given. This provides evidence of the intensity of Mill's interest in Coleridge at the time, since Sterling was one of Coleridge's disciples.

Raymond Williams in *Culture and Society* sums up the unique appeal of these essays:

> The essays bring together what Mill called 'the two great seminal minds of England in their age', but the result, quite evident in a reading of the essays, is a bringing together not of two minds but of three. For to watch Mill being influenced by, and correcting, Bentham and Coleridge is absorbing and illuminating. We see not only the working of an individual and most able mind, but a process which has a general representative importance. Mill's attempt to absorb, and by discrimination and discarding to unify, the truths alike of the utilitarian and the idealist positions is, after all, a prologue to a very large part of the subsequent history of English thinking: in particular, to the greater part of English thinking about society and culture. (Penguin, p. 65)

I would simply add that the essays look back as well as forward: they are of as much interest to the student of the Romantics as to the student of the Victorians, for it was surely in the Romantic period that the attempt to synthesise eighteenth-century rationalism and nineteenth-century idealism was first made. Bentham and Coleridge are also key figures for an understanding of all nineteenth-century critiques of society. In the essay on Coleridge, Mill wrote: 'Whoever could master the premises and combine the methods of both, would possess the entire English philosophy of his age.' Now, though such a synthesis was impossible (and Mill's great weakness lies in his inability to see that it was impossible), he was right to suggest that an understanding of the two men's work would embrace what was most important in the spirit of the age, including their radically different approaches to the criticism of society.

The nineteenth-century concern with analysing the spirit of the age was something new in the history of ideas. The actual phrase, 'the spirit of the age', so indispensable to us today, only came into use at the end of the eighteenth century. Hazlitt used it as the title for his essays on his great contemporaries, published in 1825, describing Wordsworth as a 'pure emanation' of this spirit, and regarding Bentham and Coleridge as contrasting emanations. Mill noticed the newness of the phrase, in the first of the series of essays called 'The Spirit of the Age', published in the *Examiner* in 1831.

> The 'Spirit of the Age' is in some measure a novel expression. I do not believe that it is to be met with in any work exceeding fifty years in antiquity. The idea of comparing one's own age with former ages, or with our notion of those which are yet to come, had occurred to philosophers; but it never before was itself the dominant idea of any age.[2]

It was 'an idea essentially belonging to an age of change'. One might add, belonging to an age of swift, revolutionary change. The three *Examiner* essays, written under the influence of Comtian positivism and the scientific rigour of the St Simonians, draw the distinction between *transitional* states of society, such as the one in which Mill was living, when the critical spirit was in the ascendent, and *natural* or organic states of society, when innovations had become institutionalised, state power was in the hands of the cultured, a positive era of healthy consolidation following a critical era of constant change. This rather derivative analysis, although a part of Mill's lifelong attempt to understand the spirit of his age, lacks the incisiveness and comprehensive sweep of his later and better known essays on Bentham and Coleridge.

In the opening pages of the essay on Bentham, Mill makes a number of broad comparisons between the two writers who, he says, 'have been the teachers of the teacher', the two seminal minds of their age, Bentham the representative figure of progressive philosophy, Coleridge of conservative philosophy. In the rest of the essay on Bentham, such comparisons are less frequent than in the later essay on Coleridge. Mill hails Bentham as 'the father of innovation', as the 'great subversive', 'the great questioner of things established'. He defines his special area of activity as 'the field of practical abuses,' pointing out that his great achievements had been won through his 'method of detail', which depended on the process of classification and analysis. Bentham's test of truth is to enquire what is meant by such grand phrases as Law of Nature, Law of Reason. To what do they refer that can be verified by experience? If to nothing, then they should be discarded, together with other similar 'vague generalities'. Again and again, Bentham emphasised the importance of never reasoning about wholes until they have been resolved into parts. For the Romantics, by contrast, the whole was an ideal to be pursued, not to be analysed. And the ideal of wholeness came to inspire the social criticism of many twentieth-century novelists, especially D. H. Lawrence.

Mill, having summed up the positive side of Bentham's achievement, turns to point out some of his limitations; for, by this time, he had decided that he was a man 'of remarkable endowments', but also 'of remarkable deficiencies'. Mill suggests that Bentham neither realised that man's synthesis could not be more complete than his analysis, nor understood how little of man's total experience came under his analysis. Bentham derived no light from other minds, but took the incompleteness of his own as 'a representative of universal human nature' (p. 61). He lacked poetic culture, placing poetry on a level with 'push-pin'. His only love, Hazlitt noted, was for the organ. He cared little for Imagination, either in the sense of figurative language, or as the power of entering into the minds and experiences of other people. When Mill says that Bentham 'was a boy to the last', one is irresistibly reminded of his modern counterparts for whom the highest form of cultural activity is a game of cricket, the most satisfying intellectual pursuit the theory of games. Bentham's most serious limitation of all, according to Mill, is his total neglect of man's desire for perfection and his pursuit of the ideal for its own sake. All that is best in the work of John Stuart Mill, on the other hand, arises from his understanding of the force of these two related passions, for which no room can be made in a strictly utilitarian philosophy. In recognising the pursuit of spiritual perfection as one of man's highest ends, Mill is at one with Coleridge; with Matthew Arnold in his gospel of sweetness and light and the cultivation of our best selves; with Newman in his praise of the quest of ideal perfection. The seminal idea may be found in Coleridge's *Church and State* (1830), where he speaks of 'the harmonious development of those qualities and faculties that characterize our humanity'. But Mill differs from Coleridge, Newman and Matthew Arnold in that his prose rarely glows with the fervour of these other passionate advocates of culture. His is a very cool idea of cultural perfection.

In attempting to assess Bentham's contribution to the life of the individual and the welfare of society, Mill states plainly that Bentham offers no help to the individual, since he ignores completely the whole idea of self-culture in the harmonious development of the mind, passions, and moral sense, an ideal that lies at the root of Coleridge's thought. And he can only help a society that has already attained a certain state of spiritual development, since his exclusive concern is with the protection of its material interests. His thought, says Mill, 'can teach the means of organising and regulating the merely business part of social arrangements'. And, as far as offering a theory of government that would firstly explain the source of authority in the State, secondly, explain how men are to be made to obey that authority, and thirdly, that would demonstrate how abuses are to be checked, Bentham only made a contribution to the third.

Although Mill concludes his essay by saying that Bentham's collected works should be in the hands of everyone who would understand the age (Hazlitt called them 'reference books'), it is not surprising that he thought that his essay on Bentham might possibly endanger the cause of progress. Indeed, he wondered whether it was wise to publish, and toned down some of the most critical passages when it was republished in *Dissertations and Discussions* in 1859. His main aim in writing these two essays is clear. He wanted to demonstrate the limitations of Benthamite Utilitarianism and he wanted also to convince his Radical and Liberal friends that they might 'derive most improvements' from Coleridge. At the time, he genuinely believed that an intellectual synthesis might be made; but, after the publication of the Coleridge essay in 1840, he abandoned the attempt at synthesis, retaining only one or two key ideas from Coleridge in his later works, notably the idea of the clerisy.

One of the most remarkable features of the essay on Coleridge is the number of ideas Mill advances as his own that have been unconsciously assimilated from Coleridge, for instance the idea 'that a knowledge of the speculative opinions of the men between twenty and thirty years of age is a great source of political prophecy'. Here he even reproduces Coleridge's mistake in attributing the idea to Bacon instead of to the eighteenth-century writer Sir James Steuart.[3] He takes over from Coleridge the idea that in all the controversies in social philosophy 'both sides were in the right in what they affirmed, though wrong in what they denied';[4] he also borrows the idea that to understand the difference between rival systems of thought you must use as your starting point the theory of mind on which they are based. This, in fact, is Coleridge's method in his analysis of Hobbes and of the French Physiocrats in the essays in *The Friend*.[5] These three examples point to the unique 'seminal' quality of Coleridge's writings. His writings not only contain a fund of original ideas; they possess the power to go on working in the mind of the reader long after he has put the book down, enlarging comprehension, stretching the mind to its utmost limits, modifying the whole consciousness. Thus it is with Coleridge's effect on Mill. But a rigidity of mind, product of his precocious but arid education, prevented Mill from responding to the full challenge of Coleridge's imaginative idea of a dynamic, open-society.

Some of Mill's friends, their minds fossilised in the rational strata of eighteenth-century thought, frowned on Mill's openness to Wordsworth's poetry and Coleridge's philosophy. Sir James Bowring, a collaborator on the *Westminster*, said that the reading of Wordsworth had muddled Mill, and that 'he had been in a strange confusion ever since, endeavouring to unite poetry and philosophy'. But Mill provided an answer to this charge in a letter to Carlyle: 'the same person may be poet and logician, but he cannot be both in the same composition'. The answer is not completely satisfactory. It points to a significant weakness in Mill's whole conception of poetry and the imagination. Though he recognised that Coleridge's view of man's mixed nature is truer than Bentham's simple abstraction of man as a pleasure/pain automaton, though he stressed the importance of cultivating the feelings and spoke of poetry's high powers, he was one of the first Victorians to make the disastrous division between rational and imaginative writing, assertive and expressive modes of expression, a division that by elevating poetry into a kind of religion made it less rather than more operative in the consciousness of ordinary people, so that at the end of the tradition T. E. Hulme could refer to romantic poetry as 'spilt religion'. Putting the matter very simply, the whole drift of Coleridge's work is to emphasise the unity of thought, feeling, imagination and will: the whole tendency of Mill's is to provide special reserves for feeling and imagination.[6] This is very clear in his essay, 'Two Kinds of Poetry', when he speaks of Wordsworth's 'thoughts' being 'coloured by, and impressing themselves by means of, emotions'.[7] The divisive analysis, so characteristically Benthamite, unintentionally implies what Eliot was later to call a 'dissociation of sensibility'.

It must come as a surprise to those who know Coleridge mainly as the author of the *Ancient Mariner* to find so much of the essay on Coleridge taken up with discussions of the poet's philosophy of society and psychology of government. Mill's account is unreliable in many respects. He consistently talks about the non-existent composite, 'the Germano-Coleridgean school'. There never was such a school. Certainly here was a whole that should have been analysed into its Benthamite parts. He attributes to Coleridge ideas on history that were the reverse of those he actually held. While it is true that Coleridge interprets historical development in terms of purpose – divine purpose – it is a mistake to connect, as Mill does, his work with the materialistic, cause-and-effect approach of Michelet, the historian of the French Revolution, a mistake implicitly endorsed by Dr Leavis in his edition of Mill's two essays. In the essay on Coleridge, and in his book, *Representative Government*, Mill misunderstands and simplifies the distinction Coleridge drew between the forces of progression and those of permanence. By the first, it will be remembered, Coleridge meant those forces that had not yet been given permanent form, as the result of being embodied in society's institutions; that is, forces such as commerce, industry, the press and public opinion. Indeed, one of the reasons for Coleridge's opposition to the Reform Bill of 1832 was his belief that these volatile elements already exerted sufficient power to counteract the forces of permanence. By the latter, he meant those forces that had found institutional form. Mill made the mistake of equating the forces of 'progression' with 'progress', a mistake perpetuated by many subsequent thinkers and commentators; but one looks in vain in Coleridge for such an equation.

In spite of Mill's multiple misunderstandings of Coleridge, he grasped and analysed many of the main features of Coleridge's social thought. He singles out for special praise Coleridge's 'philosophy of society'. It takes, he remarks, 'the only form in which it is yet possible, that of a philosophy of history; not a defence of particular ethical or religious doctrines, but a contribution, the largest made by any class of thinkers, towards the philosophy of human culture' (p. 130). The whole nineteenth-century debate on culture and society has its early origins in the conflict between Paine and Burke, the one wishing to ignore or re-write history, as Big Brother controls history in Orwell's *Nineteen-Eighty-Four*, the other presenting a vision of the organic life of the nation as a partnership between those dead, those living, and those yet to be born. The former is not only Paine's approach, but Bentham's also. The latter is Burke's, but it is Coleridge's, too.

Mill finds that Coleridge's view of society, unlike Bentham's atomic view, gives a convincing account of the three requisites for a stable order. These are, firstly, a system of national education; secondly, the existence, in some form or other, of the feeling of allegiance or loyalty; and, thirdly, a 'strong and active principle of cohesion among the members of the same community or state'. As Mill had pointed out in the earlier essay on Bentham, 'Bentham's idea of the world', as a 'collection of persons pursuing each his separate interest and pleasure', contributes nothing to an understanding of government and society. From a later vantage point, however, his atomic view can be seen to have been especially conducive to the *laissez-faire* economic thought of such philosophical radicals as Ricardo.

What especially interested Mill in Coleridge's last published prose work, *Church and State* (1830), was his idea of the National Church or Clerisy. As he points out, there are two views that may be taken of corrupt institutions: that they should be abolished (this is Bentham's view); or, that they should be made a reality (this is Coleridge's, in relation to the complacent Church of his own day). Coleridge's approach to all human institutions is to ask what is the idea that they have been brought into existence to fulfil. In the case of the National Church, the idea was the creation of an order that would act as a mediating power between the opposing forces of permanence and progression, thus providing that civilising influence without which neither force could contribute to the dynamic health of culture and society. Such an idea may thus act both as a guiding principle and as a measuring device for assessing how well the contemporary church fulfilled its proper functions. Naturally, as an advocate of secularism, Mill seized on Coleridge's admission that the national wealth set aside for culture need not be restricted to the clergy, since he saw in it a lever that might be used to introduce a comprehensive educational system that was purely secular. More important than the tactical advantage Mill took of Coleridge's idea of the Clerisy is his open-hearted tribute to Coleridge's philosophical justification of 'an endowed class'. If one substitutes the phrase 'endowed order' for 'endowed class', one not only comes closer to Coleridge's principle but establishes the link with nationally endowed cultural orders in modern society.

A further element in Coleridge's thought of compelling interest to Mill was his idea of landed property as a sacred trust. Once he has paid tribute to this idea, he hastens to reassure his readers that he himself must not be suspected 'of recommending a general resumption of landed possessions, or the depriving any one, without compensation of anything which the law gives him.' This was more than a sop to his radical, Benthamite, legalistic friends. It was a typical expression of his desire to synthesise what was best in two great traditions. And his account of Coleridge's fiduciary ideal exhibits his overriding concern with principles and his prophetic sense of historic development.

> Perhaps, however, the greatest service which Coleridge has rendered to politics in his capacity of a Conservative philosopher, though its fruits are mostly yet to come, is in reviving the idea of a *trust* inherent in landed property. The land, the gift of nature, the source of subsistence to all, and the foundation of everything that influences our physical well-being, cannot be considered a subject of *property*, in the same absolute sense in which men are deemed proprietors of that in which no one has any interest but themselves – that which they have actually called into existence by their own bodily exertion. (p. 158)

This, Mill saw, was one of the many contributions Coleridge had made to the liberalisation of Conservatism, and desired changes must come 'not by the impracticable method of converting them [Conservatives] from Conservatives into Liberals, but by their being led to adopt one liberal opinion after another, as part of Conservatism itself'.

It is difficult to reach a balanced judgment on Mill as a social critic and as the author of the essays on Bentham and Coleridge. According to his biographer, Michael St. John Packe,

> The permanent value of the essays rests upon their exposition of Mill's concept of synthetic truth. For him, truth was no single element, but a gem of many faces, each capable of different, even contradictory appearances. . . . That any act of vision depends at least as much upon the situation and the circumstances of the seer as upon the object seen, was Mill's position in philosophy. (*Life*, 1954, p. 246)

This is well said. But, if we go on to ask why Mill ultimately failed in this particular act of synthesis, we are forced to conclude that he was trying to reconcile the irreconcilable. If it is true that every system of thought is grounded on a particular theory of the human mind (and this was certainly Mill's declared viewpoint), then you cannot graft what is best in Coleridge's idealist critique on to a mechanistic, pleasure/pain psychology, derived from Bentham. It is equally illogical to praise Bentham for his method and to ignore the fact that Coleridge wrote a treatise on method. Mill ignored it because Coleridge's idea of method was inextricably bound up with a view of the creative powers of the human mind that could not be confined within the Benthamite processes of classification and rational analysis. Coleridge's dynamic idea of method as 'unity with progression' transcended Bentham's inflexible rationalism. Once one recognises the magnitude of these two failures of understanding, one sees why Mill gradually turned from Coleridge in his later writings. There was no possibility of constructing a permanent and durable synthesis between the idealist and utilitarian approaches.

What was most valuable in Mill's later writings arose from his critical reaction to the theory of interest between the rulers and the ruled, first adumbrated by James Mill and Bentham. Although he called the theory of 'interest-begotten prejudice' Bentham's greatest service 'to the philosophy of universal human nature', that is, Bentham's illustration of 'the common tendency of man to make a duty and virtue of following self-interest', he saw that it was the basis of class-interest and class-morality, and slowly came to realise that the theory might be used to justify various forms of tyranny. At best the Benthamite identity of interest was an unreal ideal, at worst it might lead to the tyranny of the majority, to the sacrifice of all that made life human and valuable. The anti-Utopias of Zamyatin, Huxley and Orwell present societies in which human difference has been obliterated in favour of complete identity of interest; they thus take their place in a long line of works that explore the implications of the utilitarian tradition.

Towards the end of his life Mill saw the dangers and wrote his *Essay on Liberty* to explore them. It is therefore this work rather than the essays on Bentham and Coleridge that continues to live, because it is 'a monument to belief in intellectual liberty'. According to Noel Annan,

> It is a solemn reminder how important it is to keep alive the idea of *negative* liberty, that is to say the right to allow people to go their own way even if it is to hell. For although Mill thought that it was of importance not only what men do but what manner of men they are that do it, he also thought that individual spontaneity had a value in itself and he was not prepared to coerce men to realise their better selves.[8]

As we shall see in a later chapter, these are issues that continued to haunt men and reappear in different disguises in Dostoevsky's fable of the Grand Inquisitor, for instance, and in the right to be unhappy, demanded by John the Savage in Huxley's *Brave New World.* So many works of modern social criticism seem but amplifications of Mill's warning against 'the absorption of all the principal ability of the country into the governing body' (*On Liberty*, ch. 5) and his Johnsonian utterance: 'He who lets the world, or his own portion of it, choose his plan of life for him, has no need of any other faculty than the ape-like one of imitation' (*On Liberty*, ch. 2). On the basis of Mill's 'three dimensional rounded authentic quality' Isaiah Berlin believes that we can be sure how he would have stood on the issues of our own day. From the evidence of his early protests against sexual hypocrisy and from the evidence of the essay *On Liberty*, it is certainly safe to predict that he would have supported the move to reform the law relating to conduct between consenting adult homosexuals and that he would have said that the fact that there was disagreement about the literary merits of *Lady Chatterley's Lover* was sufficient reason to justify its publication, 'since the general or prevailing opinion on any subject is rarely or never the whole truth, it is only by collision of adverse opinions that the remainder of the truth has any chance of being supplied'.

Mill's strengths and limitations are reflected in his whole manner and style of writing, just as those of Hazlitt are reflected in his essays on Bentham and Coleridge in *The Spirit of the Age*, and those of Bentham and Coleridge in their own writing. Mill's prose is the perfect instrument for dispassionate enquiry into truth, but it lacks passion and imagination. He is always lucid, possesses remarkable powers of combining summary, analysis, and apt quotation; he is never assertive, hectoring, or abusive, as Carlyle frequently is. He writes for his intellectual equals; unlike Matthew Arnold, he never patronises or condescends. From time to time, the perfectly controlled temperate tone warms into something like passion, but it is intellectual passion, not political passion – not the heat of political passion that can so often either make or mar a passage of Hazlitt's writing. Mill's patient analysis of the merits and deficiences of his two subjects in the essays on Bentham and Coleridge is beautifully poised, scrupulously fair, altogether free from those showy paradoxes that Hazlitt so loves. But his writing lacks the dramatic power of Hazlitt's prose, its volatile movement, its compressed energy, its gusto, its sudden alternations of light and shade. It lacks, too, Coleridge's genius for simultaneous surprise and revelation, his speculative daring, his brilliant flashes of metaphoric illumination. And, if we turn to Mill's *Autobiography*, we find even there a certain imaginative debility, a failure to communicate the exact quality of the great crisis in his emotional and spiritual development. Certainly, the saint of rationalism paid a heavy price in acquiring his even serenity of mind and temperate prose style. He illuminates his subject, whatever it is, but he rarely fires his reader. He analyses but cannot create the informing image. To offer a complete vision of man and society one needs to be a complete man. This Mill never was; and his vision consequently suffers a corresponding impoverishment.

4 The Comic Spirit

At the beginning of the nineteenth century three writers attempted to define the spirit of the age. They were the Romantic essayist Hazlitt, the philosopher John Stuart Mill, and the comic novelist Thomas Love Peacock. It was Mill, as we have seen in the preceding chapter, who noted the novelty of the phrase and saw that it represented a new way of looking at society. The change noted by Mill is one part of the altered attitude to society that is the subject of this book. In recent times, Humphry House was the first critic to recognize the crucial importance and interconnection of the three writers, Hazlitt, Mill and Peacock. Of Peacock he wrote that he

> was doing in his own medium the sort of thing that Hazlitt was doing in the essays that were published as *The Spirit of the Age*; and Hazlitt is the best introduction to Peacock. What neither of them could do was done by John Stuart Mill's two essays on Bentham and Coleridge. Between the three of them there was the material for a great analytical satire that none of them ever wrote; yet in a way Peacock was nibbling at it all his life (*The Listener*, vol. 42, 8 Dec. 1949, p. 998).

To call Peacock a nibbler is to miss the broad sweep and incisive bite of his festive comedy. Better than any other writer in English, he illustrates that the spirit of comedy may tell us more about man and society than the 'gloomy science' of political economy.[1] His novels offer us images of social discord resolved into harmony by the genial influence of laughter and song.

For too long Peacock has enjoyed a dubious immortality as the friend of Shelley. He has greater claims to fame than that. And yet it is undoubtedly true that the most important event in his life was his meeting with Shelley. Only slightly less important was his introduction into Bentham's and Mills' circle of philosophical radicals. Peacock first met Shelley in London in 1812; he was then 27, Shelley only 20. A visit to Shelley and his friends at High Elms, Bracknell, a little later, exerted a formative influence on Peacock's art. Peacock describes the occasion in his *Memoirs of Percy Bysshe Shelley*:

> At Bracknell, Shelley was surrounded by a numerous society, all in a great measure of his own opinions in relation to religion and politics, and a large portion of them in relation to vegetable diet. But they wore their rue with a difference. Every one of them adopting some of the articles of the faith of their general church, had each nevertheless some predominant crotchet of his or her own (*Memoirs*, ed. Brett-Smith (Oxford, 1909), pp. 29–30).

The idea of the individual crotchet, or pet hobbyhorse, provided Peacock with matter for all his novels and the title of one, *Crotchet Castle*, published in 1831.

His stay at Bracknell contributed a number of crucial elements to his comic art. It contributed the idea of the house-party as a suitable setting for his feast of laughter. It contributed a fund of challenging and eccentric ideas from the conversation of the Shelley circle. And it contributed prototypes for his comic characters. Apart from Shelley himself, who becomes Scythrop, the central character in *Nightmare Abbey*, there was J. F. Newton, an astrologer and vegetarian, a man who thought that the world had steadily deteriorated since the golden age and who saw the intervention of the devil in all things. He of course becomes Mr Toobad in *Nightmare Abbey*: 'How can we be cheerful with the devil among us.'

Peacock's friendship with the Romantic poet Shelley and the rationalists Bentham and Mill is a reminder that he had an insider's view of the two great literary and political movements that he explored through his comic art. Like Mr Crotchet in *Crotchet Castle*, he was drawn to the great ideological issues of his day. These Mr Crotchet says are: 'The sentimental against the rational, the intuitive against the inductive, the ornamental against the useful, the intense against the tranquil, the romantic against the classical.' But, unlike Mr Crotchet, who wished to see 'these great and interesting controversies' settled before he died, Peacock knew that, of their nature, they could never be settled.

Peacock laughs at the excesses of both schools of thought, but he shares a good deal of common ground with each. The portraits of Coleridge as the transcendental philosopher Mr Flosky, and of MacCulloch (the Malthusian economist) as Mr MacQuedy, ridiculous as they are, could only have been written by someone with insider's knowledge. No one has caught better Coleridge's tangential relation to ordinary life, his defensive opacities and verbal mannerisms. In *Nightmare Abbey*, the beautiful Marionetta, perturbed at her cousin Scythrop's strange behaviour, breaks in on Mr Flosky's private transcendental meditations, to ask him if he can clear up the mystery. As Mr Flosky weaves finer and finer philosophical distinctions, she becomes more and more exasperated.

Marionetta: Will you oblige me, Mr Flosky, by giving me a plain answer to a plain question.

Mr Flosky: It is impossible, my dear Miss O'Carroll. I never gave a plain answer to a question in my life.

Marionetta: Do you, or do you not, know what is the matter with my cousin?

Mr Flosky: To say that I do not, would be to say that I am ignorant of something; and God forbid, that a transcendental metaphysician, who has pure anticipated cognitions of everything, and carries the whole science of geometry in his head without ever having looked into Euclid, should fall into so empirical an error as to declare himself ignorant of anything: to say that I do know, would be to pretend to positive and circumstantial knowledge touching present matter of fact, which, when you consider the nature of evidence, and the various lights in which the same thing may be seen –

Marionetta: I see, Mr Flosky, that either you have no information, or are determined not to impart it, and I beg your pardon for having given you this unnecessary trouble.

Mr Flosky: My dear Miss O'Carroll, it would have given me great pleasure to have said anything that would have given pleasure; but if any person living could make report of having obtained any information on any subject from Ferdinando Flosky, my transcendental reputation would be ruined for ever. (*Novels*, p. 397)

Comic in tone and purpose it conveys a serious criticism of Coleridge. Several years ago I concluded a book on Coleridge's political thought with two sentences that endorse the essential rightness of Peacock's estimate.

> As long as Coleridge was sure that his words were unlikely to be fully understood he could convince himself that they contained invaluable truths. The use of a less complex style might well have attracted more readers; it would certainly have exposed him to the embarrassment of being generally understood; with what beneficial results it is perhaps idle to speculate.

Two anecdotes, outside the novels, further illustrate Peacock's insight into the blind sides of his Romantic friends and rational allies. When the youthful vegetarian Shelley was living off tea and bread and butter, occasionally drinking a sort of spurious home-made lemonade, Peacock offered to prescribe for his ill-health. 'What would be your prescription?' asked Shelley. 'Three mutton chops, well peppered.' 'Do you really think so?' asked Shelley. 'I am sure of it,' said Peacock. Shelley took the prescription: the success was obvious and immediate.

On another occasion, Peacock was dining at a country inn with the arch-rationalist, James Mill, and 'the beefsteak being very tough, came in for round abuse'. Mill gave a series of reasons that proved that it should be tender, and so declared that it was. 'Yes,' said Peacock, 'but, as usual, all the reason is on your side, and the proof on mine.' The evidence of these anecdotes, and of the novels themselves, suggests that it is unwise to label Peacock either anti-romantic or anti-utilitarian. In fact, he sought a synthesis between the two extremes, in a spirit of high comedy, a comedy in which laughter, feasting, dancing and song play an important part.

With Peacock the novel of ideas came into its own. But he was not the first to use the novel for the discussion of ideas. Thomas Day had used it for airing his views on education in *Sandford and Merton* (1783–9), and William Godwin's novels, *Caleb Williams* (1794) and *St Leon* (1799), reflect and debate political ideas; so too does Robert Bage's *Hermsprong* (1798). But in spite of these predecessors, we can say that it was Peacock who created the novel of ideas; it was with him that the *roman á clef*, the novel that refers to real people, was launched on its long career in England.

In *Headlong Hall*, the first of his novels, published in 1815, all the essential features of his art are already present. There is the house-party and convivial atmosphere, with a table groaning under the weight of good food and wine. Food and drink, we might notice, play a crucial role in Peacock's festive comedy, since they come to symbolise the well-balanced temperament, a cultivated epicureanism, the virtues represented by the jovial Mr Hilary in *Nightmare Abbey* and represented, too, by many of Peacock's accommodating divines, as ready to drink a bottle of port with squire as green tea with his lady. There is the coincidental gathering of a large group of eccentric characters, each representing some extreme oddity of behaviour – some crotchet, in other words. Mr Milestone, for instance, represents the passion for new effects in landscape gardening, a passion for rocks 'cut into the shape of a giant', and similar monstrosities. The novel is mainly in the form of dialogue and is thus set out. By all these means, Peacock creates his characters and sets in motion the clash of opinion that is the life-blood of his art. The best example of this clash comes, not from *Headlong Hall*, but from a much later novel, *Crotchet Castle*. In a chapter headed 'Theories', and prefaced by a couplet from Butler's *Hudibras*,

> But when they came to shape the model
> Not one could fit the other's noddle,

young Mr Crotchet marks the end of the dinner by initiating a lively discussion on the subject of money. In the course of the discussion, each of the characters addresses the company, oblivious of the other speakers, each pulls out a scroll, a diagram, or a paper to illustrate his point. Mr MacQuedy the Scottish Malthusian economist, Mr Toogood, the champion of Owenite cooperative distribution, Mr Skionar, the transcendental philosopher, and Mr Trillo, who, like the City Fathers of Sydney, believes that all the troubles in the world can be solved by building opera houses. With touching naivete, Mr Crotchet opens the discussion:

> Mr Crotchet, Jun.: There is one point in which philosophers of all classes seem to be agreed; that they only want money to regenerate the world.
> Mr MacQuedy: No doubt of it. Nothing is so easy as to lay down the outlines of perfect society. There wants nothing but money to set it going. I will explain myself clearly and fully by reading a paper. (*Producing a large scroll.*) 'In the infancy of society —'
> The Rev Dr Folliott: Pray, Mr MacQuedy, how is it that all gentlemen of your nation begin every thing they write with the 'infancy of society'?
> Mr MacQuedy: Eh, sir, it is the simplest way to begin at the beginning. 'In the infancy of society, when government was invented to save a percentage; say two and a half per cent. —'
> The Rev Dr Folliott: I will not say any such thing.
> Mr MacQuedy: Well, say any percentage you please.
> The Rev Dr Folliott: I will not say any percentage at all.
> Mr MacQuedy: 'On the principle of the division of labour —'
> The Rev Dr Folliott: Government was invented to spend a percentage.
> Mr MacQuedy: To save a percentage.
> The Rev Dr Folliott: No, sir, to spend a percentage; and a good deal more than two and a half per cent. Two hundred and fifty per cent.; that is intelligible.
> Mr MacQuedy: 'In the infancy of society —'
> Mr Toogood: Never mind the infancy of society. The question is of society in its maturity. Here is what it should be. (*Producing a paper.*) I have laid it down in a diagram.
> Mr Skionar: Before we proceed to the question of government, we must nicely discriminate the boundaries of sense, understanding, and reason. Sense is a receptivity — (*Novels*, pp. 685–7).

The discussion speeds up towards the end to achieve a succinct contrapuntal climax:

> Mr MacQuedy: Very true, sir (*reproducing his scroll*). 'In the infancy of society —'

Mr Toogood: The reverend gentleman has hit the nail on the head. It is the distribution that must be looked to: it is the *paterfamilias* that is wanting in the state. Now here I have provided him. (*Reproducing his diagram.*)

Mr Trillo: Apply the money, sir, to building and endowing an opera house, where the ancient altar of Bacchus may flourish, and justice may be done to sublime compositions. (*Producing a part of a manuscript opera.*)

Mr Skionar: No, sir, build *sacella* for transcendental oracles to teach the world how to see through a glass darkly. (*Producing a scroll.*)

Mr Trillo: See through an opera-glass brightly.

The Rev Dr Folliott: See through a wine-glass, full of claret: then you see both darkly and brightly. But, gentlemen, if you are all in the humour for reading papers, I will read you the first half of my next Sunday's sermon. (*Producing a paper.*)

Omnes: No sermon! No sermon!

The Rev Dr Folliott: Then I move that our respective papers be committed to our respective pockets. (*Novels*, p. 688)

Here we see Peacock's skill in arranging speeches to reflect rapidly a wide variety of views and to demonstrate that each character inhabits his own intellectual world, pursues his own line of argument with insane single-mindedness. We also notice that the arrangement, the grouping, and the timing are very reminiscent of operatic set-pieces. Peacock, like his character Mr Trillo, had a passion for opera. He was an early advocate for the complete playing of Mozart's *Don Giovanni* and an early champion of Beethoven's *Fidelio*, as 'the absolute perfection of dramatic music'.

The plot, in most of Peacock's novels, is minimal. It is a mere springboard for comic incident and good conversation. As the obituary notice in *The Athenaeum* remarked, 'he never tried for plot'. Yet *Nightmare Abbey* is an exception. The movement towards the climax reveals superb economy and comic control of plot. Throughout the novel, Scythrop is the victim of high-minded vacillation. Scythrop is a man who has written a work called *Philosophical Gas*, which has sold seven copies, just as Shelley's *Necessity of Atheism* sold only seven copies. He is an excitable and imaginative young man, who is as unable to chose between Marionetta O'Carroll and Celinda Toobad as Shelley was unable to chose between Harriet and Mary in real life. Near the end of the novel, in Scythrop's secluded and lofty tower, the two young ladies confront each other for the first time, and formally renounce the young regenerator of the world:

'He is not my choice, sir. This lady has a prior claim: I renounce him.'

> 'And I renounce him,' said Marionetta.
>
> Scythrop knew not what to do. He could not attempt to conciliate the one without irreparably offending the other; and he was so fond of both, that the idea of depriving himself for ever of the society of either was intolerable to him: he therefore retreated into his stronghold, mystery; maintained an impenetrable silence; and contented himself with stealing occasionally a deprecating glance at each of the object of his idolatry (*Novels*, p. 426).

A little later Mr Glowry asks Scythrop 'And pray, sir, who is your love?' to which Scythrop answers: 'Celinda — Marionetta — either — both.' In the final chapter, the two letters, bearing the married surnames Celinda *Flosky* and Marionetta *Listless*, signify that, even if Scythrop cannot make up his mind, the young ladies can, and have. Mr Glowry draws the obvious moral. 'And next time,' he tells Scythrop, 'have but one string to your bow.' The final paragraph marks Scythrop's ultimate rejection of romantic passion and melancholy in favour of civilised balance and convivial joy. At first, intent on suicide like the young Werter, he despatches the lugubrious butler, Raven, for a pint of port and a pistol:

> Raven appeared. Scythrop looked at him very fiercely two or three minutes; and Raven, still remembering the pistol, stood quaking in mute apprehension, till Scythrop, pointing significantly towards the dining-room, said, 'Bring some Madeira.'

Here, the last words of the novel neatly connect Scythrop's return to sanity with his return to food and drink. The comedy, which is aimed as much at Godwin's misanthropic novel *Mandeville* as against Byronic gloom,[2] restores the isolated individual to society, through a return to the festive board.

Music and dance are as important as food and drink in creating Peacock's feast of laughter. We can see this in *Nightmare Abbey*, a novel written to laugh at 'the darkness and misanthropy' of romantic literature. In this novel, the musical catch 'Seamen three! What men ye be', sung by Mr Hilary and the Reverend Mr Larynx, with its rollicking refrains, 'In a bowl Care may not be' and 'And our ballast is old wine', provides the necessary festive comment on Mr Cypress's gloomy song, 'There is a fever of the spirit/The brand of Cain's unresting doom', a parody that out-Byrons Byron in its morbid melancholy:

> There is a fever of the spirit,
> The brand of Cain's unresting doom,
> Which in the lone dark souls that bear it
> Glows like the lamp in Tullia's tomb:

Unlike that lamp, its subtle fire
  Burns, blasts, consumes its cell, the heart,
Till, one by one, hope, joy, desire,
  Like dreams of shadowy smoke depart.

When hope, love, life itself, are only
  Dust – spectral memories – dead and cold –
The unfed fire burns bright and lonely,
  Like that undying lamp of old:
And by that drear illumination,
  Till time its clay-built home has rent,
Thought broods on feeling's desolation –
  The soul is its own monument

(*Novels*, p. 414).

Byron appreciated Peacock's art and sent his congratulations, and a rosebud. In *Crotchet Castle*, a novel about schemes for regenerating the world, Mr Trillo's song comes to an end with the lines

And we'll sit till day, but we'll find the way
To drench the world with wine.

Peacock makes the single comment – it is the last sentence of the chapter – 'the schemes for the world's regeneration evaporated in the tumult of voices'. Here, music, wine and song place the romantic dream of perfectibility in its true perspective.

At times Peacock commands a robust, Shakespearean brand of humour. In the little-read *Misfortunes of Elphin*, a novel set in Wales in the time of King Arthur, he creates a magnificent Falstaffian drunkard in Prince Seithenyn. Two men enter the Welsh castle, in the middle of a drinking song, when the chief roisterer is already seeing double:

The chorus had scarcely ended when Seithenyn noticed {the two men], and immediately roared aloud, 'You are welcome all four.' Elphin answered, 'I thank you; we are but two.'
'Two or four,' said Seithenyn, 'all is one. You are welcome all. When a stranger enters, the custom in other places is to begin by washing his feet. My custom is, to begin by washing his throat. Seithenyn ap Seithyn Saidi bids you welcome' (*Novels*, p. 559).

In addition to this Shakespearean largeness of humour, Peacock also had an eye for comic gesture and movement, that is very reminiscent of the author of *Tristram Shandy*, Laurence Sterne. In *Crotchet Castle*, a heated discussion on Greek art between Mr Crotchet and the Rev Dr Folliott breaks off with a comic description.

> 'God bless my soul, sir!' exclaimed the Reverend Doctor Folliott, throwing himself back into a chair, and flinging up his heels, with the premeditated design of giving emphasis to his exclamation: but by miscalculating his *impetus*, he overbalanced his chair, and laid himself on the carpet in a right angle, of which his back was the base (*Novels*, p. 702).

The final mathematical allusion gives the farcical situation a sharpness and scholarly edge.

The most sustained piece of humour in this vein is the account of the drunken prince in *The Misfortunes of Elphin* as he 'straightens himself into perpendicularity'.

> He accomplished half his object by stiffening all his joints but those of his ancles, and from these the rest of his body vibrated upwards with the inflexibility of a bar. After thus oscillating for a time, like an inverted pendulum, finding that the attention requisite to preserve his rigidity absorbed all he could collect of his dissipated energies, and that he required a portion of them for the management of his voice, which he felt a dizzy desire to wield with peculiar steadiness in the presence of the son of the king, he suddenly relaxed the muscles that perform the operation of sitting, and dropped into his chair like a plummet. He then, with a gracious gesticulation, invited Prince Elphin to take his seat on his right hand, and proceeded to compose himself into a dignified attitude, throwing his body into the left corner of his chair, resting his left elbow on its arm and his left cheekbone on the middle of the back of his left hand, placing his left leg on a footstool, and stretching out his right leg as straight and as far as his position allowed. He had thus his right hand at liberty, for the ornament of his eloquence and the conduct of his liquor (*Novels*, pp. 559–60).

One of Peacock's favourite devices for reinforcing the point of his humour is to bring his characters into sudden ridiculous collision. This happens to good effect in *Nightmare Abbey*. Scythrop, in single-minded pursuit of the elusive Marionetta, 'at an ill-omened corner, where two corridors ended in an angle, at the head of a staircase, . . . came into sudden and violent contact with Mr Toobad, and they both plunged together to the foot of the stairs, like two billiard balls into one pocket. . . . "You see," says Mr Toobad, "my dear Scythrop, in this little incident, one of the innumerable proofs of the temporary supremacy of the devil." ' The lines cross, but each crank continues in the course of his own loquacious eccentricity.

A good deal of the humour for humour's sake arises from such farcical incidents; but, in his more serious satire, Peacock rarely invents farcical actions to satirise political events. Political ideas, not political events, are his main object; and his attack is usually oblique. Thus in *The Misfortunes of Elphin* the drunken prince's long argument that no changes should be made in the rotten embankment built to keep the waters out of his kingdom is an oblique attack on George Canning's defence of the unreformed English parliament. Seithenyn ends his speech: 'the parts that are rotten give elasticity to those that are sound: they give them elasticity, elasticity, elasticity . . . this immortal work [the embankment] has stood for centuries, and it will stand for centuries more, if we let it alone. It is well: it works well: let well alone. Cupbearer, fill.' Although the object of Peacock's satire was Canning's irrational defence of a corrupt, outworn parliamentary system, the satire rises above its local and temporary occasion. It characterises an attitude of mind, an attitude of mind which is just as likely to appear in the defence of the anachronisms of Trade Unionism or sex discrimination, as in the defence of the pre-1832 English Parliament.

Only in his novel *Melincourt* does Peacock anticipate Disraeli's method in *Sybil* (Disraeli hailed him as his master) and Dickens's method in *Hard Times*. In *Melincourt*, Peacock invented a farcical town 'the borough of One Vote' to satirise political corruption. In this novel we meet Peacock's most original creation, Sir Oran Haut-ton, a specimen of the natural and original man, who, by a fine irony, is the only Peacock character incapable of speech. The climax of the election ends thus:

> Sir Oran Haut-ton, Baronet, and Simon Sarcastic, Esquire, were nominated in form. Mr Christopher Corporate held up both his hands, with his tankard in one, and his pipe in the other: and neither poll nor scrutiny being demanded, the two candidates were pronounced duly elected, as representatives of the ancient and honourable borough of One Vote (*Novels*, p. 232).

Methods in modern elections are more complicated but the results are no less absurd.

Two of Peacock's favourite objects of ridicule were romantic excess, first encountered in Shelley, and the belief in the inevitability of progress, a belief epitomised in such phrases as 'the march of mind', and 'the steam intellect society', the latter invented to ridicule Lord Brougham's Society for the Diffusion of Useful Knowledge:

> 'God bless my soul, sir!' exclaimed the Reverend Doctor Folliott, bursting, one fine May morning, into the breakfast-room at Crotchet Castle, 'I am out of all patience with this march of mind. Here has my house been nearly burned down, by my cook taking it into her head to study hydrostatics, in a sixpenny tract, published by the

> Steam Intellect Society, and written by a learned friend who is for doing all the world's business as well as his own (*Novels*, pp. 655–6).

In view of the repeated attacks on the steam intellect society, it was a strange irony of fate that Peacock should have become the East India Company's expert on steam navigation, and filled no less than forty files on the subject. In his various novels, he ridiculed the facile belief in the talismanic effects of science, he made fun of the opponents of parliamentary reform, he laughed at the system of competitive examination in the civil service and showed that this system would have rejected all the great men of the world. But his most constant source of laughter came from lectures, lecturers, and university education. As Peacock once wisely remarked: 'Great must be his desire for improvement who can withstand an academical education.'

His last novel, *Gryll Grange*, published when he was seventy, reveals that the range and variety of genial prejudices remained as great as ever. What differentiates Peacock from his characters, however, is that he is aware of his own prejudices. His characters, on the other hand, are not and pursue their eccentric courses with relentless and ludicrous single-mindedness. The secret of Peacock's art lies in his recognition that liberal thought, which should, in theory, lead to tolerance and wide views, in fact produces a fanaticism bordering on madness. An illustration of this is Mr Fax, a Malthusian, and early advocate of Zero Population Growth.

> The cause of all the evils of human society is single, obvious, reducible to the most exact mathematical calculation; and of course susceptible not only of remedy, but even of utter annihilation. The cause is the tendency of population to increase beyond the means of subsistence. The remedy is an universal social compact, binding both sexes to equally rigid celibacy, till the prospect of maintaining the average number of six children be as clear as the arithmetic of futurity can make it (*Novels*, pp. 141–2).

If one turns up the pages of Malthus's *Essay on Population*, one finds that Peacock sticks remarkably closely to the original argument and the tone of Malthus's *Essay*: but what he does also, of course, is to exaggerate its inherent absurdities, its neglect of ordinary human nature, and then add the final epigrammatic touch with the masterly phrase 'as clear as the arithmetic of futurity can make it'. Without to-day a Peacock to laugh us back to our senses, we now idolise the writers and TV personalities who claim to be experts in the arithmetic of futurity.

Behind all Peacock's novels there lies a paradox. The world that we see is the green world of comedy, a world of idyllic seclusion; the world that we hear about is its exact opposite. It is one of conflict and activity, the busy world brought into being by industry, liberal thought, political theory, and rapid economic change. What happens in these novels is that the spokesmen for the regeneration of mankind, for Malthusian population theories, *laissez-faire* economics, Scottish philosophy, and all the other lost causes of the nineteenth century, are removed from their natural urban environment and set talking in an atmosphere in which the ideals are not progress or the creation of an ideal society, but the simple Horatian virtues: contentment, fortitude, the golden mean. Peacock's own ideal seems to be summed up by the Reverend Dr Opimian, in Peacock's last novel, *Gryll Grange*: they are 'the possession of a good library, good food, a pleasant garden and rural walks'. In the novels, the effect of placing the loquacious urban eccentrics in such an Arcadian world is to distance them and to impart an air of unreality to their serious talk, an unreality further stressed by parody, burlesque and irony. Laughter dispels their pretensions. The grim Scottish economist, Mr MacQuedy, pontificates on laughter when he says that reason is in no way essential to mirth, and when he adds that the savage never laughs he stands self-condemned. In this case, Peacock speaks through Dr Folliott and for his own art

> Rev Dr Folliott: No, sir, he has nothing to laugh at. Give him Modern Athens, the 'learned friend', and the Steam Intellect Society. They will develop his muscles.

Ultimately what does Peacock stand for? Nothing, according to one hostile critic, because he lacked a central set of values:

> To port lay the fleet of progress, to starboard the fleet of reaction; and so irresponsible was the steering of this formidable vessel that when it let off a broadside it was toss-up which of the opposing fleet took the weight of it.[3]

It was not quite toss-up, I would suggest. Peacock did have a central set of values, and he defined them in an essay on Epicurus in the *Westminster Review* in 1827: that happiness is the end of life; that there is no happiness without pleasure; and that the true and only permanent pleasure of man is peace of body and mind. He saw clearly that there was a basic incongruity in the philosophies of both the Utilitarians and the Romantics. The Utilitarians, advocates of the greatest happiness for the greatest number, believers in the pleasure/pain principle, seemed curiously unacquainted with either happiness or pleasure. And their plans seemed likely to reduce man to an anonymous economic unit. On the other hand, the Romantics, advocates of passion, imagination and freedom, often succeeded only in enslaving themselves by their plans for regenerating the world. Faced with a choice between such extremes,

Peacock rejected both, and opted for private happiness, individual liberty and festive joy. It wasn't a bad choice. In Ray Bradbury's *Fahrenheit 451*, Peacock takes his place among the immortals, sandwiched between Confucius and Thomas Jefferson. To place Peacock in the literary hierarchy, one can say that he was a Regency Rabelais, Victorian Voltaire, with all the limitations those period labels suggest. What he aspired to be was a modern Aristophanes. Only classical scholars can decide how well he succeeded. But what is certain is that his novels prove that comedy can be as effective a criticism of society as discursive prose or realistic fiction.

5 The 'Condition of England' Question

The first critics of the industrial revolution and the Condition of England were the Romantic poets, Blake, Wordsworth, Coleridge and Southey. Their actual knowledge of the details of industrialism was severely limited, but their prophetic insight into its dehumanising effects on the whole society was deep and far-sighted. Blake wrote of the 'Satanic mills', and believed that the industrial revolution was the natural consequence of the limited and perverted rationalism of the eighteenth century.

> I turn my eyes to the schools and Universities of Europe
> And there behold the Loom of Locke, whose Woof rages dire,
> Wash'd by the Water-wheels of Newton: black the cloth
> In heavy wreathes folds over every Nation: cruel Works
> Of many Wheels I view, wheel without wheel, with cogs tyrannic
> Moving by compulsion each other, not as those in Eden, which,
> Wheel within Wheel, in freedom revolve in harmony and peace
> (*Jerusalem*, plate 15, 14–20).

Here, Blake contrasts the factory cog-wheels ('wheel without wheel') with the divine harmony of Ezekial's vision ('Wheel within Wheel'), a harmony, he suggests in his work as a whole, to be achieved on earth through imagination and the four-fold vision, and not through false reason (Urizen) and single vision (Newton's sleep). Wordsworth, although he lived most of his life in the Lake District and not in industrial Manchester, wrote feelingly about the disastrous consequences of the factory system on family life and the domestic arts. His account in the *Excursion* (1814) foreshadows similar descriptions in Samuel Bamford's *Passages in the Life of a Radical*, a first-hand account of life around Manchester, and also passages in Mrs Gaskell's novel *Mary Barton*. Wordsworth's criticism in 1814 was substantiated by the circumstantial reports made by the factory inspectors and doctors in Government Blue Books, after the setting up of the Children's Employment Commission by Lord Ashley in 1841. It was on the more sensational passages in the Blue Books that Disraeli drew in *Sybil* for his account of Hatton's brutal treatment of the child workers. The evidence given by a fifteen-year-old

Willenhall boy to one of the factory inspectors supplied Disraeli with vivid details. The boy is reported as saying:

> His master beats him very much at a time, and very often; the neighbours who live agen the shop will say how his master beats him; beats him with a strap, and sometimes a nut-stick; sometimes the wales remain upon him for a week; his master once cut his eyelid open, cut a hole in it, and it bled all over his files that he was working with.

In *Sybil*, Tummas complains of Hatton's treatment at Wodgate: 'Many's the ash stick he has broken on my body; sometimes the weals remained on me for a week; he cut my eyelid open once with a nut-stick; cut a regular hole in it, and it bled all over the files I was working at.'[1]

Although the borrowed phrases give simple authenticity to these pages in Disraeli's novel, such documentary realism was not sufficient in itself to constitute a radical criticism of the industrial system.

By contrast, Coleridge's image of society was both philosophical and practical. It was philosophic in the sense that it related the dehumanising process to the current utilitarian philosophy that regarded men as means and not ends in themselves. 'But the distinction between person and thing consists herein, that the latter may rightfully be used, altogether and merely, as a *means*; but the former must always be included in the *end*, and form a part of the final cause.'[2] It was practical to the extent that it was based on the observation of sweated labour and took the form of pamphlets addressed to Sir Robert Peel the Elder, in support of his Bills to regulate child labour in the factories. Southey, for all his conversion from extreme radicalism to Toryism, was also a forceful critic of the manufacturing system. His *Letters from England*, an account of the condition of England in 1807 as seen through the eyes of the imaginary Spanish visitor, Don Manuel Espriella, gives a vivid account of child labour in Lancashire, where children, overworked and poorly fed, either die or grow up 'without decency, without comfort, and without hope, without morals, without religion, and without shame, and bring forth slaves like themselves to tread in the same path of misery' (ch. 38). In the later *Colloquies on the Progress and Prospects of Society* (1829), he summed up the malignant tendencies of the manufacturing system in vivid phrases:

> A people may be too rich; because it is the tendency of the commercial, and more especially of the manufacturing system, to collect wealth rather than to diffuse it. Where wealth is successfully employed in any of the speculations of trade, its increase is in proportion to its amount; great capitalists become like pikes in a fish-

> pond, who devour the weaker fish; and it is but too certain that the poverty of one part of the people seems to increase in the same ratio as the riches of the other.[3]

Perceptive and sometimes prophetic as the criticism of Blake, Wordsworth and Southey indeed was, it was Coleridge of all the Romantic writers who had the most pervasive and far-reaching effect on the political and social thought of the nineteenth-century. His influence came partly through such works as the *Friend*, the two *Lay Sermons*, and *Church and State*, but also as his ideas were mediated through the distorting medium of Carlyle's powerful but idiosyncratic prose.

In some respects Carlyle is a key figure in nineteenth-century intellectual history and it is fortunate that a representative selection of his writings is now available in paperback.[4] Apart from his strong influence on Disraeli, Dickens, and Mrs Gaskell (she quotes him on the title page of *Mary Barton*), his ideas form a crucial link with the organic social theories of Burke and Coleridge and also with the instinctive worship of power and authority that we meet later on in Lawrence and many crypto-fascist writers. Carlyle's worship of the hero in *Heroes and Hero Worship* (1841) is dangerously similar to the blind obedience demanded by the modern leader-principle. But it is not that side of his work that is of concern here.

The two works that had greatest influence on the Victorian Condition of England Novel were *Signs of the Times* and *Chartism*. *Signs of the Times*, reminiscent in tone and argument of Coleridge's *Lay Sermons* (1816 and 1817), was published anonymously in 1829. It may be regarded as the first sustained protest against the attitudes that were to become a dogma for Victorian materialism, anticipating such works as Ruskin's *Unto This Last* (1862) and Matthew Arnold's *Culture and Anarchy* (1869). The other powerfully influential work, *Chartism*, was written ten years later, in 1839, in response to the widespread agitation for support of the Chartists and their demand for universal suffrage, among other things. In it Carlyle analyses the causes of industrial unrest with great penetration. But he has little to offer in the way of a solution, apart from a mystique of authority and obedience, a mystique that undoubtedly seems more repellent to us today than it did to his contemporary readers.

Like Coleridge in his *Lay Sermons*, Carlyle warns the reader of *Signs of the Times* against false prophets, remarking 'At such a period, it was to be expected that the rage of prophecy should be more than usually excited' (p. 63). Apparently unaware of the inconsistency, he launches into his own prophetic analysis of the age. He writes:

> Were we required to characterise this age of ours by any single epithet, we should be tempted to call it, not an Heroical, Devotional,

> Philosophical, or Moral Age, but, above all others, the Mechanical Age. It is the Age of Machinery, in every outward and inward sense of that word; the age which, with its whole undivided might, forwards, teaches and practises the great art of adapting means to ends. Nothing is now done directly, or by hand; all is by rule and calculated contrivance. . . . On every hand, the living artisan is driven from his workshop, to make room for a speedier, inanimate one. The shuttle drops from the finger of the weaver, and falls into iron fingers that ply it faster.

Of special interest in this passage are the Coleridgean attacks upon machinery and the mechanical spirit of the age, and the use of the particular metaphor 'iron fingers', so reminiscent of the whole Coleridge habit of seeing society in contrasting vital and mechanical images. Two other features of Carlyle's *Signs of the Times* are worth noticing. The first is the general thesis that the mechanical spirit has infected not a part but every aspect of society. It has affected education, which has become mechanised instruction; religion, which has developed a vast machinery for collecting money and creating rival Bible societies; national culture, which has become devitalised; theories of government, which specifically speak of 'Society as a great Machine'; and the life of the individual, so that, 'Men are grown mechanical in head and in heart as well as in hand. . . . Not for internal perfection, but for external combinations . . . for Mechanism of one sort or another, do they hope and struggle' (*Selected Writings*, p. 67). The phrase 'in head and in heart' establishes the link with Coleridge, for whom the antithesis was a favourite, while the phrase 'internal perfection' foreshadows Arnold's ideal in *Culture and Anarchy*. What immediately strikes us, then, in *Signs of the Times* is the remarkable comprehensiveness of Carlyle's social analysis; it was his coherent structure of ideas, William Oddie suggests,[5] rather than any particular thought, that influenced Dickens, that gave him 'a nucleus around which his own ideas could form', and which provided him with 'a mirror by which to recognize their shape'. And much the same may be said of his influence on other novelists of the period.

The second major feature of *Signs of the Times* to notice is that Carlyle is not opposed to industrial progress as such, only to the total mechanisation of society. In general he accepts industrialism as one of man's heroic achievements and recognises its vast potentiality for good. In this respect he differs markedly from William Morris, who dreams of escaping into a pre-industrial society, Merry England, in his Utopian romance, *News from Nowhere.* Apologisers for Morris may claim that the dream is only a metaphor and not a vain attempt to reverse the historical process, but men find it difficult to live a whole life on a metaphor, especially one so insubstantial as Morris's.

But metaphors may become powerful agents of rhetorical persuasion.

And in *Sartor Resartus* (p. 107), Carlyle asks the rhetorical question 'what, if you except some few primitive elements (of natural sound), what is it all but Metaphors?' One critic, Mark Roberts,[6] has drawn special attention to the function of metaphor in Carlyle, and has concluded by saying that 'Carlyle's writing at its best, is always tending to the condition of symbol', and 'what I have called the "rhetoric of unreason" is in fact the rhetoric of a man who wishes, in his writing, to do what symbolism alone can do'. It is already apparent from the discussion so far that Carlyle raises the word 'Mechanical' to the level of a potent symbol and it is this metaphoric, symbolic element that links Carlyle's writing most clearly with that of Dickens in *Hard Times* and, to a lesser extent, to that of Disraeli, Mrs Gaskell, and Charles Kingsley.

Of special interest in connection with the work of these novelists are Carlyle's two prose works, *Chartism* (1839) and *Past and Present* (1843). In the year that *Chartism* appeared the Chartists presented their national petition to Parliament. Kingsley describes this in chapter 34 of *Alton Locke*. Its six points were duly rejected. These points were: universal male suffrage, equal electoral districts, removal of members' property qualifications, payment of members of parliament, the secret ballot and annual general elections. All except the last – annual elections – have now been accepted. Yet at the time, the demands seemed extreme. Until relatively recently, historians have interpreted Chartism as 'an inchoate rebellion against economic misery', instead of what it largely was, 'the response of a literate and sophisticated working class'.[7]

It is in *Chartism* that Carlyle coins the phrase 'The Condition of England Question'; and much the best parts are concerned with an analysis of the actual state of affairs in England and the ineffectiveness of such measures as the New Poor Law in bringing about an improvement. Both his paternalism and his deep humanity appear in the first chapter, in his appeal to the upper classes and in his pity for the struggles of the 'inarticulate poor' – 'dumb creatures in pain, unable to speak what is in them'. Mrs Gaskell re-echoes these exact phrases in her Preface to *Mary Barton* in saying that she is anxious to give 'utterance to the agony which . . . convulses this dumb people' (pp. 37–8). Like many subsequent writers in revolt against the Utilitarian tradition, Carlyle points out that the purely statistical approach to social problems can provide no adequate panacea, since statistics can be made to prove anything. In chapter 4, he comes near to enunciating the right to work as a sacred principle: 'A man willing to work, and unable to find work, is perhaps the saddest sight that Fortune's inequality exhibits under this sun.' Mrs Gaskell actually embodies this truth in the plight of John Barton. In chapter 10 John cries out to Mary 'I don't want money, child! D – m their charity and their money! I want work, and it is my right. I want work' (Penguin p. 159). Carlyle's comments on the effects of employing Irish labourers on the English working class are relevant to another of Mrs Gaskell's novels, *North and South.* In this novel Mr Thornton's use of Irish labour leads to the major crisis in the plot. Again, Carlyle's generous humanity and insight into essentials appears in the simple statement in chapter 5: 'It is the feeling of *injustice* that is insupportable to all men'; and he follows this with sombre reflections on the brutal injustices that working men have been driven into through union, association, and trial of members. Before condemning Carlyle as a hysterical reactionary, we need to remember what the novelists have to tell us about the effect of early unionism on the personal lives of its members, Mrs Gaskell through John Barton for example. A somewhat similar fate befalls Hyacinth Robinson in Henry James's *The Princess Casamassima*, but this time at the hands of anarchists, not unionists. It is clear that both Mrs Gaskell and James are dealing with something more universal than the function of unions or anarchists. They are exploring the most intense crisis of conscience, when political duties appear to run counter to and actually destroy our basic humanity. Shakespeare explores this universal theme in the History plays and in the Roman plays. What stands out most clearly in the whole of Carlyle's *Chartism* is his attack on the *laissez-faire* philosophy of nineteenth-century liberalism, his recognition that a philosophy of society founded on cash payment as the 'sole nexus of man to man' must inevitably lead to the debasement of all. In this section of *Chartism*, the contrast of the present with a feudal system, based on personal worth and acknowledged duties, foreshadows his method in his next book *Past and Present*, where the Abbot Samson comes to represent a social order embodying humane values. In the creation of such characters as the Abbot Samson to represent this feudal order, and Plugson of Undershot to represent the victory of the 'cash nexus', Carlyle is halfway towards becoming a novelist.

Carlyle is a central figure in any study of the writer as critic of society. His analysis is intensely powerful, and passionately conceived. He is the type-figure of the Victoria Sage.[8] He forms a link with Coleridge and Arnold; and unfortunately, through his last works, *Latter Day Pamphlets* and *Shooting Niagara*, with modern champions of the leader principle. What he says frequently parallels what the great novelists say. His influence on Mrs Gaskell, Disraeli and Dickens was great, as Cazamian fully demonstrates in *The Social Novel in England 1830–50.* In addition his works raise for us in an acute form that central problem, which has yet to be solved – how to create a society based on man's relation to man, instead of the cash nexus, without either falling into anarchy or taking refuge in totalitarian rule either of the left or the right.

When we look at the nineteenth-century novelists who used the novel as a vehicle for social criticism we see immediately that there are wide differences in many areas: in the main impulse that drew them to social criticism; in their actual knowledge of the world they criticised; in their political philosophies; and in the techniques they developed for incorporating their criticism into the imaginative fabric of their novels. These are important areas for investigation, and I propose to consider them briefly in turn. It will be a convenient and economic way of establishing broad comparisons, before looking more closely at what some of the novelists wrote, in the next chapter.

First, then, what mainly impelled Disraeli, Charles Kingsley, Mrs Gaskell, George Eliot and Dickens to write industrial, political novels? The question is most easily answered in relation to Disraeli. Disraeli conceived his trilogy, *Coningsby*, *Sybil* and *Tancred*, as a contribution to his Young England movement, a part of his programme for a revitalised Toryism. When *Coningsby* appeared in 1844, Disraeli was a relative newcomer to Parliament. The two characters, Harry Coningsby in *Coningsby* and Charles Egremont in *Sybil*, embody and propound the new Tory ideal. By contrast with Disraeli, Charles Kingsley, who was a clergyman not a politician, does not use the novel to advance the cause of a party. Nevertheless, his faith in Christian Socialism, acquired from Coleridge's disciple F. D. Maurice, and his direct experience of Chartism and industrial slums, impelled him to write a novel of social protest. The main impulse was a humanitarian desire to alleviate suffering. The motives of Mrs Gaskell, George Eliot and Dickens were rather more mixed and complicated. In the case of Mrs Gaskell it was mainly religious, an attempt to extend her charitable activities beyond her husband's northern parish. With George Eliot and Dickens, the choice of specifically political themes in *Felix Holt* and *Hard Times* represented a more intense concentration on one aspect of life that assumes some importance in their other novels. For example, George Eliot's great novel *Middlemarch* provides an unrivalled account of the actual workings of an organic society; its only rival is Hardy's *Mayor of Casterbridge*, both infused with a wonderful sense of historical chance. But *Felix Holt* is more polemical than *Middlemarch*, just as *Jude the Obscure* is more polemical than *The Mayor of Casterbridge*.

How well did these novelists know the world they described? And how did they acquire their knowledge? Disraeli is an interesting case. Actually he presents two worlds: firstly, there is the world of political debate and fashionable London life; secondly, there is the world of industrial unrest. The first he knew inside out, from personal experience. Consequently, he recreates it with a vital authenticity. The second he reconstructs secondhand from others' reports, from Government Blue Books, and similar material. As a result, it is often unconvincing, either too idyllic or, more often, too melodramatically evil. Kingsley's knowledge of the world he writes about in *Alton Locke* is also patchy. He actually attended Chartist meetings, went with a friend to watch the dismal fiasco of the presentation of the Chartists' National Petition, and spent a great deal of time in the London slums. The description, in a letter to his wife, of such a visit reveals clearly the first-hand experience he drew on for his terrifying description of the man who drowned in the ditch under the slum house in chapter 35 of *Alton Locke*. The passage in the letter runs:

> I was yesterday with George, Walsh and Mansfield over the cholera districts of Bermondsey and oh God! what I saw! people having no water to drink – hundreds of them but the water of the common sewer which stagnated full of . . . dead fish, cats and dogs under the window (*Kingsley, A Biography*, Una Pope-Hennesy, p. 90).

It is worth comparing this account with the last part of chapter 35 of *Alton Locke* with its description of 'the rotting piles over the black waters, with phosphorescent scraps of rotten fish gleaming and twinkling out of the dark hollows, like devilish grave-lights – over bubbles of poisonous gas, and bloating carcasses of dogs, and lumps of offal, floating on the olive-green hell-brake'. While this passage from the novel conveys authentic horror, there is much else in *Alton Locke* that appears too obviously fabricated and second-hand – for example, many of the details relating to sweated labour in the tailoring industry.

If we now turn to Mrs Gaskell and ask how well she knew her world, the answer would seem to be that she had a penetrating first-hand understanding of the domestic lives of the industrial poor, of the 'manners and habits of the wealthy middle class both in South and in the North of England'. Kathleen Tillotson quotes a contemporary reviewer as saying that Disraeli knew his material 'as a traveller knows the botany of a strange country', Mrs Gaskell 'as an ardent naturalist knows the flora of his own neighbourhood' (Tillotson, *Novels of the Eighteen Forties*, p. 208). But what Mrs Gaskell drastically lacked was any first-hand experience of unionism and working-class politics. But then how could a Victorian woman novelist acquire such experience? Obviously, she could not. There were exceptions, Hannah More and Harriet Martineau, for instance. In the Preface to *Mary Barton* Mrs Gaskell confesses frankly she knows nothing of political economy or theories of trade. And so, sensibly, she concentrates on those areas she knows best. And in the novel *North and South* she exploits superbly her own knowledge of what it was like to be brought up in a traditional and self-contained community and then thrown into the midst of industrial squalor and intense human suffering. Her heroine Margaret Hale undergoes a similar transformation.

What of George Eliot's knowledge of her world? It was a *past* world, not a present world. In his introduction to *Felix Holt*, Dr Leavis usefully reminds us of George Eliot's pride in achieving authenticity. She wrote to Blackwood, her publisher 'I took a great deal of pains to get a true idea of the period', and besides drawing on her own 'childish recollections' she went through newspaper accounts, and steeped herself in the first-hand account provided by Samuel Bamford's *Passages in the Life of a Radical* for her own story of a radical, Felix Holt. Mrs Gaskell also drew on Bamford for information. Conscientious as George Eliot was in assembling information about the first elections to a Reformed Parliament, the novel gains what stature it has from her intellectual grasp and her insight into character rather than from any vivid portrayal of working-class politics. However, it is a serious weakness in the novel that the spokesman for working-class radicalism, Felix Holt, should be so unreal. Dickens shows a similar weakness of characterisation in his portrayal of Slackbridge in *Hard Times*, but there is no doubt that his quick journalistic eye had seized on all the essentials of the industrial scene, as the result of his special visits to Preston to discover for himself the true realities of industrial unrest in 1854. In Italy he had read accounts in newspapers, one of his contributors to *Household Words* described conditions in 'Locked Out', and Dickens himself went to Preston later in 1854. In reading all these mid nineteenth-century novels, we need to remind ourselves how rigidly stratified English society was, and how little one class knew about another. By Dickens, the Dean of Westminster said, 'that veil was rent asunder which parts the various classes of society'.

I have taken rather long to establish these points about what impelled each writer into politics and how well each knew the world he or she chose to write about. But they are essential preliminaries to considering the kind of political philosophy we find embodied in the various novels. As one would expect from the facts already presented about Disraeli, it is Disraeli's novels that contain the most consistent and clearly defined political philosophy and Mrs Gaskell's – whose method was that of a Christian impressionist – the least. What she offered was a Christian palliative and not a very successful one at that. This does not mean that Disraeli's novels are necessarily better than Mrs Gaskell's or George Eliot's. But it does mean that they are different. Kathleen Tillotson comments:

> Mrs Gaskell differs from Disraeli and Kingsley in having no axe to grind. A wider impartiality, a tenderer humanity, and it may be a greater artistic integrity, raise this novel (*Mary Barton*) beyond the conditions and problems that give rise to it. (p. 202)

What are the essentials of this fairly systematic political philosophy embodied in Disraeli's *Sybil* and the other two novels in the trilogy? There is, first, the belief in an organic society, so that Disraeli can be seen to carry on the Burke–Coleridge tradition; second, the belief in a responsible aristocracy that would acknowledge and fulfil its duties to the rest of the nation, and that would become a champion of the poor; third, the belief in a strong monarch and an active church; and fourth, a thorough-going opposition to the worship of *laissez-faire* and the cash nexus. When Disraeli formed the Young England movement in 1841, with George Smythe (the model for Coningsby), Lord John Manners (the model for Lord Henry Sydney in *Coningsby* and *Tancred*), and Alexander Baille Cochrane (the model for Buckhurst in *Coningsby*), he planned to create a new form of radical Toryism. It may not seem as radical to us as it did to his contemporaries.

In the stagy plot of *Sybil*, we can see that Disraeli wishes to forge a natural link between the aristocracy and the working class, with the church (personified by Sybil herself) taking an active and benevolent role in creating the new society. In Book III, chapter 6, of *Sybil*, the hero, Charles Egremont, explains to Sybil that he has come to 'learn something' of the 'condition of the people'.

> 'That is not to be done in a great city like London. We all of us live too much in a circle. You will assist me . . . your spirit will animate me. You told me last night that there was no other subject, except one, which ever occupied your thoughts.'
>
> 'Yes' said Sybil. 'I have lived under two roofs, only two roofs; and each has given me a great idea; the Convent and the Cottage. One has taught me the degradation of my faith, the other of my race. You should not wonder, therefore, that my heart is concentrated on the Church and the People.'

The dialogue clarifies her symbolic role and the novel ends on a quietly prophetic note and a call to young England.

> We live in an age when to be young and to be indifferent can be no longer synonymous. We must prepare for the coming hour. The claims of the Future are represented by suffering millions; and the Youth of a Nation are the trustees of Posterity.

None of the other nineteenth-century novelists can be said to have a political philosophy in the same sense that Disraeli can. David Lodge, in his Introduction to the paperback edition of *Alton Locke*, is worth quoting in this context. It is, of course, as he himself indicates, in part a summary of Raymond Williams's thesis in *Culture and Society*. All the industrial novels, remarks Lodge

> combine a genuine, indignant sympathy for the oppressed working classes, with a reluctance to endorse political remedies, such as the Charter, and a severe disapproval of revolutionary tendencies. The intolerable situation of the underprivileged worker, dramatized in

> the person of a hero or heroine, is commonly resolved, or evaded, by death or emigration (Kingsley resorts to both expedients in *Alton Locke*), and the moral is generally that society as a whole must experience a change of heart, or suffer dire consequences.

This is well said. But there are additional points to be made and qualifications to be added. The first is that emigration was not simply a novelist's handy way out. Both Carlyle in *Signs of the Times* and Matthew Arnold in *Culture and Anarchy* recommend emigration as a solution to the problems of poverty and over-population and the policy received substantial support in Parliament. The second is that to advocate a change of heart is not as ineffective as Lodge implies. All great social reforms have been brought about as the result of changes in political consciousness (a change of heart) as well as by legislative action. Neither approach is fully effective without the other. They are *inter*dependent. And, clearly, the more appropriate area for the novelist is human consciousness not legislative reform. We may think that Dickens was unduly optimistic in his article on Strike in *Household Words*, but the emphasis on mutual explanation, forbearance and consideration between employers and employed, and the faults on both sides, at least indicates that it is a *human* as well as a political problem.

Here, then, it is appropriate to turn from the consideration of the political philosophies implicit in the nineteenth-century novelists' work to the more specifically literary question. How are these political ideas actually embodied in the artistic structure of the novels? The topic is too large to cover here and will be explored fully in the following chapter, but there are three important issues that need to be borne in mind before examining the industrial novels and 'condition of England' novels of the mid-nineteenth century.

The first is that the nineteenth-century novel was even less of a pure form than it is today. It appealed to a wide audience, both in original serial form and as a two- or three-volume hardback. For the artisan and lower-middle class reader, it supplied the instruction that the essay and serious prose work had previously supplied for the classes above. We need to bear this in mind in reading the historical explanations at the beginning of *Felix Holt*, the combined political/historical disquisitions in Disraeli's *Sybil*, the sermonising and do-goodery digressions in Mrs Gaskell, and in the purely documentary details about the tailoring trade in Kingsley's *Alton Locke*. Few of the novelists make any attempt to disguise this instructive and informative element. It's true, however, that in *Alton Locke*, Kingsley does disarm criticism to some extent by using his radical tailor as a convenient mouthpiece and descriptive eye. And his old Scots friend acts as a convenient foil.

The second thing to bear in mind, I think, is that many of the elements that seem to suggest a damaging and disabling evasion of the central human issues often occur in novels in which there are *no political issues at all*. The most obvious elements are: sensational melodrama and sudden and convenient deaths. These are the stock-in-trade of *all* nineteenth-century novelists, good and bad, political and non-political. So we need to be self-critical and we need to analyse the parts of a novel with great care before jumping to conclusions about political evasion, although, indeed, there is plenty of evasion to be found.

A third thing to bear in mind is that the nineteenth-century novel had its strict moral conventions, and these conventions were partly a reflection of the conventions of actual life. It was notoriously difficult for the novelist to present certain kinds of character and certain aspects of life. It was difficult to create women in the round and impossible to deal with sex or the fallen woman, simply and frankly. Only in Peacock, Disraeli and George Meredith, do we meet women who are men's intellectual equals. Mrs Gaskell's maudlin treatment of the fallen woman Esther in *Mary Barton* is typical of the indirection forced on her not only by the literary conventions but by the conventional morality of society. Recent books such as Steven Marcus's *The Other Victorians* and Ronald Pearsall's *Worm in the Bud*, a much less serious book but one that actually covers a wide range of Victorian sexuality, have made us aware of the striking contrast between the polite hypocritical conventions and the ugly facts, especially the details relating to mass prostitution in the cities.[9] The general theme of the effect of Victorian ideas on sexuality in the portrayal of women in fiction will be taken up in a later chapter on 'Sex, the Family and the New Women'. Here it is simply necessary to sound a note of caution before turning to look more closely at a representative selection of novels that focus attention on industrialism and the 'Condition of England'.

6 The Victorian 'Condition of England' Novel

The last chapter illustrated some of the broad differences in literary impulse, range of knowledge, political philosophy and literary technique in the work of Mrs Gaskell, Disraeli, Dickens and Charles Kingsley. There are important differences and they help to explain why the actual novels each wrote are so different. But one thing they all had in common and that was the ambition to extend the range of the nineteenth-century novel. They sought to extend it in various ways: by including the lives of the industrial poor, by portraying working-class politics, by drawing attention to a wide range of social abuses and, perhaps most important of all, by extending the range of human sensibility to embrace the thoughts and emotions of the simplest and least-educated members of society. In some respects, they were heirs to the tradition created by Wordsworth in the *Lyrical Ballads* for they were inspired by the faith Wordsworth expressed in 'The Old Cumberland Beggar': 'That we have all of us one human heart.'

In a passage in *North and South* describing what the manufacturer Mr Thornton had learnt from his relations with the mill worker, Higgins, Mrs Gaskell actually quoted this line from Wordsworth:

> He and they had led parallel lives – very close, but never touching – till the accident (or so it seemed) of his acquaintance with Higgins. Once brought face to face, man to man, with an individual of the masses around him, and (take notice) *out* of the character of master and workman, in the first instance, they had each begun to recognise that 'we have all of us one human heart' (Penguin, p. 511).

The novel, of all the literary forms, was to prove the best suited to deepen and widen the sensibility of its readers. It thus became a powerful indirect agent of social change. In *Novels of the Eighteen-Forties*, Kathleen Tillotson remarks:

> Social classes were then stratified, even isolated, not only geographically but within the limits of a single town. Some of the credit for breaking down this isolation must go to Dickens: as Arthur Stanley, the Dean of Westminster, said in his funeral sermon, 'By

> him that veil was rent asunder which parts the various classes of society' (Oxford, paperback p. 78).

Something similar might be said of most of the novelists we are about to consider in some detail.

All the works discussed in this chapter suffer as the result of being considered simply as industrial or 'Condition of England' novels.[1] They are much more than that. We need to recognise from the start that the labels are merely convenient devices for classification, for bringing together a number of novels that developed more specific criticisms of contemporary industrial society than the general run of nineteenth-century novels.

It might be useful to recall the date of the main novels before looking at them more closely. First comes Disraeli's *Sybil* (1845), preceded a year earlier by the first novel in the political trilogy *Coningsby* (1844). Next came Mrs Gaskell's *Mary Barton* (1848), then Kingsley's *Alton Locke* (1850). Four years later Dickens published his *Hard Times* (1854); and a year later came Mrs Gaskell's *North and South* (1855). It was published in Dickens's magazine *Household Words*; and when Mrs Gaskell read the serial parts of Dickens's *Hard Times*, she was afraid that he was going to give an industrial strike an important place in his novel. On 21 April 1854 Dickens wrote to reassure her:

> I have no intention of striking. The monstrous claims at domination made by a certain class of manufacturers, and the extent to which the way is made easy for working men to slide down into discontent under such hands, are within my scheme, but I am not going to strike. So don't be afraid of me.

Mrs Gaskell could therefore go ahead and present a strike in *North and South* without fear of duplicating Dickens in *Hard Times*. The last of the Condition of England novels to appear was *Felix Holt* (1866). In dealing with so many novels in a single chapter, it is impossible to offer a complete critical reading of each. Instead I shall try to indicate something of the range and quality of some of them and draw attention to some of the central critical problems. As far as possible, I shall develop my argument by means of comparison and analysis.

Two of the novelists, Disraeli and George Eliot, have a very strong historical sense. This appears immediately in the third chapter of *Sybil*, where Disraeli offers an account of Charles Egremont's ancestry to show how the Marney family had risen to power through plunder of the Church and People. He also offers a history of the political parties in England to prove that its rulers have become cut off from the people and are little better than a Venetian oligarchy. What seems improbable and melodramatic later in the novel stems from Disraeli's historical vision and exists to support and vindicate it. The plot becomes a rhetorical device for enforcing a historical myth. Thus it becomes necessary for the rightful heir, Gerard, or rather his daughter Sybil, a daughter of the Church and People, to be restored to her rightful heritage. The novel ends in a double defeat: defeat of the usurping aristocracy in the person of Egremont's brother Lord Marney; and defeat of the savage multitude personified in the Liberator of the people, 'Bishop' Hatton. In the following passage from the penultimate chapter, Disraeli brings to a climax his serious political theme:

> The Bishop was lying senseless in the main cellar, surrounded by his chief officers in the same state: indeed the whole of the basement was covered with the recumbent figures of Hell-cats, as black and as thick as torpid flies during the last days of their career. The funeral pile of the children of Woden was a sumptuous one; it was prepared and lighted by themselves; and the flame that, rising from the keep of Mowbray, announced to the startled country that in a short hour the splendid mimicry of Norman rule would cease to exist, told also the pitiless fate of the ruthless savage, who, with analogous pretension, had presumed to style himself the Liberator of the People. (World's Classics, p. 425)

A couple of paragraphs earlier, Stephen Morley had met bitter defeat, and died. ' "O Sybil!" and with this name half sighed upon his lips, the votary of Moral Power and the Apostle of Community ceased to exist.' So really it is a triple defeat: of false aristocracy (Marney); savage revolutionary action (Hatton); and radical journalism (Morley). But there is surely something very unsatisfactory about the writing in this chapter. Even granted – what of course we must grant – that Disraeli is writing symbolically not realistically, nevertheless the chapter has two faults: Disraeli's delight in the defeat of England's enemies is both cruel and superficial; and, secondly, there is a certain disparity between the subtle analytic rendering of the Condition of England in the novel as a whole and its simple melodramatic solution in the final chapters. The texture of the writing reveals limitations of sensibility. It reveals a lack of human compassion and a sadistic gloating over the sufferings of others. It also reveals a flaw in Disraeli's political thought: his tendency to believe that complex problems could be solved by a flash of genius. In this context it is worth bearing in mind what J. T. Boulton said about Burke's writing (in an article in *The Listener* 27 January 1972, pp. 110–11) since it is equally applicable to our attitude to Disraeli.

> It must become habitual for us to take account of the relationship between the ideas of a political writer and his entire literary manner.

> Then we shall have learned a lesson at least as important as any that is exclusively ideological.

It is only necessary to add that in reading Disraeli's *Sybil* we also need to take account of the novelist's philosophy of history in assessing the function and effectiveness of any single passage. Viewed in this light, the exaggeration, simplification, symbolism may be rhetorically necessary.

In George Eliot's *Felix Holt*, the importance of the historical approach to society and its problems appears immediately in the Author's Introduction. Writing on the eve of the second Reform Bill of 1867, she recreates a panoramic view of England before the first Reform Bill of 1832, from the imaginary viewpoint of an old-fashioned stagecoach, finally narrowing the focus on Transome Court, with its unexplained mysteries and secrets. The past is to play three important roles in the novel. In the plot centred on Esther, it is to prove her the rightful heiress of Treby. In the plot centred on Harold Transome, it is to produce the terrible revelation that Lawyer Jermyn, whom he hates, is his father. And, in the novel as a whole, a sense of the past, the inexorable connection of past, present and future, becomes the most distinctive element in George Eliot's vision. John Holloway remarks in the *Victorian Sage*,

> George Eliot gives expression to her 'philosophy of life' by such broad and general features of her work as its characteristic setting in the recent past; its habit of linking a particular story to known historical conditions; its meticulous charting of social and economic patterns; its interest in slow changes and events that have remote consequences; its pervasive sense of the tie of kinship; and its being rigorously confined to characters and happenings of a quite distinctive kind. (p. 123)

A natural concomitant of this emphasis upon the recent past and the relation of the story to historical conditions is an awareness of the extent to which the life of the individual is moulded by the society in which he lives, and moulded, too, by less obvious forces, arising from the immediate past. Leavis is right to say that much of the intricate plotting necessary to reveal Esther as an heiress is just a nuisance. But, clumsy as it is, it does serve George Eliot's central purpose. This is to explain the present in terms of the past. Moreover, she applies this method both to the individual and society. Neither the individual nor a society can discover its true identity or its future, except in relation to its past.

It should be clear from what has been said about Disraeli and George Eliot that each interprets the fictional present in terms of the past, that their vision of the continuity of English social life gives a special strength and solidity to their criticism of society, and that each is almost driven to using improbable plots about lost heirs and heiresses in order to demonstrate how the past stretches itself out to grasp the present, with icy or warmly loving fingers. Comparison with Hardy is illuminating. In Hardy's novels, the past certainly serves to suggest historic continuity. It also serves to suggest that man's lot has always been the same kind of elemental struggle. But the most distinctive function of the past in Hardy is to embody the incalculable interventions of fate, for example the return of the furmity woman in *The Mayor of Casterbridge*. In Disraeli and George Eliot, on the other hand, the distinctive functions of the past are moral, social and political. For all their differences in political affiliation, Disraeli and George Eliot are true heirs of Burke, inspired with a vision of a historical community in which man must find his meaning and happiness. By contrast, Mrs Gaskell's vision of society derives its characteristic strength from the closeness of present circumstances, rather than from any all-embracing philosophy of history and society, yet she, from time to time, reminds her readers that understanding of the future depends upon knowledge of the past. In *North and South* Mr Hale points out the limitations of Mr Thornton's practical approach by saying 'To be sure, he needs some of the knowledge of the past, which gives the truest basis for conjecture as to the future' (Penguin, p. 221).

Undoubtedly much of the contemporary impact of Disraeli's *Sybil*, came from its provocative sub-title, 'Or "The Two Nations" ', and from the explanatory dialogue in Book II, chapter 5, between Egremont and the Stranger. Disraeli arranges the dialogue skilfully so that the reader is held in suspense waiting for the final definition of the two nations. After Egremont has boasted proudly that the Queen reigns over the greatest nation that ever existed, the stranger asks which nation, for she reigns over two. He then proceeds to explain:

> 'Two nations; between whom there is no intercourse and no sympathy; who are as ignorant of each other's habits, thoughts, and feelings, as if they were dwellers in different zones, or inhabitants of different planets; who are formed by a different breeding, are fed by a different food, are ordered by different manners, and are not governed by the same laws.'
> 'You speak of —' said Egremont, hesitatingly.
> 'THE RICH AND THE POOR'. (p. 67)

This was deliberately provocative. It was designed to destroy complacency, to shock, and to arouse indignation and compassion. The subsequent selection of incidents serves to vindicate this division of the country into two nations. For most of Disraeli's readers, the vivid descriptions of the Butty system, the economic tyranny imposed by the

Tommy shop and the brutality of men like Hatton in the workshops, opened their eyes to the harsh injustices of the industrial system. The impact is certainly strong, but it is neither as strong nor as effective as comparable descriptions in Dickens. There are I think two main reasons. One relates to style, the other to characterisation. In describing what he has merely *read about* but not *seen* for himself, Disraeli frequently employs a flat, cumbersome, documentary prose, for example in his description of the hovels in the town in Marney, Book II ch. 3: 'These hovels were in many instances not provided with the commonest conveniences . . . , contiguous to every door might be observed the dung-heap on which every kind of filth was accumulated, for the purpose of being disposed of for manure' (p. 54). Compare this stilted, unimpassioned prose with Kingsley's impassioned description at the end of *Alton Locke* or with passages in Dickens. Elsewhere in *Sybil*, Disraeli's bright metallic prose, built up on parodox and antithesis, creates a sense of cool distance between the author and the poverty he describes. Beautifully apt for making ideas interesting and for giving epigrammatic sparkle to upper-class dialogue, his style rarely embodies genuine compassion for human suffering.

The second reason why the impact of Disraeli's novels is ultimately less strong than those of Dickens is that we care too little for the victims of the industrial system as living human beings. To take an extreme example, the boy killed in the raid on Diggs's Tommy shop is quite anonymous. Our sympathies have not been previously engaged on his behalf. His death is shocking. It is exemplary – this is what happens when crowds take the law into their own hands. But it is not deeply moving. Similarly, the transformation of Dandy Mick and Devilsdust from disgruntled workers into petty capitalists at the end of the novel is neither humanly interesting nor politically convincing. It is true that the patronising humour partly disarms serious criticism; moreover, Disraeli's contemporary readers were probably less critical of this example of social mobility than we are today. Even we smile indulgently when we are told how easily the young men and their girl friends made it into the respectable middle-class without having to alter their essential characters very much. Yet it is something of a tame ending after the provocative division of the country into the two nations, the rich and the poor. But it is an essential part of Disraeli's philosophy that the poor should find a new place under his Tory democracy. As Holloway wisely concludes in his chapter on Disraeli: 'The lighter side of Disraeli's work both interprets, and makes more sympathetic, the side which is more in earnest' (p. 110).

George Eliot's *Felix Holt* lacks any similar provocative division of the country into two nations. Its most provocative element is her dramatic presentation of the discrepancy between the ideal of a Reformed Parliament and the sordid reality of drunkeness, vote-buying and scheming by-election agents at Treby. For all its obvious melodrama, George Eliot's presentation is not without subtlety. She skilfully contrasts two kinds of radicalism, through the characters of Felix and Harold Transome, both of whom are rivals for Esther's hand. And, through Transome's motives and through his subordination to his agent, she shows that expedience, not principle, motivates the choice of the Liberal rather than the Tory colours; that whatever the choice, the prospective member is, after all, only a tool in others' hands. It is easy enough to say that her account of the Treby Riot is a rationalisation of her fear of the newly franchised classes, just as critics have said that murder and violence in Mrs Gaskell's novels are a rationalisation of a middle-class fear of organised labour. There is some truth in both views. But they are drastic over-simplifications. In the case of George Eliot, such an interpretation masks her very real understanding of mass hysteria, crowd psychology, her understanding of the ease with which the man who tries to save life in a popular demonstration is likely either to lose it, or be held responsible for the outbreak of violence itself. In trying to save the man Spratt, Felix is arrested as a leading revolutionary. Moreover, earlier in this part of the novel George Eliot carefully juxtaposes the speech of a popular demogue and Felix's speech, in order to show that the latter's is a speech by a man of culture who understands the danger of false expectations and the danger of putting one's faith in the mere machinery of voting, voting districts and annual parliaments. Here, once again, we have that attack on the mechanical spirit of the age that we have met before in Coleridge, Carlyle, and Matthew Arnold. George Eliot's *Felix Holt* offers powerful criticism of society; but as an exploration of political radicalism its success is limited by the sentimental and indulgent treatment of the two characters Felix and the Reverend Rufus Lyon.

The imaginative centre of the novel lies in the conflict of egoism between Harold Transome and his mother. The resolution of the political theme through Esther's final choice of the shadowy Felix counts for little in comparison with the tragic denouement in the mother/son relationship, so rightly praised by Dr Leavis in his introduction to the Everyman edition. It is George Eliot's great achievement in this novel to suggest, but not too strongly to enforce, the connections between private and public life. When Esther notes personal defects in Harold, we are aware that exactly similar defects make him a failure in political life. She notes:

> His very good-nature was unsympathetic: it never came from any thorough understanding or deep respect for what was in the mind of the person he obliged or indulged; it was like his kindness to his mother – an arrangement of his for the happiness of others, which, if they were sensible, ought to succeed. (ch. 43)

The greatness of *Felix Holt* lies in George Eliot's skill in making us see that such mechanical arrangements for the happiness of others cannot succeed either in private or political life. It does not lie in the explicit treatment of political radicalism.

A somewhat similar insight into the relationship of private and public life invests Mrs Gaskell's *North and South* with a distinctly modern appeal. And for this reason, and also because so much attention has always been paid to *Mary Barton*, I want to concentrate on *North and South*. But before turning to *North and South*, I should like to make three brief points about *Mary Barton*.

The first is that for all Mrs Gaskell's lack of historical perspective and coherent political philosophy, *Mary Barton* conveys wonderfully well the very texture and rhythms of a community as it is threatened by an alien system, the factory system based on the cash nexus. We can usefully apply Tönnies' distinction between the *Gemeinschaft* and *Gesellschaft* to the two different orders in *Mary Barton*. Of course it is not Mrs Gaskell's conscious purpose to contrast these two types of human organisation: such a purpose would have been utterly foreign to her whole Christian approach, which stresses unity and brotherhood, not radically opposed systems. Nevertheless, her intimate knowledge of the working class, her exact observations of their customs and simple domestic rituals, her ear for dialogue, her skill in assimilating folk dialect and traditional songs into the texture of her narrative, enable her to build up a completely authentic picture of the natural ties that bind the north of England working-class. The matter is more complicated than I have so far suggested, because in fact we are given an insight into two working-class cultures, not one. There is the old rural culture that Alice Wilson looks back to nostalgically, and there is the newer urban working-class culture that draws some of its strength from rural folk traditions but which has developed its characteristic solidarity and stoic fortitude in the face of poverty and oppression in the city. John Barton's reply to Wilson's offer of Alice Wilson's help epitomises the working-class solidarity created by urban poverty: 'She's a poor woman, and can feel for the poor.' So too can her creator Mrs Gaskell, for all her middle-class upbringing. And though her first-hand observations come to us filtered through a middle-class sensibility, the filter is almost transparent, except for those occasions when bourgeois assumptions about thrift and hard work intervene.

The second quick point I want to make about *Mary Barton* is that it is not just Mrs Gaskell's ignorance of 'Political Economy and the theories of trade' – to quote her own Preface – that limits the value of *Mary Barton* as an industrial novel, but her process of making the characters and plot conform to a pre-established view of man and society, a view based on social and religious assumptions, rather than any coherent political philosophy. Her solution to the conflict between masters and men is a Christian/humanistic one. Each must recognise the other's common humanity. Once this happens they can speak as man to man, each respecting the other's point of view. Her vision is as Wordsworthian as it is Christian: and in chapter 36 she makes a clear distinction between 'formal piety' and the 'heart's piety' (a very Wordsworthian phrase): the 'heart's piety' needs 'no garnish of texts to make it true religion, pure and undefiled'. Mrs Gaskell is wholly successful in illustrating the common bond of suffering; what she cannot portray nearly as convincingly is the actual engagement of masters and men in a man-to-man relationship. In chapter 8 she speaks specifically of the 'alienation between the different classes', but she cannot render such alienation in fully dramatic terms – the effects, yes; and she could cry: 'Why have we made them what they are?' (p. 220); but the cry locates her standpoint firmly within the compassionate but uncomprehending section of the middle class. At the end of chapter 18, she condemns old Mr Carson for demanding revenge for the death of his son and so arranges the plot that there shall be a death-bed reconciliation. But both sections, the revenge passage at the end of chapter 18, as well as the reconciliation, are too highly rhetorical; they fail to ring true. The main point to note, then, is that the weaknesses in Mrs Gaskell's criticism of industrial society are clearly reflected in weaknesses in characterisation, plotting, and the actual texture of the writing in *Mary Barton*.

The third brief point I want to make about *Mary Barton* before turning to *North and South* concerns the striking psychological insight revealed in Mrs Gaskell's rendering of the conflict between mother, son and lover. When suspicion falls on Jem Wilson for the murder of the factory owner's son, Mary visits Mrs Wilson in an attempt to establish an alibi for Jem at the time of the murder.

> She had grown – I hardly know what word to use – but, something like proud of her martyrdom; she had grown to hug her grief; to feel an excitement in her agony of anxiety about her boy.
>
> 'So, Mary, you're here! Oh! Mary, lass! He's to be tried on Tuesday.'
>
> She fell to sobbing, in the convulsive breath-catching manner which tells so of much previous weeping.
>
> 'Oh! Mrs Wilson, don't take on so! We'll get him off, you'll see. Don't fret; they can't prove him guilty!'
>
> 'But I tell thee they will,' interrupted Mrs Wilson, half-irritated at the light way, as she considered it, in which Mary spoke; and a little displeased that another could hope when she had almost brought herself to find pleasure in despair.
>
> 'It may suit thee well,' continued she, 'to make light of the misery thou hast caused; but I shall lay his death at thy door, as long as I

> live, and die I know he will; and all for what he never did – no, he never did; my own blessed boy!' (Penguin, pp. 307–8).

Nothing in Mrs Gaskell's rendering of political conflict equals this authentic portrayal of private conflict, with its vivid images of self-indulgent sorrow and its bitter recriminatory phrases. Behind Mrs Wilson's words lies her instinctive fear of being supplanted in her son's affections by Mary, a point made more powerfully later in the novel.

> 'Mother! I am going back to Liverpool to-morrow morning to see how Mary Barton is.'
>
> 'And what's Mary Barton to thee, that thou shouldst be running after her in that-a-way?'
>
> 'If she lives, she shall be my wedded wife. If she dies – mother, I can't speak of what I shall feel if she dies.' His voice was choked in his throat.
>
> For an instant his mother was interested by his words; and then came back the old jealousy of being supplanted in the affections of that son, who had been, as it were, newly born to her, by the escape he had so lately experienced from danger. So she hardened her heart against entertaining any feeling of sympathy; and turned away from the face, which recalled the earnest look of his childhood, when he had come to her in some trouble, sure of help and comfort (pp. 408–9).

For anything comparable to these two passages one has to turn to Lawrence's *Sons and Lovers*.

North and South is a more satisfying novel than *Mary Barton* in a number of respects. There is a closer interaction of public and private life and this interaction is rendered with greater psychological insight. The technique of developing the contrast between North and South in the expanding consciousness of the heroine, Margaret Hale, gives the novel a dramatic complexity that *Mary Barton* lacks. Margaret Hale begins with a contempt for people 'in trade', an attitude she has unthinkingly acquired in her sheltered, privileged upbringing in the south of England. In the painful process of acquiring self-knowledge and maturity she is forced to modify her views; and she ends up with marrying one of the new 'small princes of trade', Mr Thornton. One of the great strengths of the book lies in the dramatic rendering of the forces of attraction and repulsion at work in their relationship. While it is true that the tensions are resolved by a mechanical twist of the plot, the early exploration is almost Lawrentian in its deep understanding of sexual polarities and the subtle interconnections of conflicts in private and public life – a point well noted by Martin Dodsworth, the Penguin editor. Yet although his remarks on the sexual implications of

Margaret's intervention in the strike scene and on her brother's action in attacking Leonards at the railway station are perceptive, they are couched in such modern terms that they give a quite mistaken impression of the actual imaginative impact of these scenes.

Where *Mary Barton* has virtually a single setting, *North and South* has three: rural Helstone in the south of England, London, and Milton-Northern, the northern industrial city based on Manchester, where most of the action takes place. The South occupies too small a part in the book to serve as a wholly effective contrast. The brief scenes in London, although they are not representative of metropolitan life and were not intended to be, very neatly suggest the pointless life that many young women lead there. The Hales leave Helstone at the beginning of chapter 8, and Margaret only returns briefly near the end of the book (when the very external and satirical presentation of the new clergyman and his wife seems at odds with the more 'internal' presentation of events through Margaret's maturing consciousness elsewhere in the novel). The main point about the three settings, however, is that we need little direct knowledge of two of them, Helstone and London. When Margaret moves North, she takes with her part of her southern experience. It is, then, as the South continues to exist in her consciousness and influence her reaction to Northern people that it counts. She comes to understand that 'one had need to learn a different language, and measure by a different standard, up here in Milton' (p. 212). Mrs Gaskell succeeds in making us feel that it does count, that it does need to be modified in the light of the wider experience Margaret gains in Milton-Northern. Martin Dodsworth remarks that she comes eventually to reject the South not on ideological grounds, but because she has outgrown her childhood (p. 26). It is noticeable, too, how skilfully descriptions of houses, interior furnishings, meals, manners, and rhythms of life offer critical and contrasting views of cultural values. Once again, because these descriptions are rendered through Margaret's expanding consciousness, the novel remains fairly free from moral and aesthetic dogmatism and from overt commentary.

Two of the older characters occupy important contrasting places in the story. These are Mrs Thornton, the factory owner's proud, ambitious, wilful mother and Mrs Shaw, Margaret's aunt. Both are women of aggressive nature and limited sympathies, but radically different in temperament and social origin. Mrs Thornton seeks only to forward her son's fortunes and might be compared with Mrs Transome in *Felix Holt*. Mrs Thornton represents the successful vulgarian in the newly rich mill-owning class. But she is more interesting as an acutely observed psychological study than as a representative social figure. Her powerful influence on her son (occasionally reminiscent of Mrs Morel's in *Sons and Lovers*) increases his difficulty in establishing relations with Margaret. The triple relationship of mother and son and

Margaret is very Lawrentian, both in its intuitive understanding of subconscious elements and in its recognition of the intimate connections between the health of the individual and the health of society.

The sub-plot is only partially integrated into the fabric of the novel through Margaret's lie to Mr Thornton. She lies to save her brother Frederick, who risks his life to be at his mother's death-bed. Thornton suspects an unknown suitor. But the sub-plot could have served the main plot even more effectively if Mrs Gaskell had drawn more attention to the common themes of justice and the relations between masters and men. Margaret's brother Frederick had been involved in a mutiny at sea. His justification lies in his championing of justice against injustice. Clearly the sub-plot could have been brought into closer harmony with the main plot, concerned with justice and injustice, with the relations between masters and men. As it is, it is something of a melodramatic excrescence.

The plot in *North and South*, as in *Mary Barton*, imposes too simple a solution on complex social issues. Mrs Gaskell presents two industrial crises. The cause of the first is a down-turn in trade and the refusal of the workers to accept the necessary reduction in wages. To avoid capitulating to the Union's demands Mr Thornton employs Irish immigrants. Much is made of Thornton's knowledge of the hard facts of economic competition and, subsequently, of the importance of man-to-man understanding between masters and men; but nothing in the plot recognises that it is large-scale economic forces (over which neither masters nor men have control), that bring about the crisis. In the last chapter Thornton speaks of wishing to cultivate some intercourse with 'hands' beyond the mere 'cash nexus', but the final solution in the novel is simply more cash, conveniently supplied by Margaret.

The cause of the second crisis is even more explicitly a change in the condition of international trade, specifically the effects of American competition. Thornton is faced with the choice of staking all (including the welfare of his men) in risky speculation, or selling up with honour (apparently the welfare of the men is no longer important where the honour of a gentleman is concerned). He chooses the latter. But, in the very last chapter, he is rescued from financial failure and unhappiness by the intervention of Margaret, who can lend him the money to go on working Marlborough Mills. The weakness here is not just the fairy god-mother element in the plot (Bell's legacy to Margaret is another); but that the solution is no solution. Margaret's gift suggests that Thornton's only trouble was lack of capital. But the novel itself has made it clear that his troubles arose from an economic blizzard. Thus, we have to admit, the novel offers rather unsatisfactory solutions to both social and romantic themes. But perhaps in the nineteenth-century novels, as in Shakespearean comedy, we should be prepared to accept somewhat arbitrary group resolutions.

The number of specific references to class warfare in *North and South* are an indication of Mrs Gaskell's recognition of the bitterness of nineteenth-century industrial strife. She frankly accepts class difference, but fails to give sufficient emphasis to its economic basis. Instead, she stresses that the classes are mutually interdependent. In her technique as an imaginative novelist, she has a style and manner all her own, but in her criticism of society she is clearly a spokesman of the middle-class religious moderates, whose interests (apart from their religious ideas) prompted them to analyse the industrial situation in basically humanistic rather than economic terms and to propose enlightened christian management with a modicum of subservient worker-participation as a complete solution. This is what the chastened Mr Thornton proposes at the end of the novel:

> I have arrived at the conviction that no mere institutions, however wise, and however much thought may have been required to organize and arrange them, can attach class to class as they should be attached, unless the working out of such institutions bring the individuals of the different classes into actual personal contact. Such intercourse is the very breath of life. A working man can hardly be made to feel and know how much his employer may have laboured in his study at plans for the benefit of his workpeople. A complete plan emerges like a piece of machinery, apparently fitted for every emergency. But the hands accept it as they do machinery, without understanding the intense mental labour and forethought required to bring it to such perfection. But I would take an idea, the working out of which would necessitate personal intercourse; it might not go well at first, but at every hitch interest would be felt by an increasing number of men, and at last its success in working come to be desired by all, as all had borne a part in the formation of the plan; and even then I am sure that it would lose its vitality, cease to be living, as soon as it was no longer carried on by that sort of common interest which invariably makes people find means and ways of seeing each other, and becoming acquainted with each other's characters and persons, and even tricks of tempers and modes of speech. We should understand each other better, and I'll venture to say we should like each other more. (Penguin, p. 525)

Thus, the economic status quo is maintained and the hardships of the workers alleviated, always provided that the masters themselves can keep in business (which Mr Thornton cannot), and provided that they can afford to treat the workers humanely (which Mr Thornton finds he cannot do and has to employ Irish immigrants at cut rates).

The minor characters serve varying roles in developing Mrs Gaskell's criticism of society. Bessy Higgins, a victim of the industrial machine who has contracted card-room asthma, or byssenosis, from the fluff inhaled in the carding-room, not only exemplifies the human waste involved in gaining industrial wealth but serves to give Margaret her first actual insight into the lives of the cotton workers. By casting Bessy's account of her work and the possible means of preventing card-room asthma into simple uneducated speech, Mrs Gaskell fuses social documentation and fictional reality:

> 'Fluff,' repeated Bessy. 'Little bits, as fly off fro' the cotton, when they're carding it, and fill the air till it looks all fine white dust. They say it winds round the lungs, and tightens them up. Anyhow, there's many a one as works in a carding-room, that falls into a waste, coughing and spitting blood, because they're just poisoned by the fluff' (Penguin, p. 146).

The authentic flavour of Bessy's speech here and elsewhere in the novel effectively counteracts the somewhat sentimental and lachrymose scenes invented to portray her plight. Similarly, the convincing quality of her father's speech makes us less conscious that he has been created as the instrument for educating Mr Thornton in humane relations between masters and men. Nicholas Higgins has the simple dignity that John Barton lacks in *Mary Barton*; there is genuine tension between Higgins and Thornton, brought about by a clash of proud wills and class conflict, so that the final resolution of their differences represents a gain in both political and human understanding for each. By contrast the shadowy and insubstantial Mr Bell not only fails to come alive as a character but fails to sustain his representative role. As an Oxford don, whose source of wealth lies in Milton-Northern, Mr Bell is intended, through his character and his action in the plot, to suggest the need for the combination of culture and commerce, the past and the present, so that in some respects what we have is an interesting anticipation of the main theme of Forster's *Howards End*. In chapter 40 of *North and South* there is a conversation between Thornton and Bell that reveals the impossibility of transposing Arnoldian Oxford ideals of sweetness and light to the strenuous life of the North. Already, in chapter 10, Thornton has recognised that 'the whole machinery' – using that phrase in its extended Arnoldian sense to apply to a whole way of life – is too new to have developed its own scale of humane values. Where the conversation in chapter 10 turns on the question of legislative intervention, that in chapter 40 turns on the relevance of the wisdom of the past to present conditions in the North. Defending Milton from Bell's charge that its inhabitants look back to a violent pagan past and seeking to show the irrelevance of Bell's Oxford culture, Thornton gives his own account of the value of the past:

'If we do not reverence the past as you do in Oxford, it is because we want something which can apply to the present more directly. It is fine when the study of the past leads to a prophecy of the future. But to men groping in new circumstances, it would be finer if the words of experience could direct us how to act in what concerns us most intimately and immediately; which is full of difficulties that must be encountered; and upon the mode in which they are met and conquered – not merely pushed aside for the time – depends our future. Out of the wisdom of the past, help us over the present. But no! People can speak of Utopia much more easily than of the next day's duty; and yet when that duty is all done by others, who so ready to cry, "Fie, for shame!" '

'And all this time I don't see what you are talking about. Would you Milton men condescend to send up your to-day's difficulty to Oxford? You have not tried us yet.'

Mr Thornton laughed outright at this. 'I believe I was talking with reference to a good deal that has been troubling us of late; I was thinking of the strikes we have gone through, which are troublesome and injurious things enough, as I am finding to my cost. . . .' (Penguin, p. 414).

Such passages make explicit Mrs Gaskell's recognition that the cultural values of the South cannot simply be imposed on the North and that the North will have to work out its own pattern of humane values. But the structure of plot suggests something further; it suggests that the wealth made in the North needs to travel South, acquire wisdom from an older culture, and then return to save the proud Northern manufacturers from disaster. It is Milton-Northern money that enables Mr Bell to enjoy Oxford culture; it is Mr Bell's money that comes to save Thornton, when Margaret, as the mediator between North and South, offers him the money from Bell's legacy. Mrs Gaskell's strength arises from her direct observation of cultural differences between the North and the South and of the clash between masters and men, but her frankly acknowledged lack of interest in political economy leads her to relegate the relation between culture and money to a minor character and the mechanics of the plot.[2]

Although it is a less satisfying novel than *North and South*, Kingsley's *Alton Locke* presents a much more critical view of the church and the ancient universities in nineteenth-century industrial England, and of the conflict between masters and men. It does so because its basic premise is the need for Christian Socialism. As a disciple of Carlyle and F. D. Maurice (the founder of the Christian Socialist Movement), Kingsley used the novel as a means of reaching a wider audience than was possible through sermons and such pamphlets as *Cheap Clothes and Nasty*. But it is clear that Kingsley's Socialism was diversionary in effect if not in purpose. His main aim seems to have been to use the powers of Christianity to bridge the gulf between Disraeli's two nations, the Rich and the Poor, rather than to create a genuine Socialist society in which there would no longer be two nations but one, a single classless society. For a vision of such a society we have to turn from Kingsley to William Morris's *News From Nowhere* and Robert Tressell's *The Ragged-Trousered Philanthropists*, or in our own century, Lewis Grassic Gibbon's trilogy *A Scots Quair*.

In form *Alton Locke* is an autobiography, but in effect it is a political tract. It is presented as the story of the chartist 'Tailor and Poet' Alton Locke, written aboard the boat that is taking him to Texas, a few months after the failure of the Chartist Petition on 10 April 1848. Had the work as a whole rendered the developing consciousness of its hero more consistently, it would have been a finer and more unified novel. In chapter 6, the hero writes: 'This book is the history of my mental growth; and my mistakes as well as my discoveries are steps in that development, and may bear a lesson in them.' But Kingsley has insufficient faith in the exemplary quality of this 'mental growth' and frequently intervenes to address and admonish society, while retaining the formal pretence that it is Alton Locke who speaks. This is especially evident in the caustic reflections on society's faith in political economy in the chapter called 'The Men Who Are Eaten':

> You know how to invest your capital profitably, dear Society, and to save money over and above your income of daily comforts; but what has [the labourer] saved? – what is he profited by all those years of labour? He has kept body and soul together – perhaps he could have done that without you or your help. But his wages are used up every Saturday night. When he stops working, you have in your pocket the whole real profits of his nearly fifty years' labour, and he has nothing. (Cassell, paperback, p. 259)

This, and the subsequent rejection of 'that same snug competitive and property world of yours' might have come straight from the pages of Coleridge's *Lay Sermons* or one of the Christian Socialist political pamphlets. Yet the fact that Alton's account of his struggles to realise his latent creative powers and help his fellow-workers is cast in a retrospective mould goes some way to making allowance for the sermonising and superior tone: 'I tell my story, not as I saw it then, but as I see it now.' The method, in theory if not wholly in practice, combines the immediacy of present observation with the superior wisdom gained through hindsight.

Compared with any of the other Victorian 'Condition of England' novels, *Alton Locke* is more loosely structured and episodic, but the various incidents in the hero's life all contribute something to Kingsley's vision of society, casting a critical light on education, nonconformity, the church, radical journalism, working conditions in small workshop industries, city slums, agricultural poverty and, above all, the two kinds of Chartism: 'revolutionary' Chartism and 'moral force' Chartism. The sections in the novel that describe a poor man's struggle to obtain education and recognition for his literary talents, and those that portray his envy of his more fortunate cousin at Cambridge, foreshadow the theme of Hardy's *Jude the Obscure* and much twentieth-century fiction. Alton's reluctant agreement to exclude passages of social criticism from his poems in order to have them published through the good offices of the Dean, and his contempt for the 'immoral' advertising and sensationalism in radical journals, exhibit a concern with the state of literature in society comparable with Gissing's in *New Grub Street* many years later.

The hero's father, a small retail tradesman, dies when the boy is young and he is brought up in a strict calvinistic atmosphere, the very narrowness of which makes him acutely sensitive to the beauties of the natural world. But apprenticeship to a tailor soon confines him to a dark, narrow, airless prison: 'The windows were tight closed to keep out the cold winter air; and the condensed breath ran in streams down the panes, chequering the dreary outlook of chimney-tops and smoke.' These appalling conditions in a high-class tailor's establishment are nothing to those in the 'sweat-shop', from which Alton and his Scots mentor, Mackaye, rescue a boy in the chapter called 'The Sweater's Den'. The visit to Cambridge and the Cathedral City of D., which not only enables Kingsley to develop the romantic elements in the plot but also to satirise the worldliness of the church, marks a false step in the hero's 'mental growth' and he returns to London, his artistic integrity compromised, and in debt. As the result of listening to arguments, Alton becomes a convinced Chartist, but his speech delivered to a crowd of angry starving agricultural labourers is misunderstood and leads to riot and rick burning. From the time of his trial and his three years in prison, Alton begins to reconsider the meaning of his experiences and to plan his autobiography. The three main episodes in the last third of the novel are the rejection of the Charter, the death of the drunken Downes in the foul water beneath his 'sweater's den', and the long dream sequence, the product of a fever caught during Alton's visit to the den. During the latter, Alton relives the history of life on earth, taking in turn the identity of all primitive forms of life, madrepore, crab, remora, ostrich, mylodon and ape. He wakes to find the imperious Eleanor at his side and is now in the light of his evolutionary dream vision able to explain that 'moral' Chartism is preferable to 'revolutionary' Chartism.

> If by a Chartist you mean one who fancies that a change in mere political circumstances will bring about a millennium; I am no longer one. That dream is gone – with others. But if to be a Chartist is to love my brothers with every faculty of my soul – to wish to live and die struggling for their rights, endeavouring to make them, not electors merely, but fit to be electors, senators, kings, and priests to God and to His Christ – if that be the Chartism of the future, then am I sevenfold a Chartist, and ready to confess it before men, though I were thrust forth from every door in England. (p. 387)

The part of the plot that concerns Alton's love for the unattainable Lillian, a figure from fairyland who first appears to him as a vision of beauty in an art gallery and who subsequently marries his shallow worldly cousin, contributes very little to the serious social themes of the novel. The lofty Eleanor, who marries Alton's early patron and becomes Lady Ellerton, proves to be his real friend. She also serves the role of rescuer, sympathetic listener and nurse in the final stages of Alton's life. Kingsley lacks altogether Mrs Gaskell's psychological insight into the connections between personal and public life; consequently the romantic elements remain peripheral to the meaning of the novel and are seen for what they are – sops to convention and unconscious revelations of Kingsley's admiration of female dominance. Carlyle, apart from disliking the 'treatment of my own poor self', in the character of Mackaye, recorded that he 'found plenty to like, and to be grateful for in the book: abundance, nay exuberance of generous zeal; headlong impetuosity of determination towards the manful side on all manner of questions', but felt bound 'to say, the book is definable as *crude*'. It is a judgment impossible to deny.

The best-known of the Victorian 'Condition of England' novels, Dicken's *Hard Times*, was dedicated to Carlyle, and in many respects is the most Carlylean of all; yet, although Carlyle read Dickens with enjoyment, he always regarded him as an entertainer and not as a serious critic of English society. This, however, must be seen not so much as a judgment on Dickens as on the novel as a means of communicating ideas. Dickens's seriousness of purpose is obvious in every page of *Hard Times*; it is also damaging to its success as a novel. The change from long monthly-part serialisation to brief weekly instalments, and the determination to expose the connection between utilitarianism and industrialism, drastically hampered the novelist's expansive genius. The central weakness of *Hard Times* arises from the curious parodox that in designing a work to expose the malign effects of the mechanical spirit, Dickens chose a form of expression that was in itself too mechanical and programmatic. In comparing it with *North and South* we can see that curiosity, exact observation, flexibility of mind, are as important qualities for the 'Condition of England' novelist as an organising framework of ideas.

Hard Times presents an intensely and coherently imagined fictional world in which there is seen to be an integral relationship between the main characters and the cultural and physical environment they inhabit and which they have been partly responsible for bringing into being. As F. R. Leavis has remarked, Dickens's 'intention is peculiarly insistent, so that the representative significance of everything in the fable – character, episode, and so on – is immediately apparent as we read',[3] yet the consistency is not achieved at the expense of delicacy or depth. The connection between the education in facts, portrayed in Mr Gradgrind, 'with a rule and a pair of scales, and the multiplication table always in his pocket, sir, ready to weigh and measure any parcel of human nature', and the circumstantial but symbolic description of Coketown, 'a town sacred to fact', strikes the reader in the opening chapters of the novel. As the story develops, the carefully prepared climaxes enforce the meaning of the moral fable, especially as it relates to the ruin of Gradgrind's system, founded exclusively on facts and the development of the mind at the expense of the emotions. At the end of the second book, Louisa Gradgrind who has been prudentially married off to the coarse wealthy manufacturer, Bounderby, discovers that another kind of man exists in James Harthouse.

> 'All that I know is, your philosophy and your teaching will not save me. Now, father, you have brought me to this. Save me by some other means!'
>
> He tightened his hold in time to prevent her sinking on the floor, but she cried out in a terrible voice, 'I shall die if you hold me! Let me fall upon the ground!'
>
> And he laid her down there, and saw the pride of his heart and the triumph of his system lying, an insensible heap, at his feet. (Bk. II, ch. 12)

Next morning Gradgrind reflects that some persons hold 'that there is a wisdom of the Head, and that there is a wisdom of the Heart',[4] although he had not supposed so, but that now he must mistrust his belief that the head was 'all sufficient'. The other prepared climax is the exposure of Mr Gradgrind's son, Tom, for bank robbery, by the inflexible product of the Gradgrind system, Bitzer. The indictment of the system is compelling and complete, but it does not amount to a philosophic exposure of the main tenets of utilitarianism, as has sometimes been claimed by later writers, nor was it intended to be so by Dickens. The Utilitarian philosophy was more humane and less inflexible than Gradgrind's system, and the objects of Dickens's attack are so various they could never be brought within the bounds of any single philosophy. The alternative that Dickens offers to the bleak and stunted form of life at Coketown centres on Sleary's circus and involves joy, make-believe and entertainment. There is little justification in the text for equating it with any Blakean or Coleridgean faith in the imagination, although perhaps John Holloway overstates the opposite point of view when he says that 'the creed which Dickens champions in the novel against Gradgrind's, seems in the main to be that "all work and no play makes Jack a dull boy".'[5] This is perhaps in line with the novelist's *Household Words* article on 'Frauds upon Fairies' and his plea in that article, and in a letter to Angela Burdett-Coutts on 18 September 1853, for 'a little more fancy among children and a little less fact'. Two principles enunciated in Dickens's speech in the Birmingham Town Hall on 30 December 1853 came closest to stating the positives offered in *Hard Times* to the dehumanising Gradgrind and Bounderby system. There he held up the ideal of 'the fusion of different classes . . . the bringing together of employers and employed . . . the creating of a better common understanding among those whose interests are identical', and secondly the creation of a great educational institute for 'the education of the feelings as well as of reason'.

The title and many chapters of the story, so Dickens claimed in a letter to Peter Cunningham on 11 March 1854, existed before his visit to Preston to observe the strike. He feared that the statement in the *Illustrated London News* that the 'recent enquiry into the Preston strike is said to have originated the title, and, in some respects, suggested the turn of the story' would 'localize' the meaning of the novel, whereas it had 'a direct purpose, in reference to the working people all over England'. In a letter to Mrs Gaskell, as we have already seen, he reassured her that she need have no worries about *North and South*, as he had no intention of making *Hard Times* a novel about the strike. And yet the strike does occupy an important part in the novel, and it is impossible to consider Dickens's vision of the creation 'of a better understanding among those whose interests are identical' without considering his presentation of the strike, union activity, and the characters who represent the conflict between masters and men.

Dickens shows a much more sympathetic understanding of the common sense and organising power of the unionists in his *Household Words* article 'On Strike'.[6] In the article, he praises 'their astonishing fortitude and perseverance; their high sense of honour among themselves; the extent to which they are impressed with the responsibility that is upon them of setting a careful example'. In the novel, he polarises workers into the loud-mouthed Unionist, Slackbridge, and the hapless, bewildered martyr, Stephen Blackpool. The structural principle of startling opposites upon which the whole novel is based necessitates such a polarity, but it works against the novelist's intention of offering a vision of conciliation and brotherhood between men with identical interests. Moreover, although Stephen Blackpool does in fact develop a very Carlylean view of economic *laissez-faire* and the characteristic weakness of masters and men, he is not a sufficiently articulate or powerful force in the novel; it is only when his speeches have been paraphrased and expressed in normal prose, as they are by William Oddie in his *Dickens and Carlyle*, that we recognise the potential cogency and force of his ideas in the novel.[7]

Dickens's broad and comprehensive vision in *Hard Times*, although it brings into a single unity a mass of social problems, including even the class differences in the divorce laws, does make it difficult for him to treat individuals as individuals, to credit them with powers to resist an alien system of values, or to be self-critical and capable of change. Since the plot requires that both Gradgrind and Bounderby should alter as the result of added experience, it is necessary that from the start we should believe that each possesses at least a rudimentary inner life and is capable of self-criticism. But the bold lines of representative characterisation do not permit such complexity. The whole man is expressed through external details of appearance and speech. Bounderby, when we first meet him, has no internal life, seems incapable of self-doubt:

> He was a rich man: banker, merchant, manufacturer, and what not. A big, loud man, with a stare, and a metallic laugh. A man made out of a coarse material, which seemed to have been stretched to make so much of him. A man with a great puffed head and forehead, swelled veins in his temples, and such a strained skin to his face that it seemed to hold his eyes open, and lift his eyebrows up. A man with a pervading appearance on him of being inflated like a balloon, and ready to start. A man who could never sufficiently vaunt himself a self-made man. A man who was always proclaiming, through that brassy speaking-trumpet of a voice of his, his old ignorance and his old poverty. A man who was the Bully of humility (Bk. I, ch. 4).

The later pricking of the balloon, especially when it is as large as this one, is an impressive part of Dickens's deflationary technique; but it is useless to look for the internal causes of collapse. In contrast to Bounderby, Mrs Gaskell's master manufacturer, Mr Thornton, has an inner life and is capable of self-criticism. Like many other Manchester employers who have risen swiftly, he realises that his education is incomplete and employs Mr Hale to remedy this deficiency. Mrs Gaskell creates a dynamic tension between the individual and the total environment. Mr Thornton's internal reactions to people and to changes in industrial society are consistently subtle and convincing. Until the closing pages of the novel, when the conveniences of the plot take over, we have the sense of an individual re-making himself as he comes to see the need to remake the world of things and human relations about him. Immensely powerful though *Hard Times* is as an indictment of the mechanical spirit – and this is what links it most closely to Carlyle – it is less impressive as a fictional plea for flexibility of mind, the cultivation of the feelings, and joy. Dickens creates a world of mechanical monsters and passive victims dominated by inflexible economic and psychological laws. It is therefore illogical of him to suppose that the interests of monsters and victims are identical; and it is both illogical and inartistic to suppose that the mechanical monsters are capable of inner development and change. Significantly he has to create his world of feeling and spontaneous joy outside the mechanical system altogether. Sleary's circus serves in the novel as a reserve area of somewhat trivial culture just as Dickens's surreptitious visits to places of low entertainment with Mark Lemon and Wilkie Collins served as a release from the conventions of Victorian society.

While it is true, as Louis Cazamian has suggested,[8] that 'taken as a group, Dickens, Disraeli, Mrs Gaskell, and Kingsley had one common ideal: an efficient, paternalistic philanthropy, in which the State, or the great traditional estates of Church and nobility, carefully supervised social ills', there are in fact significant differences in emphasis and wide variations in fictional technique. In all its many manifestations, the Victorian 'Condition of England' novel reflects the moral conscience of the age struggling to humanize an alien system and finding in the novel the richest resources for expounding ideas, eliciting compassion, and advocating reform. What necessarily remained abstract in the prose pamphlets and treatises of the day became concrete in the pages of *Sybil*, *North and South*, *Felix Holt*, *Alton Locke* and *Hard Times*. By reliving the immediate past, by exploring the teeming present, the Victorian novelists helped to mould the future.

7 Political Action and the Crisis of Conscience

The title of this chapter describes exactly Henry James's major theme in *The Princess Casamassima*; if, mentally, we add a subtitle 'Anarchy and Social Order', the combination conveniently embraces Dostoevsky's *The Possessed*, Conrad's *The Secret Agent* and *Under Western Eyes*, as well as *The Princess Casamassima*, first published in 1885–6. They form a coherent group of major novels, all deeply concerned with the implications of political action, all rendering in fictional form the threat that secret societies pose to the individual consciousness and to the established social order. What, we may ask, is their special value? What do they tell us about anarchism that we could not find out equally well if not better by studying the growth of secret societies in Europe and the political philosophy of anarchism?

The chief difference between the political philosopher and the novelist is that the first seeks to establish which theories are valid and which are not, whereas the second explores the full human implications of attempting to carry a particular theory into action. The novelist characteristically traces the consequences of action both in relation to the individual who decides to act and in relation to the society in which the action takes place. And the novelist's unique strength lies in his capacity to reveal what it feels like to be involved in political action: what it feels like to experience the contrary pulls of public and private duty, to experience the disparity between theory and practice, intention and effect, and to experience the conflict between the quest for social justice and the quest for individual happiness and fulfilment.

In *The Possessed*, Dostoevsky explores this complex of problems through a fairly large group of characters, all of whom, however, radiate around the twin centres formed by Stavrogin and Pyotr Verkovensky. 'Do you think that nihilists cannot love beauty?' Verkovensky asks Stavrogin. 'It is only idols that they do not love, but I love an idol. You are my idol.' As typical Dostoevskian 'doubles' in a novel in which 'doubles' proliferate to suggest similitude within dissimilitude, both characters embody the daemonic released from all moral limits. With an intuitive insight into the destructive consequences of moral nihilism even greater than Turgenev's in *Fathers and Sons*, and with an imaginative grasp of political anarchy far wider than that of any other writer, Dostoevsky has written the greatest ideological novel in world literature – ideological, not in the sense of enforcing a particular political theory, but in the sense of dramatising a conflict of ideas.

By contrast, James's novel *The Princess Casamassima* is not an ideological novel at all. Moreover, unlike Dostoevsky's *The Possessed*, it centres its interest mainly on one character, Hyacinth Robinson. It is in Hyacinth that the crisis of consciousness and conscience is enacted. And the circle of London anarchists serves chiefly as a background to give authenticity to Hyacinth's moral dilemma. In Conrad's *The Secret Agent*, the world – or rather underworld – of London anarchism occupies an altogether more important role, although even Conrad is more concerned with the effect of anarchism on individuals than on society as a whole. Yet the novel does not concentrate on the single figure of Mr Verloc, the epitome of idle bumbling inefficiency. The novel includes a varied assortment of anarchists and explores in detail the consequences of Verloc's actions: for himself, for the simple-minded victim, Stevie, and the dutiful Winnie Verloc. In the other secret society novel, *Under Western Eyes*, Conrad is as interested in rendering 'the psychology of Russia' as he is in the crisis of conscience experienced by the central character, Razumov, who like James's Hyacinth Robinson has a political duty forced on him that is more than he can bear. Conrad is also concerned with presenting the cross-currents of European anarchism in this novel, written in the Dostoevsky manner. He tells his readers that he aimed at a 'scrupulous impartiality' and certainly contemporary critics were puzzled by his ironic detachment and failed to perceive the subtlety of Conrad's political vision. A later critic, Irving Howe, in *Politics and the Novel*, seriously undervalues Conrad because the revolutionaries are not made positive enough in *Under Western Eyes* and the anarchists are made to look silly in *The Secret Agent*. At the root of Howe's objections lies an unwillingness to forgive Conrad for not being (a) politically committed; and (b) an extreme left-wing socialist.

As readers and critics, it is doubtful if we have a right to demand of an author either political commitment or adherence to a specific political theory or party. It is more interesting and valid to examine the precise relationship between political vision and literary form and to see how well each supports the other. Thus, it is important to notice the connection between Dostoevsky's politics of salvation and his daemonic, messianic form; to notice the connection between Conrad's conservative, pessimistic political vision and his heavily ironic, detached style. It is also especially illuminating to consider how much of the actual complexity of political action gets into a particular novel. And to ask: How does it do so? Is it mainly through the complexity of the plot? Is it mainly through the depth of characterisation? Is it mainly through the author's commentary? Or is it through the balance between the moral vision of the characters and the overall moral vision of the author? Christopher Cooper's main thesis in *Conrad and the Human Dilemma*, that we must see that the overall morality is quite different from the moral vision of any one of the characters, is a useful reminder to see novels as artistic wholes and not to seize on single characters, episodes, set speeches or comments as conclusive evidence of what the author thought. It is a useful reminder not to use the parts of a novel as if they were historical documents containing indisputable facts.

A close examination of Henry James's *The Princess Casamassima* reveals particularly well the exact relation between political vision and literary form. It also reveals that the central theme of the novel is 'Political Action and the Crisis of Conscience'. *The Princess Casamassima* is a novel about an anarchist cell in London. It is a novel about the duty of assassination laid upon the youthful hero, Hyacinth Robinson. And it is a novel about the vast seething mass of the London poor, a novel about London, 'the great, indifferent city' (ch. 47).

But, how did Henry James, the scholarly recluse and great diner-out in London's most fashionable houses, come to know anything about the political underworld of secret societies, or the life of the London poor? For an answer to that question, we have to go to James's Preface. There he gives his own account of the novel's origin.

> The simplest account of the origin of *The Princess Casamassima* is, I think, that this fiction proceeded quite directly, during the first year of a long residence in London, from the habit and the interest of walking the streets. . . . It is a fact that, as I look back, the attentive exploration of London, the assault directly made by the great city upon an imagination quick to react, fully explains a part of it.

This, then, was one germ of the novel. James describes the other in a later paragraph:

> It seemed to me I had only to imagine such a spirit intent enough and troubled enough, and to place it in presence of the comings and goings, the great gregarious company, of the more fortunate than himself – all on the scale of which London could show them – to get possession of an interesting theme. I arrived so at the history of little Hyacinth Robinson – he sprang up for me out of the London pavement.

Well, perhaps he sprang up less simply than that. James had recently read and reviewed Turgenev's *Virgin Soil*; and the hero of that novel, Nezhdanov is, like Hyacinth Robinson, a 'person in a false position . . . not of his own making'. And, again like James's hero, he too commits suicide as a way out of his tormented circumstances.

In his Preface, James goes on to explain exactly what qualities such a figure as Hyacinth must have. Although a poor London artisan, he must not be coarse, or stupid, or blind. He must possess 'the power to be finely aware and richly responsible'. And yet his awareness must be limited by circumstance and other people. For Hyacinth there must be plenty of bewilderment, 'and plenty of slashing out in the bewilderment'. And the whole success of the novel would depend on the quality of that bewilderment. 'The picture of the exposed and entangled state' of Hyacinth's experience renders in the most intense fashion the conflict between two worlds, without false heroics or sentimentality. If we are drawn to compare Hyacinth with E. M. Forster's Leonard Bast, immediately, I think, we recognise that Leonard is too limited, too shallow a consciousness, with his pathetic attempt to imitate Ruskin, and his Edwardian nature-yearning centred on the 'Open Road'.

Most of Henry James's heroes suffer from some obscure hurt, some fatal impairment of mind or body that prevents them from achieving final fulfilment, some secret that they carry within themselves that contains the seeds of their own destruction. Needless to say, psychological and biographical speculation has come up with various explanations, based on the author's own mysterious references to an obscure wound that prevented him from serving in the Civil War with the other young men of his generation. It seems to have been nothing more romantic or mysterious than a slipped disc. But upon this slender – one might say tender – foundation wonderful theories of impotence and castration complexes have been built.

Hyacinth Robinson, the hero of *The Princess Casamassima*, carries with him no less than two guilty secrets. One is the guilty secret of his birth; the other is the guilty secret of his indissoluble association with Hoffendahl and the gang of anarchists. In the case of the latter, he actually carries the guilty secret in his pocket in the later stages of the novel. This takes the form of the letter instructing him to assassinate a member of the English peerage.

It is convenient for the purpose of analysis to deal with these two guilty secrets separately, although of course they are connected in the novel. First, then, the guilty secret of Hyacinth's birth. Some features of James's presentation have been highly praised, others have come in for a good deal of criticism. Most critics have praised the scene describing the visit to the prison. Reservations have been made about its melodrama. It has been called Dickensian pastiche, based on books not life, in spite of the fact that we know that a boyhood visit to the notorious Sing Sing gaol produced a traumatic effect on the young James, and that at the time of composing *The Princess Casamassima* he visited Millbank Prison. What happens in the novel, it will be recalled, is that Miss Pynsent, Hyacinth's guardian, takes the young boy to see his dying mother in the prison hospital. Glowering in the background is the massive and muscular Mrs Bowerbank, a kind of prison procuress. Years before, Hyacinth's mother, Florentine Vivier, a French milliner, had murdered her aristocratic English lover, the shadowy 'Lord Frederick'. The boy Hyacinth knows nothing of this. But he had always been made to feel special. Miss Pynsent 'had made him feel there was a grandeur in his past'. But the details had remained secret. The lurid prison scene, shot through with irony, ends with the little boy being made to kiss the terrible dying woman.

> Amanda caught the child with an eagerness almost as great as Florentine's and, drawing him to the head of the bed, pushed him into his mother's arms. Kiss her – kiss her well, and we'll go home! she whispered desperately while they closed about him and the poor dishonoured head pressed itself against his young cheek. It was a terrible, irresistible embrace, to which Hyacinth submitted with instant patience. . . . What thoughts were begotten at that moment in his wondering little mind his protectress was destined to learn at another time. (ch. 3)

There are three features of this passage that deserve special attention. The emphatic phrase, 'terrible, irresistible embrace' foreshadows the whole horrible but compulsive fascination of Hyacinth's dedication to a popular cause (his French mother is a woman of the people). The use of the phrase 'strange ordeal' marks out this visit to prison as the first stage in Hyacinth's 'ordeal of consciousness', the first of many initiation ceremonies. The mysterious, proleptic sentence ('What thoughts were begotten at that moment in his wondering little mind his protectress was destined to learn at another time.') prepares the reader for the gradual unfolding of Hyacinth's destiny in relation to his early traumatic experience. The somewhat lurid, melodramatic quality of the scene (which is not, as has often been suggested, Dickensian) is wholly justified, since the scene is mediated through the distorting medium of the young boy's consciousness.

Just as it is irrelevant to ascribe James's sombre evocation of nineteenth-century prison life to Dickens, so too it is almost as irrelevant to ascribe the theme of guilty birth to Zola's deterministic theories of the novel. In chapter 2 of *The Experimental Novel*, Zola defines the role of the novel as demonstrating 'the way in which intellectual and sensory processes . . . are conditioned by heredity and environment', and his own novels *The Drunkard* and *Nana* are examples. There are traces of Zola's genetical determinism in *The Princess Casamassima*, certainly, but these are relatively insignificant and work against the deeper meanings of the novel. James's purpose is not to trace the inevitable effects of heredity on Hyacinth; it is to use his hero's humble origins symbolically, thus linking personal and public themes. In doing so, he enormously expands the significance of the novel, giving it a mythic dimension. The clash between the rich and the poor, the contrast between the aristocracy and the people, mirrored in every detail of London life, has its counterpart in Hyacinth's parents, in the passionate affair between the poor French woman and her aristocratic English lover. French, of course, to link her with the revolutions of 1789 and 1848. That passionate affair ends in brutal murder, the birth of Hyacinth, and finally the death of his mother. We are not, I think, intended to see Hyacinth's subsequent suicide as absolutely predetermined by his guilty ancestry. (And yet this is partly suggested at the end of the novel.) What we are meant to see is that the unravelling of this secret, and the understanding of its personal and social implications, is part of Hyacinth's ordeal and initiation into life.

A man may triumph over one guilty secret. But to load him with two is to weigh the scales heavily against him. And this is what James does in bringing his hero into association with the group of anarchists as part of his initiation into the life of the great city. It is possible, as Lionel Trilling has suggested in *The Liberal Imagination*,[1] to see *The Princess Casamassima* as belonging to a great line of novels that runs through the nineteenth century, the heroes of which may be described as the 'Young Man from the Provinces'. Such a tradition includes Stendhal's *Scarlet and Black*, Balzac's *Père Goriot*, Dickens's *Great Expectations*, and Flaubert's *Sentimental Education.* Indeed, it is particularly illuminating to compare Flaubert's Frédéric with James's Hyacinth. In *The Princess Casmassima*, there is a centrally important passage that clearly establishes Hyacinth's role as a young man from the provinces.

> In such hours the great roaring indifferent world of London seemed to him a huge organisation for mocking at his poverty, at his inanition; and then its vulgarest ornaments, the windows of third-rate jewellers, the young man in a white tie and a crush-hat who dandled by on his way to a dinner-party in a hansom that nearly ran over one – these familiar phenomena became symbolic, insolent, defiant, took on themselves to make him smart with the sense that *he* was above all out of it. He felt, moreover, that there was neither consolation nor refutation in saying to himself that the immense majority of mankind were out of it with him and appeared to put up well enough with the annoyance. That was their own affair; he knew nothing of their reasons or their resignation, and if they chose neither to rebel nor to compare he at least, among the disinherited, would keep up the standard. . . . Everything which in a great city could touch the sentient faculty of a youth on whom nothing was lost ministered to his conviction that there was no possible good fortune in life of too 'quiet' an order for him to appreciate – no privilege, no opportunity, no luxury to which he mightn't do full justice. It was not so much that he

> wanted to enjoy as that he wanted to know; his desire wasn't to be pampered but to be initiated. Sometimes of a Saturday in the long evenings of June and July he made his way into Hyde Park at the hour when the throng of carriages, of riders, of brilliant pedestrians was thickest; and though lately, on two or three of these occasions, he had been accompanied by Miss Henning, whose criticism of the scene was rich and distinct, a tremendous little drama had taken place privately on the stage of his inner consciousness. He wanted to drive in every carriage, to mount on every horse, to feel on his arm the hand of every pretty woman in the place. In the midst of this his sense was vivid that he belonged to the class whom the 'bloated' as they passed didn't so much as rest their eyes on for a quarter of a second. They looked at Millicent, who was safe to be looked at anywhere and was one of the handsomest girls in any company, but they only reminded him of the high human walls, the deep gulfs of tradition, the steep embankments of privilege and dense layers of stupidity fencing the 'likes' of him off from social recognition. (ch. 11)

This densely metaphoric passage powerfully renders the 'little drama' that has taken place 'privately on the stage' of Hyacinth's 'inner consciousness'; it expresses the desire of the 'disinherited' for a full initiation into the life of riches and pleasures and the recovery of a cultural heritage that is his by right of a superior sensibility.

If the novel can be seen as a novel about a young man from the provinces, it can also be seen as a novel structured on a series of initiation ceremonies, each with its appropriate test, task, or ordeal. And it is Hyacinth's misfortune to be initiated into the life of a secret society, a society of anarchists, that exacts complete obedience and the loss of personal liberty and life, if necessary. It is a further misfortune that soon after this fatal initiation he should receive his first initiation into the life of European culture. He has glimpsed it at Medley, with its English country house splendour and charm, but it is in Paris that he has a sudden vision of the sweetness of not dying, and a little later in Venice that he achieves happiness.

It is a happiness that logically demands a drastic revision of his reforming zeal. In simple terms his situation is that he has fallen in love with the world that he has agreed to blow sky high – the world of inherited riches, aristocratic culture, a civilisation based on cruelty, thoughtlessness and exploitation. Hyacinth records this crisis of consciousness and of conscience in his long letter to the Princess. The ending is one of the key passages in the novel. Like Keats and in words that strike us as almost an echo of Keats, he explains that he has come to see that 'want and toil and suffering are the constant lot of the immense majority of the human race'. He goes on to explain that what has struck him is 'the great achievements of which man has been capable', 'in spite of this great burden of misery':

> the splendid accumulations of the happier few, to which doubtless the miserable many may have also in their degree contributed. The face of Europe appears to be covered with them and they've had much the greater part of my attention. They seem to me inestimably precious and beautiful and I've become conscious more than ever before of how little I understand what in the great rectification you and Poupin propose to do with them. Dear Princess, there are things I shall be too sorry to see you touch, even you with your hands divine; and – shall I tell you *le fond de ma pensée*, as you used to say? – I feel myself capable of fighting for them. You can't call me a traitor, for you know the obligation I supremely, I immutably recognise. The monuments and treasures of art, the great palaces and properties, the conquests of learning and taste, the general fabric of civilisation as we know it, based if you will upon all the despotisms, the cruelties, the exclusions, the monopolies and the rapacities of the past, but thanks to which, all the same, the world is less of a 'bloody sell' and life more of a lark – our friend Hoffendahl seems to me to hold them too cheap and to wish to substitute for them something in which I can't somehow believe as I do in things with which the yearnings and the tears of generations have been mixed. You know how extraordinary I think our Hoffendahl – to speak only of him; but if there's one thing that's more clear about him than another, it's that he wouldn't have the least feeling for this incomparable, abominable old Venice. He would cut up the ceilings of the Veronese into strips, so that every one might have a little piece. I don't want every one to have a little piece of anything and I've a great horror of that kind of invidious jealousy which is at the bottom of the idea of a redistribution. You'll say I talk of it all at my ease while in a delicious capital I smoke cigarettes on a magenta divan; and I give you leave to scoff at me if it turns out that when I come back to London without a penny in my pocket I don't hold the same language. I don't know what it comes from, but during the last three months there has crept over me a deep mistrust of that same grudging attitude – the intolerance of positions and fortunes that are higher and brighter than one's own; a fear, moreover, that I may in the past have been actuated by such motives, and a devout hope that if I'm to pass away while I'm yet young it may not be with that odious stain upon my soul. (ch. 30)

There will always be readers who are more interested in the political implications of this passage than in its function in relation to Hyacinth's crisis of conscience. It does raise radical questions about the price society pays to support what Veblen calls a 'leisure class culture', a culture characterised by 'conspicuous leisure', 'conspicuous consumption', and 'conspicuous waste'. And James's position – in this novel and most of his novels – is patently ambivalent. But it is precisely this ambivalence that enables him to dramatise the inherent contradictions in his characters, and in nineteenth-century society. Had he been a more committed political writer, it is likely that he would have falsified these contradictions in terms of some simple political panacea. Duality lies at the heart of James's fictional universe: duality of daemonic artist and ironic observer; duality of allegiance to the Old World and to the New; duality of attitude to money, as both necessary for high civilisation and as a blighting curse. It is worth keeping this idea about duality in mind when one reads good left-wing liberals like Lionel Trilling, who though they may illuminate the social background, tend to distort the novels to make them conform to their own radical ideologies. James is the complex chronicler of a bourgeois society. His values are basically those of that society. But certain gifts enabled him to see the internal contradiction of that society more clearly than his contemporaries and to disengage himself from conventional bourgeois values. These gifts were: the gift of a complex inheritance that almost demanded that he should see with a double vision and therefore attempt to do justice to the contrary elements within himself and his society; the gift of psychological insight that always took him below the surface appearances; and the gift of a superb irony, an irony that constantly undermines the too confident assertion of *positive* values by any of his characters. With James – as with Keats and Shakespeare – we have to be content with uncertainties, 'without any irritable reaching after fact and reason'.

The Princess Casamassima would be a thin and shallow book if the conflict between the rich and poor were reflected *only* in the consciousness of the hero Hyacinth. But this is not the case. It also includes a large number of finely observed and delicately rendered characters. They cover the whole spectrum of English life in the 1880s. Each of the characters achieves a representative quality without losing individuality. James often stresses this representative quality when he first introduces the character, but never with the patent obviousness of Dickens in *Hard Times*. On the whole James's method is to accumulate a mass of significant detail (only the details of the cockney accent strike a wrong note). He then places the character with a single defining sentence. This he does with Millicent Henning. But the defining comes not from James as omniscient author, but from the 'finely aware and richly responsible' consciousness of Hyacinth, who registers his impressions of her thus:

> She summed up the sociable humorous ignorant chatter of the masses, their capacity for offensive and defensive passion, their in-

stinctive perception of their strength on the day they should really exercise it. (ch. 10)

Such definitions do not have the effect of reducing the characters to mere social paradigms, because they are subject to constant revision and modification, partly from the reader's greater understanding, partly through the hero's growing awareness, and partly through the inclusion of a rich profusion of complicating detail. This detail makes the characters as complicated, inconsistent and unpredictable as people in real life.

The characters represent the main varieties of Victorian social reform. By this means, James places Hyacinth against the background that is felt to be richly and complexly *there*. Paul Muniment represents the rather coarse-grained North country radical: good humoured, limited in sensibility, easily tempted to place self-advancement before devotion to a cause. Hyacinth's growing disenchantment with Paul is part of his (and our) political education. Lady Aurora represents the aristocratic lady who finds her mission in life in slumming (a sort of early Beatrice Webb). And the mention of Beatrice Webb is a reminder that the first volumes of her autobiography *My Apprenticeship* give an unrivalled account of the London poor in the year James wrote his novel, the 'constantly decomposing mass of human beings' she saw in her long trudges through the East End of London, an account comparable with Mayhew's for the London poor of the 1850s and 1860s; and Charles Booth's for the London of the 1880s and 1890s. Lady Aurora is saved from becoming simply a social stereotype, the slumming aristocrat, by being seen through Rose Muniment's romantic sensibility, a sensibility distorted by gratitude and reverence. And also through James's rendering of her personal oddities of speech and behaviour. The Princess Casamassima, whom we meet as Christina Light in the early novel *Roderick Hudson*, represents the type of woman who is drawn to social problems as an escape from boredom. She hopes to find in serving others' misery the excitement or satisfaction that her luxurious life denies her. And it becomes apparent to us (as it only very belatedly becomes evident to Hyacinth) – even though he is warned by Paul, Mr Vetch, Sholto and then Grandoni – that her attitude to her helpers and intermediaries is as selfish and callous as her attitude to the poor. 'She plays with life, but she plays audaciously.' In the theatre scene, when the Princess Casamassima commissions Captain Sholto to bring Hyacinth to her box, the reader immediately recognises Sholto's abject position in relation to the Princess. It is only a matter of time before Hyacinth comes to occupy a similar position. And yet the Princess is capable of deep feeling of loyalty to a person as well as to a cause; she is capable of generous self-sacrifice. At the end of the novel, when she says she can easily find out the great house where Hyacinth is to fire his pistol shot, Schinkel asks her if she plans to warn the victim. She answers: 'No, I want to do the business myself first, so that it won't be left for another.' In other words, it won't be left for Hyacinth. She is prepared to assassinate the peer herself.

The main characters, then, have a firm representative quality which does not obliterate the more personal qualities that establish the personal identity of each. Not only do the main characters have this representative social quality; the places where they live and the debates they take part in have a similar dimension. James achieves this generic dimension without resorting to the kind of rhetorical devices Dickens employs in *Hard Times*, a novel that imposes social significance on the characters, the places where they live and the debates they take part in with a much heavier and more emphatic hand.

It is not necessary to have first-hand knowledge of London to sense the representative quality of the various settings: Millicent's little back room near the Edgware Road, Poupin's anarchist cell in Lisson Grove, Paul Muniment's dingy nook in Audley Court, a nook brightened by vulgar prints and the presence of his invalid sister Rosy, who is a reminder of the strange power that the Victorian invalid wielded from her bed (one thinks of Florence Nightingale and Elizabeth Barrett Browning). Lady Aurora's house in Belgrave Square stands utterly remote from London's seething underworld of misery. So, too, does the Princess in South Street. And occupying something of the symbolic function of Forster's house, Howards End, in the novel of that name, is Medley, where the Princess entertains her little book-binder, Hyacinth, and first introduces him to 'a world enchantingly new'.

> There was something in the way the grey walls rose from the green lawn that brought tears to his eyes; the spectacle of long duration unassociated with some sordid infirmity or poverty was new to him. (ch. 22)

This is Hyacinth's initiation into the life of the English gentry. It represents a ripe civilisation and ultimately he dies to ensure that it survives. His visit to Medley is an initiation ceremony. James actually uses the word 'initiation'. The glories of Medley are seen through the expanding vision of the young book-binder. But the reader notes that the Princess only *rents* Medley. It represents a culture that can neither be bought by money, nor acquired by the dispossessed. Neither the Princess nor Hyacinth, therefore, is really at home at Medley, though they respond to its appeal. And its pervasive and universal influence remains with Hyacinth. In later novels James was to write of the English country house with a more ironic eye, aware of ostentation, isolation and touches of vulgarity.

If the houses in which the characters live come to embody different cultural values, the number of scenes set in the London parks on a Sunday also come to embody complex truths about London life in the 1880s. The prisoners of industrialism have their one day of freedom. Milly, thoroughly conventional, unthinking in her acceptance of inherited religious values, insists on taking Hyacinth to church before walking in the park with him. The Princess wanted to destroy society and Millicent to uphold it, Hyacinth reflects. These walks in the London parks suggest a temporary escape into a diminished Eden for the London poor; and not even James's own fastidious distaste as he describes how 'the young of both sexes, hilarious and red in the face, roll in promiscuous accouplement over the slopes', destroys the sense of a poignant tarnished pastoral. If we set against this the central image of Hyacinth seeing 'life through the glass of the pastry-cook's window', we have the two essential features of James's vision of the yearning impoverishment of city life.

Characters, houses, London's parks have their representative quality as they do in Forster's *Howards End*. But so, too have the set-pieces of conversation. They never become formal debates, they never become rhetorical, but they serve to define exactly the main varieties of social reform. And the arguments about levelling up and levelling down still retain their interest for us today.

The ending of *The Princess Casamassima* has been interpreted in a variety of ways. Hyacinth thinks he has been deserted by Paul Muniment and the Princess. He receives his instruction to kill the duke. But he decides to kill himself instead. He visits Milly's shop, as a last refuge in his friendless, deserted state. There he is confronted with the brutal evidence of Milly's frailty, as Captain Sholto silently proclaims his sole rights in her. It is one of James's great scenes. At the moment his friends are marshalling to rescue him, Hyacinth locks his door and shoots himself – with the revolver provided for the duke. He is discovered by the Princess, initiator into the world of art, and by Schinkel, one of his initiators into the world of politics; a fine symbolic touch.

According to Lionel Trilling, Hyacinth 'dies of the withdrawal of love'; his death is 'not his way of escaping from irresolution' but 'an act of heroism'. Such an interpretation ignores much in the text and is more typical of Trilling's liberal idealism than James's complex vision. Louise Bogan, in what is otherwise one of the best brief essays,[2] can give no satisfactory account of Hyacinth's act, because she regards Hyacinth's consciousness as a cool and undistorting mirror, shining between the dark and violent world of the disinherited on the one hand and the preposterous world of privilege on the other. But to regard it as an undistorting mirror is to equate it with the author's undistorting consciousness and to miss the point of the book. The whole point of the book is that Hyacinth's limited understanding of events and people leads him to tragic errors of judgment. He doubly misunderstands

Paul: first seeing in him the religion of friendship and then a code of self-seeking and brutal desertion. In fact, Paul had never been the fond friend Hyacinth imagined, and he has not deserted him. He merely wishes to leave Hyacinth free. And the hero doubly misunderstands the Princess also. His earlier view of the Princess is heavily idealised. Once he has experienced the 'rage of jealousy', as he and the Prince watch Paul and the Princess descend from a hansom and enter her house together, he feels betrayed and deserted. Thus, he does not tell the Princess that his call has come. Had he done so, the outcome might have been different. He does not tell her because he has already judged her, and is overwhelmed by self-pity. In fact, the Princess would have saved him by carrying out the task of assassination herself.

What many readers and critics would prefer to forget when trying to answer the question why Hyacinth should shoot himself is the part played by the memory of his mother. This is the least satisfactory part of the book. It would be absurd to say that Hyacinth shoots himself because he wishes to avoid repeating his mother's crime of shooting an aristocrat:

> This loathing of the idea of a *repetition* had not been sharp, strangely enough, till he had felt the great, hard hand on his shoulder. . . . Yet now the idea of the personal stain made him horribly sick; it seemed by itself to make service impossible. (ch. 47)

Yet we cannot ignore the evidence of the text in the last chapter, where the element of biological determinism, the Zola element, is given a psychological dimension. To my mind this is the least satisfactory part of the whole novel. But it is unmistakably there and stressed at a structurally crucial point.

Why did Hyacinth kill himself? There is no simple answer. Three main influences may be seen to be at work. There is the hero's loss of faith in the political cause, as the result of a new insight into civilisation and European culture, which in the terms of the novel is a genuine insight. There is his loss of faith in his friends, which is seen by the reader to represent a tragically limited understanding of their natures and their actions. And there is his desire to avoid repeating his mother's crime by resorting to violence to restore the moral order. All three contribute something vital to the tragic pattern. The first, the conflict between reforming zeal and the discovery of European culture, provides a genuine tragic conflict. The second, Hyacinth's fatal errors of judgment in relation to Paul, Milly and the Princess, give the novel a subtle psychological dimension, and James presents the judgments so that the reader is made painfully and tragically aware of the discrepancy between Hyacinth's limited consciousness and the facts as they are. The third and least satisfactory of all, but nevertheless contributing to the sense of inescapable tragedy, is the element of biological determinism, that suggests man's powerlessness in relation to predetermined events.

Ultimately, what prevents *The Princess Casamassima* from being the great tragic work it might have been are the sensational elements of Hyacinth's early life and the intrusive deterministic element. But these are small flaws in an otherwise wonderfully mature exploration of the conflict between public and private life, in a limited but amazingly sensitive consciousness, the consciousness of Hyacinth Robinson. Yet in all this we must never forget the importance of the consciousness of the author himself. As James himself wrote in the Preface to *The Portrait of a Lady*:

> The spreading field, the human scene, is the 'choice of subject'; the pierced aperture, either broad or balconied or slit-like and low-browed, is the 'literary form'; but they are, singly or together, as nothing without the posted presence of the watcher – without, in other words, the consciousness of the artist.

In *The Princess Casamassima*, it has been seen, James's political vision is inseparable from his literary form. His criticism is embodied in the structure of the novel as a whole and in every detail of its imaginative organisation. His main theme is political action and the crisis of conscience, not 'the death of a society', as Stephen Spender has claimed.[3] Only by attending closely to his precise method of narration can we be sure that we have understood his criticism of society.

8 Sex, the Family and the New Woman

The large family in the nineteenth century was both a potent myth and an economic necessity. It was a potent myth, in that it conveniently embodies many essential features of conventional Christianity: it was an economic necessity, in that it maintained social stability in a period of rapid economic change and provided a large enough work force for England's industrial success at home and commercial expansion abroad. But there was a wide gap between the myth of the united, happy, Christian family and the actual reality. At what cost was this happiness bought? What lay behind the decorous façade?

It was bought at the expense of the subjection of the woman in the home and the denial to her of an equal right to sexual happiness; and current medical theories conveniently supported this denial.[1] It was bought at the cost of child brides, the cult of the innocent maiden, as a counterweight to the massive prostitution in all the great cities. In *The New Machiavelli*, H. G. Wells refers to the city prostitutes as the 'doomed safety valves of purity'; but no Victorian novelists were equally outspoken, and it needed the sensational journalism of W. K. Stead's exposure of the White Slave traffic in the *Pall Mall Gazette* to prepare the way for the franker treatment by the Edwardian novelists.[2] It is now apparent that the myth of the happy Victorian family was bought at the expense of monstrous hypocrisy, stunted emotional growth, and sexual deviation. In *David Copperfield*, both David's mother and his first wife are child brides. It is not until nearly the end of the century that Ibsen exposes the status of the wife as a doll. Although the final slamming of the door, as Nora leaves her husband, shocked many of Ibsen's contemporaries and offered a promise of freedom to others, *The Doll's House* provided no convincing solution to the inequality of the sexes in marriage. Even though the whole plot turns on money and shows the subterfuges woman are driven to, neither Nora nor her foil Mrs Linde attain complete financial and sexual independence. With Ibsen and Shaw, the theatre became a centre of lively debate on women's status, on marriage and the family. In contrast with such serious 'problem plays' as *The Doll's House* and *Getting Married*, there was a spate of less serious works that attracted wide audiences because of their dash of daring. But such popular plays as Pinero's *The Second Mrs Tanqueray*

(1893) and *The Notorious Mrs Ebbsmith* turned serious questions about marriage into melodramatic situations and satisfied the audiences with safe conservative endings. Something of the same pattern appears in the popular novels of the day. Although Grant Allen's *The Woman Who Did* (1895) championed the rights of women, it conveniently satisfied conventional morality by ensuring that the heroine died for her defiance of Victorian sexual morality. If such moral endings were repugnant to some, so too was the conventional ending, a happy marriage. In a paper on 'Pessimism in Modern Literature',[3] Forster pointed out that for at least three writers (Zola, Ibsen and Tolstoy) such an ending was a lie; 'we of to-day know that whatever marriage is, it is not an end . . . how can the novelist to-day, knowing this, end his novel with marriage?'

What actually lay behind the decorous façade of the Victorian family, it is difficult to say, but an ironic passage in Mark Rutherford's fine novel *Clara Hopgood* describes one aspect of polite male hypocrisy:

> A man determines that he must marry; he makes the shop-girl an allowance, never sees her or her child again, transforms himself into a model husband, is beloved by his wife and family; the woman whom he kissed as he will never kiss his lawful partner, withdraws completely, and nothing happens to him. (ch. 25)

To decide what Victorian sex life was really like, it is fashionable to adduce the evidence assembled by Steven Marcus in *The Other Victorians*, but we need to be on our guard. Much of the so-called documentary material quoted from *My Secret Life* may be as fictional, as much a piece of wish fulfilment, as the passages quoted from the pornographic section at the end of the book, works such as the *Romance of Lust*, with its monstrous feats of multiple copulation.[4] There is certainly a remarkable similarity. Moreover, the author of *My Secret Life* can hardly be taken as a representative Victorian male. But there is a mass of rather better authenticated material to suggest that behind the polite façade of Victorian family life there was great diversity of human behaviour. The Benson family provides an example. E. W. Benson, a handsome Adonis in clerical cloth, who became Archbishop of Canterbury, began making advances to the little girl who became his wife when she was only eleven. They later produced a family of sons, none of whom married, all of whom became homosexuals. And the mother found happiness and fulfilment, not with her husband, but in passionate Lesbian relations. Havelock Ellis's autobiography, *My Life*, apart from giving a most moving account of the discovery of his true self, when he was working as a bush schoolmaster at Sparkes Creek in New South Wales, provides a tolerant and sympathetic account of his life with his Lesbian wife, and their intimate relations with the South African novelist, Olive Schreiner, who wished she had been born a man, but who struggled to work out patterns of happy relations with both men and women.

In all ages there have been women who wished to enjoy the same freedom as men. It was especially difficult for them to achieve this ideal in the nineteenth century, but many tried; and gradually, as the century advanced, the cause of women's emancipation attracted greater support, not only from women, but also from men, from Edward Carpenter, for instance, and from Bernard Shaw, and H. G. Wells. The 'New Woman', as she was called, has a long and interesting history.

If we look at some of the ways open to women to break out of the stultifying limits of the conventional Victorian family, we may perhaps understand the literature of 'The New Woman' rather better. The first thing to say, of course, is that the whole problem was a middle-class problem. Working-class women were not confined to their homes. They worked. They had to. And their families suffered, as novelists as different as Mrs Gaskell and Zola pointed out. For example Mrs Wilson, in *Mary Barton*, has never learnt to cook properly, because she had been obliged to go out to work as a child. And, in fact, much the same situation still exists in most of the undeveloped countries of the Third World. In Victorian England, though the women and children from the poor worked, they worked from necessity and were treated as economic inferiors.

For the classes above, the escape-routes from the respectable Victorian marriage were limited. Florence Nightingale pioneered two, as Lytton Strachey reminds us in *Eminent Victorians*. In early life, by her example and her administrative skill, she made nursing a respectable profession for middle-class girls. In later life, as one of the many pampered Victorian invalids, she proved that the sick-bed could rival the throne as a centre of tyrannic power.

> Lying on her sofa in the little upper room in South Street, she combined the intense vitality of a dominating woman of the world with the mysterious and romantic quality of a myth. She was a legend in her lifetime, and she knew it. She tasted the joys of power, like those Eastern Emperors whose autocratic rule was based upon invisibility, with the mingled satisfactions of obscurity and fame. And she found the machinery of illness hardly less effective as a barrier against the eyes of men than the ceremonial of a palace. Great statesmen and renowned generals were obliged to beg for audiences; admiring princesses from foreign countries found that they must see her at her own time, or not at all; [5]

Elizabeth Barrett Browning discovered the same source of power, and so did the sickly Rose Muniment in James's *The Princess Casamassima*.

Sex was a potent instrument. If the members of the great demi-monde enjoyed a range of freedom utterly denied to the respectable, the moral seemed obvious. Emulate the great London courtesans. Use your sex to hook the biggest fish, make the hardest bargain possible within the polite conventions, and then negotiate from strength. It was disgust with this approach that made Mrs Lynn Linton the harshest critic of the Girl of the Period. She severely criticises the girl who dyed her hair, threw off the veils of maidenly modesty, and went out to get her man.

> But the Girl of the Period does not please men. She pleases them as little as she elevates them; and how little she does that, the class of women she has taken as her models of itself testifies. All men whose opinion is worth having prefer the simple and genuine girl of the past, with her tender little ways and pretty bashful modesties, to this loud and rampant modernization, with her false red hair and painted skin, talking slang as glibly as a man, and by preference leading the conversation to doubtful subjects. She thinks she is piquante and exciting when she thus makes herself the bad copy of a worse original; and she will not see that though men laugh with her they do not respect her, though they flirt with her they do not marry her; she will not believe that she is not the kind of thing they want, and that she is acting against nature and her own interests when she disregards their advice and offends their taste. We do not understand how she makes out her account, viewing her life from any side; but all we can do is to wait patiently until the national madness has passed, and our women have come back again to the old English ideal, once the most beautiful, the most modest, the most essentially womanly in the world.[6]

Education was an equally powerful and more respectable instrument of change. Because of the limited education available to young girls, there were almost no jobs they were qualified to take. Even as late as the end of the century, Gissing's novel *The Odd Women* shows that acting as a governess or lady's companion was almost the only thing most women could do when thrown into the employment market. This novel, and *New Grub Street*, paint a sombre picture of the plight of the semi-genteel women from professional families, unexpectedly forced to earn their own living, or supplement a tiny annuity.

But the situation improved as the result of a few pioneers in women's education. The founders of Cheltenham College for Ladies, Miss Buss and Miss Beale, set out to provide a first-class education for well-born ladies. But it was an education that neglected the emotions:

> Miss Buss and Miss Beale
> Cupid's darts do not feel.
> How different from us
> Miss Beale and Miss Buss.

In Ford Madox Ford's *Some Do Not*, the New Woman – Valentine Wannop – knows Greek and Latin and can correct Christopher's schoolboy translations. Inevitably, the newly educated young woman becomes an object of fun in much nineteenth-century literature – and probably with good reason. This is not restricted to English literature and the pages of Punch – in many ways the most accurate guide to what the average Englishman of the nineteenth century found funny. It appears in European literature, as well. A typical instance is the woman Bazarov and Arcady visit near the beginning of *Fathers and Sons*. Madame Kukskin's table groans under the weight of political pamphlets and scientific textbooks, her room is in disarray, and her conversation full of silly affectation and irrelevance. However, it was not necessary to resort to such broad satire to make the point that education was a mixed blessing. More sympathetically presented characters, Gissing's Rhoda Nunn, Ford's Valentine Wannop, Lawrence's Ursula, not to mention Hardy's Tess and Sue Bridehead, make the point more effectively, because they are treated in the round and are not simplified targets for social satire.

Another pathway to greater emancipation lay through the movement for free love, taken up rather uneasily and self-consciously by Wells for example. A more public approach came through the suffragette movement, which finally produced votes for women, after women had chained themselves to railings and thrown themselves under a Derby race horse. The movement left in its wake a litter of minor novels and plays, plays such as Elizabeth Robbins's *Votes for Women*, put on at the Court Theatre in London in 1907. In the suffragette movement, we see the same division as in Women's Lib today, a division into male-hating extremists and moderates who claim equality with men, seek their support and strive for community, not isolation and separatism. But Women's Lib today has made two new contributions to the problem: it has exposed the male chauvinism of our major novelists and also the insidious tyranny exerted by the commercial exploitation of sex. Clearly neither the vote, as the suffragettes thought, nor a private income and 'a room of one's own', as Virginia Woolf thought, has proved an adequate solution.

The serious novelists who took up the theme of the New Woman in the 1890's and in the Edwardian Age, served a most valuable function as critics of society by using the novel to reveal more clearly three rather neglected aspects of the whole problem, aspects that public opinion found it convenient to ignore. These three aspects were: the connection between the opposition to female emancipation and some rather ugly features of male sexuality; the connection between female emancipation and the quest for fulfilment, for both women and men; and the connection between sexual harmony and social harmony, between the private and the public life.

A striking instance of the first, the connection between male attacks upon the New Woman and ugly aspects of male sexuality, occurs in the first part of Ford Madox Ford's novel *Some Do Not*, published in 1924, but relating to suffragette activities before the first World War. It offers a particularly good example of the difference between the writer as propagandist and the novelist as penetrating critic of social and sexual mores working through selective rendering and ironic juxtaposition. Ford does not argue the case; he renders; but behind the subtle rendering lies profound psychological analysis. In this novel the hero, Christopher Tietjens, meets a young suffragette just at the moment he has decided to return to Sylvia, his promiscuous wife. He thus becomes caught between two codes. The young suffragette, Valentine Wannop, together with a friend, are demonstrating, distributing pamphlets, and trying to lobby Liberal support. They find themselves pursued, like animals, by their opponents, and also by the unwilling village policeman. The scene is a golf links. The players form a representative cross-section of upper-class English society. Ironically, it is the Old Tory, Christopher Tietjens, who, by tripping up the policeman, causes a diversion, and allows the girls to escape.

Ford Madox Ford's method of exposing one of the ugly features of the opposition to the suffragette movement is very subtle, though it loses some of its subtlety in being reduced to commentary and quotation. In the golf club scene, Ford begins by juxtaposing Christopher's honourable thoughts about his estranged wife against the lewd conversation of two business men, who are looking forward to their sexual adventures on a forthcoming business trip. One of them has kept a mistress, Gertie, for five years:

> The man with the oily hair said in a sickly voice that Gertie was hot stuff, but not the one for Budapest with all the Gitana girls you were telling me of! Why, he'd kept Gertie for five years now. More like the real thing! His friend's voice was like the voice of indigestion. Tietjens, Sandbach and the General were stiff like pokers.

A little later, Ford describes the scene on the golf links itself:

> 'A regular rat-hunt,' the girl [Valentine] said; she was counting. 'Eleven and two more caddies! . . . I headed them all off except two beasts.'

Then her companion appears.

> A little young woman, engrossed, like a hunted rat, came round the corner of a green mound. 'This is an assaulted female!' the mind of Tietjens said to him. She had a black skirt covered with sand, for she

> had just rolled down the sandhill; she had a striped grey and black silk blouse, one shoulder torn completely off, so that a white camisole showed. Over the shoulder of the sand-hill came the two city men, flushed with triumph and panting; their red knitted waistcoats moved like bellows. The black-haired one, his eyes lurid and obscene, brandished aloft a fragment of black and grey stuff. He shouted hilariously: 'Strip the bitch naked! . . . Ugh . . . Strip the bitch stark naked!'[7]

Through his brilliant impressionistic technique, through ironic juxtaposition, Ford suggests the basic connection between the men's depraved sexuality, their attitude to women as sex-objects, to be bought and used for their lewd gratification, and the cruel sadistic pleasure they derive from hunting the two young suffragettes. The whole scene is registered on the horrified sensibility of the hero, Christopher Tietjens, for whom it is a terrible revelation. Putting it very simply, this part of *Some Do Not* enforces the idea that opposition to women's freedom arises from man's inability to rise above his instinctive bestiality. In fact, Valentine refers to the men as 'those two beasts'.

The second major achievement of the novelists was their success in revealing that the pursuit of happiness and individual fulfilment must involve some radical reassessment of sex, marriage, and the status of men and women in society. Strictly speaking, the theme of the New Woman is only *one* aspect of this much wider and all-embracing theme. Not the least of their contributions, then, was the demonstration that it was not a *separate* problem that could be solved once for all by giving women the vote, or by other legislative action. The novelist's unique contribution as a critic of society is to reveal complexity and interrelatedness. He makes us see deeper and he makes us more sceptical of easy solutions.

The writer who was most pre-occupied with this whole complex of problems was H. G. Wells. But partly because the pre-occupation arose from the failure of his own emotional life and partly because of his tendency to *talk* about problems instead of *exploring* them, his novels move us less deeply than do those of Ford, or Forster, or D. H. Lawrence. They are full of information for the social historian, because Wells has his fingers on the pulse of the nation and writes directly and openly about social problems. This is especially true of *Tono Bungay* and *The New Machiavelli*. But the illumination they provide is limited. It is limited by the sensibility of the author and the intrusive polemical impulse. For the literary critic, as opposed to the social historian, Wells's treatment of women in *Tono Bungay* reveals an unresolved conflict between a desire for freer sexual relations and an ingrained acceptance of male superiority. We are certainly made to see how George's marriage to the shallow, conventional Marion, became 'at last like a narrow, deep groove in the broad expanse of [his] interests'; but the self-justifying stance provides no insight into her side of the marriage. Eight years after the divorce, George records 'I do not know where she is or what she is doing. I do not know whether she is alive or dead. It seems to me utterly grotesque that two people who have stood so close to one another as she and I should be so separated, but so it is between us.' This complacent insensitivity is not placed in a critical context; it is difficult to separate it from the author, and the treatment of the other relations with Effie, and with Beatrice, reveals a sensibility that oscillates between coarse sensuality and unrealized romantic idealism. The false romanticism may be seen in the passage that is clearly intended to mark the turning point in the hero's experience of love:

> and we wandered into the night together and Beatrice talked to me of love . . . I'd never heard a woman before in all my life who could talk of love, who could lay bare and develop and touch with imagination all that mass of fine emotion every woman, it may be, hides.'

In reading Wells, one comes to the conclusion that he knew remarkably little about 'all that mass of fine emotion', remarkably little about women at all, as emerges most clearly from the story of his relations with the gifted and sensitive writer, Rebecca West. Consequently, his whole treatment of the New Woman, in *Tono Bungay*, in *Ann Veronica* and in *The New Machiavelli*, suffers. So, too, does his account of the individual's pursuit of fulfilment and happiness in an imperfect, not yet socialised, society. The conclusion to *Ann Veronica* indicates clearly enough how he maintains male dominance in a supposedly emancipated world '[A woman] wants to be free – she wants to be legally and economically free, so as not to be subject to the wrong man; but only God, who made the world, can alter things to prevent her being the slave to the right one.' Wells believed that woman could be fulfilled only in such a relation; consequently, he identified the suffragette movement with women's failure to find the right kind of husbands. But so, too, did Lawrence, as may be seen in his portrait of Clara Dawes in *Sons and Lovers* and his portrayal of the lesbian schoolteacher in *The Rainbow*.

The third special contribution the novelists made was to reveal the reciprocal relationship between a revitalised conception of love and a revitalised society. For Lawrence, Mellors, in *Lady Chatterley's Lover*, acts as a spokesman for a society redeemed through tenderness and bodily awareness.

> 'I stand for the touch of bodily awareness between human beings,' he said to himself, 'and the touch of tenderness. And she is my mate. And it is a battle against the money, and the machine, and the insentient ideal monkeyishness of the world.' (Penguin, 292).

In Forster's *Maurice*, the final coming together of Maurice Hall and Alec Scudder in a union that combines 'toughness and tenderness' offers a long-term promise of a classless society redeemed by the love of 'comrades'. In Ford Madox Ford's novels there is an integral relationship between sexual and political values. But Lawrence, Forster and Ford Madox Ford were not the only novelists to explore the connection. H. G. Wells, in his open, programmatic fashion, speaks of the connection in the opening pages of *The New Machiavelli*. Richard Remington, a modern statesman whose career has been destroyed by his scandalous affair with the one woman who could have inspired in him a new vision of society, meditates, in retirement in Italy, on the differences between his ideas and Machiavelli's, including their ideas on women.

> He left the thought of women outside with his other dusty things when he went into his study to write, dismissed them from his mind. But our modern world is burthened with its sense of the immense, now half articulate, significance of women. They stand now, as it were, close beside the silver candlesticks, speaking as Machiavelli writes, until he stays his pen and turns to discuss his writing with them.
>
> It is this gradual discovery of sex as a thing collectively portentous that I have to mingle with my statecraft if my picture is to be true, which has turned me at length from a treatise to the telling of my own story. In my life I have paralleled very closely the slow realizations that are going on in the world about me. I began life ignoring women, they came to me at first perplexing and dishonouring; only very slowly and very late in my life and after misadventure, did I gauge the power and beauty of the love of man and woman and learnt how it must needs frame a justifiable vision of the ordered world. Love has brought me to disaster, because my career had been planned regardless of its possibility and value. (Penguin, pp. 13–14).

What is of special interest here is not only Wells's simple explicitness, but the representative significance of his choice of form: not a treatise, but a confessional novel. In the novel, as Lawrence saw, 'you can develop an instinct for life . . . instead of a theory of right and wrong, good and bad'. In Wells's slightly earlier confessional novel, *Tono Bungay*, there is an equally explicit statement about the connection between love and society.

> Love is not only the cardinal fact in the individual life, but the most important concern in the community; after all, the way in which

> young people of this generation pair off determines the fate of the nation.

Yet, Wells lacked the sensitivity to establish the importance of love and sex as creative forces – the phrase 'pair off' is typical of the superficial, matter-of-fact, sociological tone that alternates awkwardly with lush romantic tributes to the transfiguring power of love.

In a penetrating analysis of the Edwardian Woman Question, Samuel Hynes has drawn attention to the extensive ramifications of the changing relations between the sexes

> This social revolution had many implications beside the sexual: it also involved legal, political, and economic issues, and touched on property ownership, the franchise, higher education, the birth rate, laws of marriage and divorce, the protocol court, and the future of the Empire – in short, on nearly every aspect of Edwardian society. In all these aspects, the question asked was, what should be the role of women here? (Or by Tories, what is the trouble with women *now*?) Before the Edwardian years were past, the trouble with women had been blamed on everything from contraceptives to bicycles and had been the subject of novels, poems, and plays, of debates in the Lords and the Commons, and of rallies in Trafalgar Square. (*The Edwardian Turn of Mind*, 1968, p. 172)

Of the literary forms Hynes mentions, undoubtedly the novel was best suited to explore the full implications of this social revolution. Its unique function, in Lawrence's words, was 'to reveal the relation between man and his circumambient universe, at the living moment' (*Selected Literary Criticism*, London, 1955, p. 108).

Two of the best novels that explored the wide ramifications of Women's Emancipation were not Edwardian novels at all, but were written before the turn of the century. These were Gissing's *The Odd Women* (1893) and Henry James's *The Bostonians* (1886).[8] Both illustrate the superiority of subtle artistic rendering over direct sociological commentary and the advocacy of reform. *The Odd Women* tells the story of what happens to three doctor's daughters when, as the consequence of their father's sudden death, they are thrown on the employment market, without specific talents or specialised training. 'Now could one have a better instance than this Madden family of the crime that middle-class parents commit when they allow their daughters to go without rational training', observes one of the spokeswomen for women's emancipation. The title, *The Odd Women*, perhaps embodies a pun, since the women Gissing portrays are both odd statistically (they are the excess women who can never hope to marry) and odd psychologically, since the lack of suitable marriage partners and the limited opportunities for a career in a male-dominated society frustrate the normal development of the personality. Of the three Madden sisters, Monica becomes the main focus of interest. Her marriage to Widdowson, a dreary man of small independent means, offers an escape from being a shop-girl or a secretary. When she falls in love with another man, Bevis, she comes to realise that she has never loved Widdowson. She visits Bevis, at his flat, and declares her love for him

> I love you, and in that there is nothing to be ashamed of; but what bitter shame to be living with *him*, practising hypocrisy. He makes me hate myself as much as I hate *him*. (Doughty Library ed., p. 229)

But she has misjudged the man and her feelings. A superficial sentimentalist, he is embarrassed at this open and passionate declaration of love and promises half-heartedly to send for her once he has found a suitable place for the two of them abroad. When Widdowson discovers that his wife is pregnant, he believes that she has been unfaithful but the child is his, as she establishes on the night she dies in child-birth. Monica's story illustrates the strong forces of circumstance that draw a well-born but poorly educated young woman first into a loveless marriage and then into a fleeting but disastrous affair. The pessimism is only slightly relieved by the hope that Monica's child may be better prepared for life, although that is only likely if she is educated by champions of women's independence and not by the simpering and untrained Agnes and Virginia – 'as soon as baby can walk we are going to think very seriously about the school . . . here is one pupil growing up for us' (p. 336).

Much of the interest of *The Odd Women* centres not on Monica, nor her two elder sisters, Alice and Virginia, both of whom have been reduced to genteel invalidism and middle-aged childishness, but on the two champions of women's emancipation, Rhoda Nunn and Mary Barfoot. Miss Barfoot runs a school to train middle-class girls to become secretaries and therefore to achieve economic independence. Questioned on one occasion by an interfering and overbearing person, Miss Barfoot defines the scope of her work

> 'But surely you don't limit your humanity, Miss Barfoot, by the artificial divisions of society.'
>
> 'I think those divisions are anything but artificial,' replied the hostess good-humouredly. 'In the uneducated classes I have no interest whatever. You have heard me say so.'
>
> 'Yes, but I cannot think – isn't that just a little narrow?'
>
> 'Perhaps so. I choose my sphere, that's all. Let those work for the lower classes (I must call them lower, for they are, in every sense), let those work for them who have a call to do so. I have none. I must keep to my own class.' (p. 53)

Her close helper, Rhoda Nunn, shares these views but otherwise differs greatly in character and outlook.

> It was clear that Miss Barfoot stood in some danger of becoming subordinate to her more vehement friend. Her little body, for all its natural dignity, put her at a disadvantage in the presence of Rhoda, who towered above her with rather imperious stateliness. Her suavity was no match for Rhoda's vigorous abruptness. (pp. 51–2)

Around these two contrasting figures the theme of the education of the new woman revolves. Mary typifies the patient, long-suffering, compassionate approach, while Rhoda, in her angry outbursts and uncompromising adherence to abstract principle, represents the militant approach. Their differences come to a head over the question of accepting a former pupil back after a moral lapse. Rhoda's strong moral rectitude prevails. But the pupil's subsequent suicide brings about a silent tension in their relations. In the end, the 'joyous confidence in themselves and their cause' prevails over such clashes of temperaments and differences of views.

In the novel Rhoda is presented with a symbolic choice – marriage to an intellectual champion of women, Everard Barfoot, at the cost of 'unconditional surrender', 'complete subjugation', or continued devotion to the cause of the New Woman. She chooses the latter. In three memorable scenes the battle of the two proud wills is superbly presented, as is the disparity between Everard Barfoot's intellectual acceptance of women's equality with men, and his emotional need to assert male dominance. The first of these scenes takes place at night on a beach in the Lake District, when Barfoot is determined to persuade Rhoda to give herself to him without going through the formality of marriage. For Barfoot the question is one of male vanity and sexual possession; for Rhoda it involves ideals of personal relationship as well as consequences for the public cause, since her entering into a conventional marriage would be interpreted as an admission that women were incapable of independence. In fact, she would be willing to live with Everard, but decides to insist on marriage; and, when he accepts these terms, he feels that he has been weak and lost the battle.

> 'Yielding in one point that didn't matter to you at all? It was the only way of making sure you loved me.' Barfoot laughed slightingly.
> 'And what if I needed the other proof that you loved *me*?' (p. 267)

The second of the three great scenes occurs next morning when Rhoda receives a letter that seems to establish beyond any doubt that Everard has been having an affair with a married woman. In Rhoda's subsequent confrontation with Barfoot, he is too proud to substantiate his denial of the affair; 'the battle was declared. Each stood at full height, pertinacious, resolved on victory.' The much later third scene in London brings to a conclusion the battle of wills and multiple misunderstandings. Afterwards, Everard Barfoot goes off to marry the tame and conventional Agnes Brissenden, and Rhoda emerges the finer of the two proud spirits, superior in insight and capacity for selfless love. She turns her back on the illusory private happiness once offered her and dedicates herself once more to the public cause. On the last page of the novel, as she holds Monica Widdowson's baby in her arms, she tells Agnes and Virginia Madden of the success that she and Mary are making of their education of women for independence: 'We flourish like the green bay-tree. We shall have to take larger premises . . . Miss Barfoot was never in such health and spirits – nor I myself. The world is moving!' Like the heroine of Mark Rutherford's novel *Clara Hopgood*, Rhoda Nunn finds her fulfilment in public service, not in private relations.

But it is not only the plot-line that suggests that conventional marriage is not the solution for the problem of the statistically 'odd women'. The attacks upon the false romanticism kept alive by bad fiction are also important, for instance Rhoda's expression of disgust in chapter 6:

> Love–love–love; a sickening sameness of vulgarity. What is more vulgar than the ideal of novelists? They won't represent the actual world; it would be too dull for their readers. In real life, how many men and women *fall in love*? Not one in every ten thousand, I am convinced. Not one married pair in ten thousand have felt for each other as two or three couples do in every novel. There is the sexual instinct, of course, but that is quite a different thing; the novelists daren't talk about that. (p. 58)

Gissing's two major preoccupations as man and artist, the falsity of popular literature and the disasters of marriage, combine admirably in this novel, *The Odd Women*, thus relating it to his other work; but it achieves its unique power from its intensely honest and comprehensive picture of the plight of women at the end of the nineteenth century in England.

The Odd Women ends with the triumph of a public cause over private happiness; Henry James's *The Bostonians*, a novel about the Women's Liberation Movement in America in the 1880's, ends with the victory of the private, and a partial reconciling of the contrary claims of public and private life. Like *The Princess Casamassima*, it deals with that 'strained human anguish between the conception of a political ideal and its execution in the face of contrary impulses'. Like many other serious novels, it reduces to a democratic level the strained human anguish that

Shakespeare's kings experience, as they struggle to achieve their public ambitions, while striving to retain their basic humanity. In *The Bostonians*, the conflict is finally resolved when Verena Tarrant, the eloquent spokeswoman for woman's rights, abandons the cause and opts for private happiness and sexual fulfilment with the upright Southern gentleman Basil Ransom. But it is by no means a conventional happy ending. Verena weeps in her lover's arms; and the last sentence of the novel offers no radiant vision of the future:

> 'It is to be feared that with the union, so far from brilliant, into which she was about to enter, these were not the last [tears] she was destined to shed.'

The action does not centre exclusively on Verena in *The Bostonians*; James creates an extensive gallery of portraits to illustrate the variety of forms that humanitarian zeal may take in American provincial life. He is clearly fascinated by the ironic perversion of the human spirit, fascinated by the high-minded charlatanism and political quackery that devotion to a public cause can breed. It appears in the theatrical opportunism of Dr Tarrant, the mesmerist; in Mrs Farrinder, the professional orator; and in that early epitome of the brash, vulgar, American journalist, the ineffable Mr Matthias Pardon. It is against this background of eccentric Bostonians, a background that includes the elderly feminist, Miss Birdseye, that James sets his two main female characters, Olive Chancellor, and her beautiful red-headed protégée, Verena Tarrant: Olive, 'who would reform the solar system if she could get hold of it'; Verena, a passive receptacle for others, first for her mesmerist father, next for Olive, and finally for Basil Ransom.

In *The Princess Casamassima*, it is the public theme that is secret, submerged, subterranean. In *The Bostonians* it is the private. Throughout *The Bostonians* we are made aware of intensely strong undercurrents of emotion. The white-faced, angular feminist, Olive Chancellor, and the passively appealing Verena Tarrant soon become involved in a demanding lesbian relationship – a relationship that demands a subjection for Verena almost as servile as the one the Bostonian feminists protest against, and almost as servile as that against which John Stuart Mill had earlier protested in his famous pamphlet, *On the Subjection of Women*. That is one irony. But we feel a similar ironic undercurrent of emotion in the relation between the Southern gentleman Basil Ransom and Verena. Although the overt subject of conversation in chapter 34 is woman's place in society, 'damnable feminization', in Ransom's phrase, it is clear that Verena's cold despair arises from her recognition of Ransom's inadequacy as a lover rather than from any ideological difference. 'She felt cold, slightly sick, though she replied that now he had summed up his creed in such a distinct, lucid way, it was much more comfortable – one knew with what one was dealing, a declaration much at variance with the face, for Verena had never felt less gratified in her life' (Penguin, p. 290). And a little later, in the scene in Central Park, James makes the specific point that general ideological questions provided a refuge from painful private issues.

Much of the strength of *The Bostonians* comes from the extreme simplicity of its basic structure. The structure serves to bring into brilliant and agonising contrast the call of duty and the call of the heart. The call of duty – women's emancipation – is public, plausible and defensible on rational grounds; but, ironically, it involves compromise, vulgarity, prostitution of one's talents in the attempt to win popular support. The call of the heart, on the other hand, is private, implausible, and indefensible on rational grounds. And yet the heart is stronger and wins in the end.

Yet what kind of victory is it? The answer to this question points immediately to the central irony of *The Bostonians*. Verena's victory leads not to emotional freedom and fulfilment, but to possession by Basil. Olive Chancellor, the intense champion of female rights and Basil Ransom, the upright Southern lawyer, battle for possession of Verena's soul. She is inescapably victim. Basil and Olive are both too inflexibly egotistical, too much the victims of their limited creeds to be able to imagine a human relationship based on equality and independence. And so, when Verena frees herself from the bondage of her Lesbian relationship with Olive, when she releases herself from the dubious freedoms promised by the Women's Emancipation Movement, what she enters is not a relationship based on independence and mutual self-respect, but (one is led to suppose by James) a typically nineteenth-century marriage. James makes it quite clear that Basil visits the little New England seaside village, Marmion, with the specific intention of taking 'possession' of Verena.

> The hotel itself offered few resources; the inmates were not numerous; they moved about a little outside, on the small piazza and in the rough yard which interposed between the house and the road, and then they dropped off into the unmitigated dusk. This element, touched only in two or three places by a far-away dim glimmer, presented itself to Ransom as his sole entertainment. Though it was pervaded by that curious, pure, earthy smell which in New England in summer, hangs in the nocturnal air, Ransom be-thought himself that the place might be a little dull for persons who had not come to it, as he had, to take possession of Verena Tarrant. (Penguin, pp. 300–1)

Temporarily he fails, because Verena has been recalled to a sense of public duty by Mrs Birdseye's moving death speech:

> 'It isn't much – only I tried to take hold. When I look back from here, from where we've sat, I can measure the progress. That's what I wanted to say to you and Mr Ransom – because I'm going fast. Hold on to me, that's right; but you can't keep me. I don't want to stay now; I presume I shall join some of the others that we lost long ago. Their faces come back to me now, quite fresh. It seems as if they might be waiting; as if they were all there; as if they wanted to hear. You mustn't think there's no progress because you don't see it all right off; that's what I wanted to say. It isn't till you have gone a long way that you can feel what's been done. That's what I see when I look back from here; I see that the community wasn't half waked up when I was young.' (Penguin, pp. 344–5)

But Basil wins in the end. And not by argument, not by rational persuasion. At first, Verena leaves Marmion, she accepts the re-call to duty, she agrees to Olive's proposal to address a large public meeting in Boston. This is to be her personal triumph. And it is to be Olive's too, a supreme proof of her faith in Verena's 'magnetic powers' (we note the ironic equation with her father 'specious mesmerism'). It is also to be the supreme proof of Olive's control over her destiny. But it ends not in triumph, but in failure. Why? Quite by chance, Verena sees Basil in the audience, as she enters the hall. The mere sight of him, reminiscent of his immediate physical presence, his strong masculinity, his self-sufficiency and the call of heart to heart, felt by the sea at Marmion, is sufficient. It convinces her that her future (and, one supposes, James suggests, the future of all women), lies with her lover.

This drastically simplified account is a travesty of a richly complex novel. But even in so simplified an account there appears to be a certain ambiguity in James's vision. On the one hand, he seems clairvoyantly aware that most forms of love are only a disguised form of possession and subjection. And, on the other, he is sufficiently a man of his age to believe that the subjection of a Victorian marriage was preferable to the illusions of female emancipation and all the compromises of integrity the campaign involved: and preferable, too, to the perversities of an intimate Lesbian relationship. Did he, as an artist, explore this relationship more deeply than he was aware? His judgment – if that is not too strong a word – is psychological rather than social or moral. But the novel, as a whole, develops a powerful and comprehensive criticism of society.

The central theme of *The Bostonians* is not the Women's Emancipation Movement, but something larger and more all-embracing. It is the sacrifices exacted as the result of entry into public life. For each character the sacrifices are different; and the anguish of conscience is defined by differences in temperament, environment and moral sensibility. But, it is the champion of women's emancipation, Olive

Chancellor, who most *fully* reflects the agonized tension between fastidious idealism and the vulgar corruptions, compromises and deceits of public life. What is most disturbing and most original for its time is James's intense insight into that profound sexual disorientation of America, noted earlier by De Tocqueville, and later by Walt Whitman and Henry Adams, 'the sacrifice of sexuality to business and the machine, the blighting effect of public causes on sexual life and moral sensibility'. Putting the matter simply, what we have in *The Bostonians* is a set of moral cripples, each in origin a solitary, with no healthy social relations, each claiming to know how to cure society, but each seeking in social reform an escape from solitude and a substitute for normal living. It is a novel with grave moral and social implications, especially for some modern champions of Women's Lib.

9 Continuity and Change

The phrase 'Condition of England', first coined by Carlyle in *Past and Present* (1853) and used much later by the liberal statesman C. F. G. Masterman as the title of a book he published in 1909, neatly establishes the connection between Victorian Sages and Edwardian Prophets. In a great variety of ways, especially through their concern with harmonious development and their opposition to the mechanical spirit, the modern critics of society continue the tradition created by Coleridge and the great Romantics at the beginning of the nineteenth century and carried on by the Victorian Sages, who although they may not have been capable of influencing the main course of events, provided for the age, as George Watson has suggested, 'a counterpoint of ideas which otherwise would be lacking'. In the Edwardian Period, the centres of preoccupation remained much the same. The main objects of attack continued to be the neglect of ideas, the worship of materialism, the evil effects of industrialism, and the disintegration of the organic community. But there was change as well as continuity. The problems raised by the rapid growth of science and technology, the sudden explosion of urban population, the emergence of popular newspapers and mass advertising, the vast increase in social mobility, charted for example in *Tono Bungay*, gave a special urgency to later writings. One of the advantages of coming to the modern critics of society after reading some of the great nineteenth-century writers is that we are better able to see their ideas in proper historical perspective. The continuity is particularly evident in two areas of thought: the criticism of the city and the discussion of women's place in society.

T. S. Eliot's sombre evocation of London in the *Waste Land* as the 'unreal city' – 'terrible city' in an earlier manuscript version – has often been mistaken for a startlingly original attack upon the sterility of urban life by those unfamiliar with the tradition to which it belongs. This tradition begins with Wordsworth's picture in the *Prelude* of solitary desertion in the midst of meaningless movement, a wonderful anticipation of the sociologist David Reisman's phrase, 'the lonely crowd'.

> How often in the overflowing Streets,
> Have I gone forwards with the Crowd, and said

Unto myself, 'the face of every one
That passes by me is a mystery'.
(*Prelude*, 1805, Bk. VII, 594–7)

The tradition includes De Quincey's descriptions of lonely people in empty houses, Dickens's image of London as both a source of depravity and of potential redemption, Thomson's unrealised but profoundly melancholy 'City of Dreadful Night', Gissing's city drained of life and hope, Gustave Doré's Dantesque pictures of bustling crowds and human derelicts, Baudelaire's 'fourmillante cité', James's evocation of 'the deep perpetual groan of London misery' in *The Princess Casamassima*, Wells's capturing, in *Tono Bungay*, of the individual's fear that he would 'drop into and be swallowed up sooner or later by this dingy London ocean', and Forster's vision of the 'abyss' that awaits the Leonard Basts of the Edwardian age, and of London as the outward expression of a 'civilization of luggage'.[1]

The literature on woman's place in society has a similar long tradition. It takes its origin from the writings of the eighteenth-century blue stockings, it achieves its first aggressive articulation in Mary Wollstonescraft's *Vindication of the Rights of Women* (1798) – a typical product of the French Revolution – acquires male support in John Stuart Mill's *On the Subjection of Women* (1869), and becomes one of the main themes of much popular nineteenth-century literature and journalism, in the novels and essays of Mrs Lynn Linton, for example.[2] Although she became a bitter critic of what she called the 'shrieking sisterhood', her *Saturday Review* essays in the 1860's, subsequently published as *The Girl of the Period and Other Essays*, indicate the lively interest taken in women's role in society long before the Edwardian suffragette movement or the later Women's Lib. Together with James's *The Bostonians*, Mrs Linton's writings deserve to be read with attention, since they establish the continuity of the Victorian and Modern tradition in this field of thought.

But there was change as well as continuity. What, we might ask, were the distinctively new elements that gradually changed man's vision of himself, the universe, and the society in which he lived – elements that therefore profoundly modified the critical literature from about 1860 onwards? We can, I think, point to four.

The first was the theory of evolution. The publication of Darwin's *Origin of the Species* in 1859 is a vital event in the history of ideas. On the one hand, it destroyed faith in the Biblical account of creation, already eroded by both geologists and German theology, and thus intensified religious doubt. On the other hand, it created faith in the future, faith in evolutionary progress both for the individual and for mankind. It is hardly coincidental that Samuel Smiles's *Self Help* appeared in exactly the same month as Darwin's *Origin of the Species* and not at all surprising that the former proved the more popular book. For the average Victorian, the evolution of the individual towards prosperity and absolute respectability along the lines laid down by Samuel Smiles was of more immediate concern than Darwin's visions of geological time and the long evolution of man. Butler, in *The Way of All Flesh*, makes a gallant but finally unconvincing attempt to infuse Darwinian evolutionary theory with creative purposefulness. 'All our lives long', he says in chapter 69, 'every day and every hour, we are engaged in the process of accommodating our changed and unchanged selves to changed and unchanged surroundings.' This statement has a historic importance, since many novelists ever since have been concerned with exploring this process of accommodating the Self to the Other, although of course their idea of the Self has been less fixed than was Butler's.

The second new element that changed the whole tone and temper of the critical writings on man and society was closely connected with Darwinian theory. This was the growth of agnosticism. It was T. H. Huxley, one of Darwin's champions, who coined the word. With the growth of agnosticism, men learnt to live without God. They also learnt to explain man and nature without recourse to a divine creation. For some the sense of release was tremendous, the promise seemed infinite. In time science would explain all. For many Victorians, the process of learning to live without God also involved learning to dispense with his earthly substitute, the pater familias, the father of the earthly family. Such otherwise dissimilar works as Turgenev's *Fathers and Sons* (1862), Butler's *The Way of All Flesh* (1903) and Edmund Gosse's *Father and Son* (1907) derive much of their vigour and power from their rejection of the authoritarian father figure and from their critical attitude towards the family. Lawrence's *Sons and Lovers*, so revolutionary in some respects, comes at the end of this Victorian tradition. To appreciate the full force of this tradition we need to recall that for the Victorians the family was an image of heavenly order. The image is consecrated in the pages of Dickens and George Eliot, and repeated with sickening inevitability in the painting of the period. It needed Butler's mocking irreverence to shatter this pious respect for the family. A passage under the heading 'The Family' from his *Note-Books* makes explicit the master theme of *The Way of All Flesh*:

> I believe that more unhappiness comes from this source than from any other – I mean from the attempt to prolong family connection unduly and to make people hang together artificially who would never naturally do so. The mischief among the lower classes is not so great, but among the middle and upper classes it is killing a large number daily. And the old people do not really like it much better than the young. (*Selections from the Note-Books of Samuel Butler*, The Travellers' Library 1950, p. 33)

If Butler's iconoclasm was mainly directed at the private heroes of the home, the new biography, initiated by Lytton Strachey's irreverent *Eminent Victorians* (1919), pulled the Victorian public heroes down from their pedestals and viewed them 'dispassionately, impartially, and without ulterior intentions'. Strachey's scepticism towards the popular heroes of Victorian England, his mocking treatment of Cardinal Manning and Dr Arnold of Rugby, were but late manifestations of Victorian agnosticism, involving the rejection both of the father figure and of the family as an image of heavenly perfection.

The third new element that offered a revolutionary way of looking at man and society was Marxist theory. Marx offered a new view of man's relation to society, to history, and to the future. The proletariat, he argued, by taking over the means of production would bring into being a new classless society. Marx significantly redirected attention from political institutions to radical economics. Whereas in the past England had supplied the whole of Europe and the New World with political theory and institutions of government, mainly but not exclusively through the writings of John Locke, now she was the fearful beneficiary of European political thought. Marxist theory threatened to destroy the established social hierarchy. And the tradition of 'high culture' developed and championed by Coleridge and Arnold embodied that hierarchical scale of values. So, at every level, Marxist theory constituted a threat, or a promise, or a challenge. But there was nothing in England at the turn of the century to compare with the agonised Marxist revisionism in Europe; there was nothing comparable with the intense conflict between Bernstein's gradualism and the orthodox Marxism expressed in Rosa Luxemburg's *Reform and Revolution* (1899). By contrast, in England there was the peaceful creation of the Fabian Society out of the New Fellowship and the slow growth of the English Labour Party, with Keir Hardie as the first of its members to be elected to Parliament in 1900. Shaw, Wells and Edward Carpenter were early members of the Fabian Society, attracted by its declared faith in progressive gradual reform, and approach comparable with the Bernstein model. Although there were frequent clashes of opinion among its members, on the whole the characteristic spirit of compromise prevailed. When Wells resigned from the Fabian Society, he neither started a new society nor promulgated his revisionist views. He put his opponents, Beatrice and Sidney Webb, into a novel called *The New Machiavelli* and got his revenge that way. How quiet and insular it all is and how characteristically English. Yet this is also the period in which James and Conrad were sniffing out dangerous anarchists in *The Princess Casamassima* and *The Secret Agent*, when London was the centre of European anarchy, not France, as Zola mistakenly suggests through the character of Etienne in *Germinal*. Although Marxist theory never produced the ideological debates and revolutionary action in England that it produced on the Continent, it added a new dimension to man's thoughts about society. Moreover, it was not necessary to espouse Marxist doctrine, as William Morris did in *News from Nowhere*, to achieve this new dimension. A deeper insight into the economic basis of society and some notion of the potential revolutionary role of the proletariat became part of the intellectual equipment of a host of writers who owed no formal allegiance to Marxism.

The fourth element that profoundly changed the writer's views on man and society the reader will already have guessed. In time it was the latest. It was Freudian theory. Freud's theories of the unconscious constituted an obvious challenge to the ideal of rationalism on which the whole of nineteenth-century society had been built. Freudian ideas eroded the whole notion of a stable personality, as may be seen from Lawrence's letter to Edward Garnett on 5 June 1914.

> You mustn't look in my novel for the old stable *ego* of the character. There is another *ego*, according to whose action the individual is unrecognizable, and passes through, as it were, allotropic states which it needs a deeper sense than any we've been used to exercise, to discover are states of the same single radically unchanged element. (Like as diamond and coal are the same pure single element of carbon . . .)'[3]

But, most important of all, in *Civilization and its Discontents*, Freud offered an interpretation of the evolution of society that united the new sciences of psychology and sociology in a fresh and illuminating manner. In both individuals and societies, he argued, there is a strong instinct for self-destruction as well as creation. With all the confidence of a new messiah, he wrote:

> And now, I think, the meaning of the evolution of civilization is no longer obscure to us. It must present the struggle between Eros and Death, between the instinct of life and the instinct of destruction, as it works itself out in the human species. This struggle is what all life essentially consists of, and the evolution of civilization may therefore be simply described as the struggle for life of the human species.[4]

George Steiner adapts this thesis in his book *In Bluebeard's Castle* to explain the coexistence of high culture and concentration camps in Nazi Germany. There is, he argues, an extinct theology at work in our world views. Although we no longer believe in a heaven above or a hell below, we continue to yearn for both. And it has proved easier, allowing the death wish to triumph, to create our living hells than our ideal heavens. They are not in Buchenwald only. They lie around us everywhere.

The vision of apocalypse is always more urgent at the end of centuries, as Frank Kermode has pointed out in *The Sense of An Ending*. Why, however, did apocalyptic literature continue almost unabated after the 1890s? Two reasons may be suggested. The first is that the pace of change had become so accelerated that man could no longer feel he was in full control and came to sense that the outcome must be universal destruction – the First World War provided a partial confirmation. The second is that Freud's ideas gave new life to the *fin de siècle* sense of apocalypse, by enunciating as a major principle the drive towards destruction. There are Freudian overtones to be heard in what I would call, using a conscious pun, Mellor's 'apocalyptic cock' in chapter 15 of *Lady Chatterley's Lover*. His passionate attack on the destructiveness of money and machine culture ends with the scornful irresponsibility of 'pay 'em money to cut off the world's cock. Pay money, money, money to them that will take spunk out of mankind, and leave 'em all little twiddling machines.' What alone calms him is a thought akin to Kurtz's 'exterminate the brutes', in Conrad's *Heart of Darkness*: 'To contemplate the extermination of the human species and the long pause that follows before some other species crops up.' When Connie asks him why he is so bitter, why, we might say, he is so full of apocalyptic frenzy, he answers: 'I'm not! If my cock gives its last crow, I don't mind.' For all his occasional absurdity, Lawrence alone of the twentieth-century novelists seems to have realised that for some men wholeness of being can only come after accepting the idea of death, as in the case of Mellors, or the core of darkness, as in the case of Will Brangwen in *The Rainbow*, and that Eros or the flame of love can alone triumph over the forces of disintegration and destruction, in man and in society.

These, then, are four of the main new elements that came to transform the direction and the tone and temper of the earlier nineteenth-century criticism of society: evolution; agnosticism; Marxist theory; and the ideas of Freud. All four came to challenge and disrupt the Victorian picture of the world, based as it was on belief in God, the importance of the family, stability of character, and England's imperial mission to bring Christian civilisation to the world. But, as we have already seen, many of the greatest Victorian writers had already attempted to redraw this picture. Indeed, much of their greatness arises from their clear-sighted criticism of Victorian assumptions. Carlyle criticised the implicit acceptance of the 'cash nexus' as the main bond linking men in society, Arnold questioned the current faith in mere machinery, Ruskin and Morris protested against the dehumanising of men and art by a materialistic society; but they all, like most critics of Victorian society, accepted unquestioningly certain values of their age. What were these values? How well did they resist later attack? How were they modified and assimilated by later writers?

The chief Victorian values were a belief in the efficacy of reason, the power of law, the value of culture, the inevitability of progress, the virtue of tolerance (in this respect, the Victorians were, as G. M. Young once remarked, the disappointed heirs of the French Revolution) and, finally, faith in Christianity, or if not in Christianity, faith in what came to be called 'the Religion of Humanity'. The latter secular faith had its roots in the eighteenth-century Enlightenment; it burst into vigorous life during the French Revolution and produced rather unexpectedly sombre blossoms in the later nineteenth century, in the works of Auguste Comte and Herbert Spencer, and in the novels of Spencer's friend and disciple, George Eliot.

The values just enumerated survived later attacks remarkably well; and it is perhaps only comparatively recently that we have become aware of the unstable basis of the Victorian order, of the glaring inconsistencies that it succeeded in reconciling or quietly obscuring. Attacks on the decorous façade began during the Victorian period itself, but they reached their climax in the twentieth century in Lytton Strachey's witty but malicious portraits of Cardinal Manning, Florence Nightingale, Dr Arnold, and General Gordon in *Eminent Victorians* (1918), a work that turned Carlyle's faith in heroes and hero-worship upside-down. For any radical attack on the Victorians' deeply held faith in culture and material progress, however, we have had to wait until today. We now see that the extension of culture and education to all does not produce the fruits the great Victorians hoped; it produces only new problems and fresh discontents. We see too that high culture is based on an economically stratified society, that its hierarchical values accurately reflect belief in an aristocracy of talent (Coleridge had been quite specific about this when he stressed the importance of the philosophic few and stoutly resisted the 'plebification of knowledge'). And we see, as neither the Victorians nor the early writers of Utopian fiction like Bellamy saw, that material progress, far from inaugurating an ideal society, dehumanises man and irreparably pollutes the environment. Looking at the abandoned house his uncle had begun to build for himself as the successful inventor of the quack medicine Tono Bungay, the narrator of Wells's novel sees in it 'the compactest image and sample of all that passes for Progress, of all the advertisement-inflated spending, the aimless building up and pulling down, the enterprise and promise' of his age.

> 'Great God!' I cried, 'but this is Life?'
> For this the armies drilled, for this the Law was administered and the prisons did their duty, for this the millions toiled and perished in suffering, in order that a few of us should build palaces we never finished, make billiard-rooms under ponds, run imbecile walls round irrational estates, scorch about the world in motor-cars, devise flying-machines, play golf and a dozen such foolish games of ball, crowd into chattering dinner parties, gamble and make our lives one

> vast dismal spectacle of witless waste! So it struck me then, and for a time I could think of no other interpretation. This was Life! It came to me like a revelation, a revelation at once incredible and indisputable of the abysmal folly of our being. (Bk. Four, ch. 1, §2)

The tasteless and amoral displays of the Edwardian plutocracy led H. G. Wells and his generation to call in question the myth of progress that had sustained the Victorian age. Today, living in what has been called a 'post-cultural period', we not only reject the myth of progress; we are also more sceptical of the rewards of culture than either the Victorians or Edwardians, perceiving that culture may as easily become the instrument of tyranny as of freedom. In modern literature, idealistic utopias are replaced by anti-utopias, or to use Zamyatin's terminology, plus utopias give way to minus utopias, like Orwell's *Nineteen Eighty-Four*, in which history and culture are controlled to maintain central power.

The transition from the apparently stable Victorian world to an age of agony and existential crisis is an enormously complex process, as John Lester and Samuel Hynes have amply demonstrated in *Journey Through Despair* and *The Edwardian Turn of Mind* respectively.[5] Essentially it was a transition from a religious to a secular age. In *Religious Humanism and the Victorian Novel*, Knoepflmacher has illustrated the ways in which George Eliot, Pater, and Samuel Butler transmuted religious prophetic zeal into secular forms, into prophecies of art. The process of continuity and change is embodied in the very language used by these and other writers. The late-Victorian and Edwardian novelists took over many of the key religious terms of the preceding age and by using them in specifically secular contexts gave them not only new currency but fresh meaning and significance.[6] The best known example is 'epiphany', because of Joyce's use of this religious term to describe 'a sudden spiritual manifestation, whether in the vulgarity of speech or of gesture or in a memorable phase of the mind itself', upon which his art in the *Dubliners* and *A Portrait of the Artist as a Young Man* is based. Two other religious terms play an equally important part in modern fiction; these are 'salvation' and 'transfiguration'. All Forster's early novels revolve round the idea of salvation.[7] In *Where Angels Fear to Tread*, for example, two ideas of salvation are played off ironically against each other, both secular, but the one is concerned with preserving one's inner integrity, while the other with saving face. Yet it was not only Forster (for whom 'being saved' was an idiom of the Cambridge of his youth) who saw life as the search for a secular salvation. Wells, characteristically, discusses the whole question openly in *Tono Bungay*, saying 'men find their salvation nowadays in many ways', and going on to consider socialism and science as two of the commonest. If we look at the whole body of late-Victorian and Modern fiction we can see that salvation might ultimately be in origin religious, ethical, or it might come through nature, through art, through love and friendship, or through society. A number of writers retained sufficient Christian faith to make salvation for the individual a specifically religious issue, as it is for Zakariah Coleman in Mark Rutherford's *The Revolution in Tanner's Lane* (1887). In *Adam Bede* salvation comes from conversion. But more normally in George Eliot's novels the context of salvation is ethical and consists of a battle between blind egotism and altruism (culminating in and related to a 'religion of humanity'). Meredith's *The Ordeal of Richard Feverell* provides a good example of the hero who is 'saved' through some quasi-mystical experience of nature; Richard is saved as the result of his Rhineland forest encounter, a piece of fashionable pantheism that Forster at first imitated in *The Longest Journey*, but later omitted in the published text. Salvation through art is common to the novels of Hawthorne, James, Wilde and Forster. The hero or heroine enjoys a vision of truth through contemplating a picture or statue or through looking at the world as if it were a picture. Finally, G. E. Moore gave philosophic authority to this mode of apprehension by declaring that aesthetic experience is one of the paths to personal 'salvation'. Moore also gave his philosophic blessing to friendship as a path to salvation, regarding it as one of the undefinable absolutes. In modern fiction, where the psychological idea of self-fulfilment takes the place of earlier religious or ethical goals, love and friendship become not only desirable ends, but the means of personal 'salvation'. The notion of 'comradeship' provided a number of writers, such as Edward Carpenter, D. H. Lawrence, and E. M. Forster, with a convenient means of linking salvation through friendship with salvation through society. The link between the salvation of the individual and the reform or redemption of society is of course Romantic in origin. It provides the whole schema of Wordsworth's *Prelude*, while Coleridge, in advising Wordsworth how to complete the poem, spoke of the whole society being subject to a 'vast redemptive process'.

We think of the Victorian Age as an age of Prophets or Sages. But the Edwardian period had its prophets too. Shaw and Wells immediately spring to mind. Most of the Edwardian prophets were inspired by a faith in four things: democracy; science; socialism; and the rationalisation of personal relations. Just as our understanding of the Victorian 'Condition of England' novel was enlarged through reference to the Victorian Sage, Carlyle, so too our understanding of the modern 'Condition of England' novel may be deepened as the result of reading the works of a neglected prophet of the late-Victorian and Edwardian period. That prophet was Edward Carpenter.

Through his ideal of wholeness and his crusade for sexual liberation, Carpenter forms an interesting link between Coleridge and D. H. Lawrence. Born in 1844, he came under the Coleridgean influence of F.

D. Maurice, whose curate he became for a short time. For Carpenter as for G. Lowes Dickinson and E. M. Forster, Cambridge became a symbol of the perfect union of beauty and comradeship, yet the true nature of the comradeship had at first to remain secret because of the taboo against homosexuality. A passage that G. Lowes Dickinson quotes from Carpenter's autobiography *My Days and Dreams* makes this clear.

> What a curious romance ran through all that life – and yet on the whole, with few exceptions, how strangely unspoken it was and unexpressed! This succession of athletic and even beautiful faces and figures, what a strange magnetism they had for me, and yet all the while how insurmountable for the most part was the barrier between! It was as if a magic flame dwelt within one, burning, which one could not put out, and yet whose existence one might on no account reveal.[8]

To everyone's surprise, Carpenter gave up a Cambridge Fellowship to live the simple life, to cultivate a few acres, be economically self-sufficient, design and make his own rational clothes, mix with working men, give lectures to them, and make a homosexual marriage with a working man, George Merrill, a marriage that lasted for over twenty years and was only ended with Merrill's death. It was during a visit to their smallholding at Millthorpe near Chesterfield that Forster was inspired to write his homosexual novel *Maurice.* Forster describes in the 'Terminal Notes' to that novel how George Merrill touched his 'backside – gently and just above the buttocks –', and how 'at that precise moment' he had 'conceived' the idea of *Maurice.* Forster was not the only novelist to be influenced by Carpenter's socialism and homosexuality. It is almost certain that Lawrence read his voluminous works at a formative stage in his career, as Emile Delavenay has suggested. The musicologist Edward J. Dent, who was the prototype for Philip Herriton in Forster's *Where Angels Fear to Tread*, summed up Carpenter by saying that 'he simplified life by abandoning everything that was not beautiful, and he was prepared to see beauty not merely in works of art but in all aspects of daily life'. In his emphasis on cosmic consciousness, self-sufficiency and the simple life, Carpenter might be regarded as the prophet of the modern commune, but beneath his primitive communism there was a strong autocratic element, and beneath his championing of the wisdom of the body there was a strong ascetic streak.

The work by which Carpenter achieved fame in his own day was the long poem *Towards Democracy*. It has been described rather cruelly and unfairly as 'Whitman and water'. It is better than that, as Havelock Ellis, who coined the phrase, soon realised. Carpenter called the poem 'the starting-point and kernel' of all his later work. Written in the little wooden sentry box that he made for himself as an outdoor study at Bradway and which he later transported to Millthorpe, it communicates his joy in the unity of nature and the comradeship of man.

> What sweet times were those! all the summer to the hum of the bees in the leafage, the robins and chaffinches hopping around, an occasional large bird flying by, the men away at work in the fields, the consuming pressure of the work within me, the wonderment how it would turn out; the days there in the rain, or in the snow; nights sometimes, with moonlight or a little lamp to write by; far far away from anything polite or respectable, or any sign or symbol of my hated old life. Then the afternoons at work with my friends in the fields, hoeing and singling turnips or getting potatoes, or down in Sheffield on into the evenings with new companions among new modes of life and work – everything turning and shaping itself into material for my poem. (*My Days and Dreams*, 1918, p. 107)

Carpenter continued to add to the poem from 1883, when the first edition was published, until 1905, when it had swollen to more than four times its original length. Although it is excessively long, uneven in quality, repetitive in phrase and sentiment, and diffuse in imaginative impact, it offers a vision of industrial England redeemed through imaginative love that is occasionally moving, especially to readers more familiar with Lawrence's poetic vision of Albion than Blake's.

Ah, England! Ah, beating beating heart!
No wonder you are weary! weary of talk!
Weary seeking amid the scramble, amid the scramble of words
  and the scramble of wealth,
Amid the fashionable, the scientific, the artistic, the
  commercial, the political, the learned and literary scramble –
  weary,
....
O rivers and hills of Albion, O clouds that sail from the
  Atlantic to the North Sea, and wrinkled old Abbeys and modern
  towers and streets of heavily laden drays,
Behind your masks I am aware of an imperceptible change;
  surely it must be the appearance of a Face. (Part One, XXXV and
XLI)

Even the author himself recognised that its form was 'open to question', but was content that it 'should go its own way quietly, neither applauded by the crowd, nor barked at by the dogs, but knocking softly here and there at a door and finding friendly hospitality' (*My Days and Dreams*, p. 201). Mrs Havelock Ellis confessed that she had never gone to the poem *Towards Democracy* and come away in the same mood. 'It is surely the epistle of a life, and the gospel of a life to be, when love has solved the difficulties of pain, jealousy, separation, and death, and when great Mother Nature is recognized as the real Healer.'[9]

It is not *Towards Democracy*, but *Civilisation: Its Cause and Cure* and *Love's Coming of Age* that deserve special attention today.[10] *Civilisation: Its Cause and Cure* is the title essay of a collection that first appeared in June 1889 and was frequently reprinted. It occupies a special place in the history of the literature on culture and society on account of its cogent restatement of Coleridge's original distinction between culture and material civilisation. But, far more important, it offers definitions of wholeness as an ideal both for the individual and society that strikingly foreshadow the writings of Forster and Lawrence. 'Health', Carpenter insists, 'in body or mind – means unity, integration as opposed to disintegration' (p. 21). Asking himself what is the cause of the loss of this unity, he answers that it lies in the excessive growth of self-consciousness, and goes on to speak of 'the frightful struggle of self-consciousness, or the disentanglement of the true self from the fleeting and perishable self' (p. 24). It is precisely such a disentanglement of the two selves that has become the central preoccupation of the twentieth-century novelist. Fusing a Coleridgean analysis of the disintegrating effect of civilisation with a pre-Lawrentian vision of sacramental sex, Carpenter writes:

> it has been the work of Civilisation – founded as we have seen on Property – in every way to disintegrate and corrupt man – literally to corrupt – *break up* the unity of his nature. It begins with the abandonment of the primitive life and the growth of the sense of shame (as in the myth of Adam and Eve). From this follows the disownment of the sacredness of sex. Sexual acts cease to be a part of religious worship; love and desire – the inner and the outer love – hitherto undifferentiated, now become two separate things. (pp. 25–6)

Carpenter argues that property draws man away from nature, from his true self, and from his fellows. Man, he claims, 'has sounded the depth of his alienation from his own divine spirit'. On the basis of the old magical formula, 'Man clothes himself to descend, unclothes himself to ascend', he proffers a lyrical appeal to spend as much time as possible in the open in touch with nature, to be naked in the sun (he was an early advocate of sunbathing), to eat only vegetarian diet, and to observe a ritual of cleanliness in all things. Like Forster later, he assimilates the religious idea of 'transfiguration' into a secular context. 'And thus', he writes 'the whole human being, mind and body, becoming clean and radiant from its inmost centre to its farthest circumference – "transfigured" – the distinction between the words spiritual and material disappears' (p. 38).

Where does the hope of the future lie if so-called civilisation has destroyed this wholeness of being? His answer at the end of the essay is curiously 'Lawrentian'. 'It is in these two movements', he writes

> towards a complex human Communism and towards freedom and Savagery – in some sort balancing and correcting each other, and both visibly growing up within – tho' utterly foreign to – our present day Civilisation, that we have fair grounds I think for looking forward to its cure. (p. 49)

In many ways, Carpenter's criticism of late Victorian society foreshadows the critical temper of much twentieth-century fiction, but nowhere more obviously than in his ideal of wholeness, his rejection of the material trapping of modern civilisation, his opposition to industrialism, and his vision of the liberating powers of sex.

For his ideas on sex, for his frank championing of homosexuality, one needs to turn to another work, to the collection of essays called *Love's Coming of Age* (1896). In all it contains nine essays: on sex, the position of women in society, marriage, homosexuality (or 'the intermediate sex' to use Carpenter's phrase), and the free society. Some of the essays had already been issued as pamphlets by the Labour Press Manchester, and the notoriety they achieved made it difficult for Carpenter to find a publisher for both his long poem *Towards Democracy* and *Love's Coming of Age*. As Carpenter remarked in connection with Fisher Unwin's withdrawal of his agreement to publish *Towards Democracy*, 'the Wilde trial had done its work; and silence must henceforth reign on sex subjects'. But the Labour Press Manchester came to the rescue and published *Love's Coming of Age*, and, when it proved a success, it was later issued by major publishers and translated into many foreign languages.

The first essay, 'The Sex-Passion', turns immediately to the difficulty of speaking frankly about sex at the end of the nineteenth century.

> The subject of Sex is difficult to deal with. There is no doubt a natural reticence connected with it. There is also a great deal of prudery. The passion occupies, without being spoken of, a large part of human thought; and words on the subject being so few and inadequate, everything that *is* said is liable to be misunderstood. (p. 1)

What is of chief interest in this opening essay is the connection established between attitudes to sex and the state of society. Carpenter prophesies that 'with the regeneration of our social ideas the whole conception of sex as a thing covert and to be ashamed of, marketable and unclean, will have to be regenerated'. Yet, in this essay, as in all his writings on sex, Carpenter strikes a distinctly ascetic note; he complains that everywhere sex 'is slimed over with the thought of pleasure' (p. 15), and clearly regards physical union as an 'allegory and expression of the real union', which is spiritual. In his autobiography, Carpenter confessed that some of the essays in *Love's Coming of Age* should have been written by a woman, but that he could not get any of his women friends to take up the task. Certainly, the essays, 'Woman, the Serf', 'Women in Freedom', 'Marriage: A Retrospect' and 'Marriage: A Forecast' exhibit a remarkable intuitive sympathy with women's nature and women's needs. Because sex is more of a 'constructive instinct', less of 'an unorganized passion', than in man, a woman should be free 'to work out the problem of her sex relations as may commend itself best to her – hampered as little as possible by legal, conventional or economic considerations, and relying chiefly on her own native sense and tact in the matter' (p. 62). The whole conception of 'a nobler Womanhood', he argues depends on 'her complete freedom as to the disposal of her sex'. It must be freed from the 'cash nexus to a husband', the 'money-slavery of the streets' and 'the nameless terrors of social opinion'. She must cease to be a doll; human love must from now on be based on 'that entire refusal to "cage" another person, or to accept an affection not perfectly free and spontaneous'. In his 'Forecast' of what marriage might become in the future, Carpenter prophesies that it will be based on greater freedom for the woman, saner education for boys and girls as a preparation for marriage, a less exclusive attachment allowing greater variety of loves and affections and, finally, a complete abandonment of the notion of the irrevocable bond of marriage: 'there is something quite diabolic and mephistophelian in the practice of the Law' which 'claps its book together with a triumphant bang, and exclaims: "There now you're married and done for, for the rest of your natural lives"' (pp. 106–7). Daring as such views were at the time, it was the essay called 'The Intermediate Sex' that gained Carpenter greatest notoriety. In it he sketches in what he calls 'the extreme types and the more healthy types of the "Intermediate" man and woman' and moves towards a fully developed theory of the androgynous nature of the great artist similar to Virginia Woolf's and G. Wilson Knight's.[11] Like Shaw, Carpenter was a bit of a crank, but his essays now seem to have a surprising modernity. They deserve to be read for their own sake as well as for the light they throw on the transition from Victorianism to Modernism.

George Gissing was certainly neither a Victorian Sage nor an Edwardian Seer or Prophet, but one of his novels, *New Grub Street* (1891), possesses a prophetic insight into the patterns of continuity and change, especially into the corruptions of literary culture brought about by the new journalism and the widespread commercialism of literature.

New Grub Street belongs to a tradition of critical writing that includes Pope's *Dunciad*, Wordsworth's *Prefaces*, with their reflections on the multitude of causes operating to blunt discrimination and produce an almost 'savage torpor', Coleridge's *Biographia Literaria* and *Lay Sermons*, and Arnold's *Culture and Anarchy* and *Essays in Criticism*, all works that in some degree see the state of literature as an accurate index of the cultural health of society. But, whereas these works expound abstract principles about the relationship between literature and society, Gissing's novel actually renders this relationship through plot, characters and imagery. As a struggling and disappointed author himself, he knew the literary world of London from the inside, although the very intensity of his sufferings led him to distort some of its worst features. In *New Grub Street*, he presents an extraordinarily comprehensive picture of the impact of modern commercialism on literature. The major characters have obvious representative functions. Milvain and Whelpdale represent the literary tradesmen, adept in knowing what the public wants and skilled in supplying it for a price. Reardon and Biffen represent the genuine artists, both failures, neither very gifted, and neither able to make a decent living without compromising their artistic integrity, which Biffen is certainly not prepared to do and therefore commits suicide. As P. J. Keating has remarked,[12] it is the final irony of the career of Biffen, the author of the realist novel *Mr Bailey Grocer* 'that his suicide is ultimately inspired by Amy Reardon who, although Biffen will never believe it, has long since become a spokesman for the commercial ethic'. To complete the picture of London literary life there is Alfred Yule, Marian's selfish, tyrannical father, who typifies the vain, devious Man of Letters. What unites the separate fragments of London's literary underworld of striving writers and journalists, apart from the network of personal relations that constitutes the plot, is the British Museum. It is there where most of them carry on their sorry hackwork, there that they intrigue, there that Marian sees herself and other researchers as 'hapless flies caught in a huge web, its nucleus the great circle of the Catalogue'; it is there that the courtship of Marian Yule and Jaspar Milvain is largely conducted. Clearly, there is a studied irony in Gissing's use of the Museum as the central symbol of the novel. The vast circular reading room of the Museum that ought to be a great beacon of intellectual light becomes instead an image of a great spider's web that traps the hapless victims, all examples of the impoverished specimens of London literary life. Moreover, the various characters define themselves through their different attitudes to the reading room and all it stands for.

In the histories of English Literature, *New Grub Street* is often praised almost exclusively for its violent attack on the three-decker novel kept in being by the circulating libraries for which Milvain designs an allegorical cartoon, a 'triple-headed monster, sucking the blood of the

English novelist'. But the novel is more appropriately praised for its comprehensive rendering of a whole society's response to literary culture. Parts foreshadow similar passages in Wells's slightly later novel, *Tono Bungay*, for example the sections satirising the new popular journalism, with its ready appeal to the quarter-educated, through such magazines as *Chit-chat*, based obviously on the real magazine *Tit-Bits*. The critical spirit in which the whole was conceived seems to look forward to Mrs Leavis's pioneering work of literary sciology, *Fiction and the Reading Public* and to Orwell's novels and essays on popular journalism. The last decade of the nineteenth century was a crucial period in the disintegration of a single unified reading public. It marks the real beginning of the division into mass and minority culture. Among the major novelists both James and Hardy realised that they must now appeal to a minority audience, while newcomers like Bennett and Wells believed that it was possible to appeal to a mass audience and remain a serious novelist. In his early works Gissing extracts a gloomy satisfaction from being a lone exile addressing a few readers, and this phase reaches its culmination in *New Grub Street*, but thereafter, as Adrian Poole has pointed out,[13] he discovered a sense of community as an exile among other exiles.

> Here, therefore, is the radical ambiguity about the condition of exile from which his writing is drawn. For on the one hand, it can be conceived as solitary and fixed, conferring the dignity of achieved independence as well as the stigma of rejection. But on the other hand, it can be transformed into an image of a shared or shareable experience through which the writer can connect with the element of 'exile' in every reader, and thereby create the more difficult and valuable imaginative community that must precede physical community. It was to the first notion that Gissing the man was deeply attracted, but to the second that Gissing the creative writer aspired.

As a forceful criticism of society, *New Grub Street* is a deeply moving book. But ultimately Gissing can offer neither solution nor effective protest. As Bernard Bergonzi has remarked, it is 'a novel of resentment rather than of protest'.[14] And because it is infused with a myth of catastrophe, personal rather than social in origin, its picture of the sudden, rapid decline in literary standards exaggerates the actual situation. Gettman's research on literary life in the London of the 1830's reveals that many of the corrupt features of London literary life that Gissing ascribed to the 1890's were already in existence sixty years earlier. Raymond Williams, too, in *The Long Revolution*, has shown that there was no sudden decline in standards at the end of the century. Nevertheless the novel communicates its own authentic picture. It is a terrible and terrifying picture of what happens when the spirit of commerce comes to dominate and control the cultural life of a nation. When the citadel of culture has surrendered its defences what hope is there for the modern 'Condition of England'?

10 The Modern Condition of England Novel

When C. F. G. Masterman revived the phrase 'Condition of England' for the title of his political tract in 1909, he did so at a time when contradictory views of the immediate future of England were current and were often entertained by one and the same man. The advent of a Liberal Government that was committed to ambitious measures of social reform inspired optimistic visions of the future, and Masterman himself was briefly a member of the Liberal Cabinet. It was widely believed that a more rational, statistical approach to poverty and unemployment would inaugurate a new era of social justice. Of the two young men that we meet in the opening scene of Ford Madox Ford's *Some Do Not*,[1] the small, dark, ambitious Scotsman, Vincent Macmaster, works for the Imperial Department of Statistics and is busy collecting the statistics on which the new legislation will be based. But dark clouds are already gathering and the train in which we meet Macmaster and Christopher Tietjens is not a train running from London to Rye, as its occupants think, but, as Robie Macauley has remarked in his introduction to *Parade's End*, running 'from the past into the future, and ahead of them on their one-way journey is a chaotic country of ripped battlefields and disordered towns'. Even when Masterman's *The Condition of England* was published in 1909, the growing might of Germany and the decline in the imperial ideal awoke an almost apocalyptic sense of national disaster. Much of the popular fiction of the Edwardian period reflected the growing fears of invasion and national collapse.[2] Erskine Childers' *The Riddle of the Sands* (now thought of only as a boys' spy story), warned the country of the danger of German invasion. There are even faint echoes of the German threat in Forster's *Howards End.* But the oddest treatment of this theme occurs in Saki's novel *When William Came*, when the Boy Scouts' refusal to parade defeats the German conquerors of England.

One of the special interests of Masterman's book *The Condition of England* lies in its representative character, as an analysis of 'some, at least, of the characteristics of the various classes of Society today in England', and as a diagnosis of the social maladies of the country. Perhaps better than any other single work of the period, it expresses the special blend of Christian humanism and liberal idealism that inspired many reformers of both the Victorian and Edwardian Age. It is infused by a noble ideal of man and his potentialities for good. Masterman's chief thesis is that modern urban civilisation, a civilisation symbolised by the glaring disparity between rich and poor in London, everywhere thwarts and frustrates this development. The dominant tone of the later sections of the book is a combination of righteous indignation and passive bewilderment and regret. To man's neglect of the spirit in an overwhelmingly materialistic age, this undecided prophet attributes the root cause of most of the nation's ills.

> Fulness of bread in the past has been accompanied with leanness of soul. And the modern prophet is still undecided whether this enormous increase of life's comforts and material satisfactions has revealed an equal and parallel advance in courage and compassion and kindly understandings. The nations, equipped with ever more complicated instruments of warfare, face each other as armed camps across frontiers mined and tortured with the apparatus of destruction. A scared wealthy and middle class confronts a cosmopolitan uprising of the 'proletariat', whose discontent it can neither appease nor forget. The industrious populations which have been swept into masses and congestions by the new industry have not yet found an existence serene, and intelligible, and human. No one, to-day, looking out upon a disturbed and sullen Europe, a disturbed and confident America, but is conscious of a world in motion: whither, no man knows. (*The Condition of England*, 5th ed. 1911, p. 177)

As a work, *The Condition of England* still lives, because of the author's sincerity, humanity, and passion for social justice. But even the most sympathetic reader must be aware that the combination of vague Liberalism and evangelical Christianity forms an unstable basis for a valid criticism of Edwardian society. In some sense, then, Masterman's *The Condition of England* represents the bankruptcy of the English liberal tradition.

Discredited though liberalism was as a coherent political philosophy, exhausted as an active political force, much of its idealism and many of its humane values were assimilated by the Edwardian novelists, especially by E. M. Forster, who wrote his first stories and essays for *The Independent Review*, with which Masterman was closely connected. Liberal values also inspired Ford Madox Ford, who, though a high Tory, was a close friend of Masterman. They also inspired Galsworthy, and even Wells. Both Forster and Wells, especially in *Howards End* and *Tono Bungay*, illustrate how easy it was to combine socialist sympathies with the older ideals of English liberalism. Although Forster's connections with the Labour paper the *Daily Herald* and with the *New Statesman* point clearly to his socialist sympathies, his actual novels belong more obviously to the liberal tradition, often gently exposing some of the characteristic weaknesses of that tradition.[3] Wells, too, for all his membership of the Fabian Society and authorship of Socialist tracts, assimilated many of the values and assumptions of that older liberal tradition. This helps to explain why Masterman thought so highly of Wells's novel *Tono Bungay*. Wells's regret for a passing order and his inclusive attack on the materialism that characterised the Edwardian plutocracy made the novel especially congenial to the prophet of a dying liberalism. D. H. Lawrence – whose first three novels appeared before the First World War – however, owed little to either socialist or liberal tradition. The novelist who came closest to presenting the end of the old liberal order and the agonising creation of the new was Ford Madox Ford. His attitude to the two orders was sufficiently ambivalent for him to present their interaction and conflict in all their full complexity. Moreover, he had worked out an aesthetic of the novel that supplied theoretical support for his practice of rendering the totality of social tension through brilliantly selected detail and the choice of the representative 'affair'. He and Conrad agreed that the novelist should not seek to impose an orderly pattern on events, but rather reflect the impressions that life makes on the mind; the novelist's art, they believed, depends on his skill in selecting impressions. Only those things (characters, incidents, phrases) will be included that carry the story a stage forward to its inevitable end, and it was essential, Ford thought, that it should be carried forward faster and faster, with greater and greater intensity, a procedure he referred to as *progession d'effet*. The choice of the Affair is important because the right choice will ensure the maximum concentration of effect. The Affair should be some small-scale incident which, to the perceptive eye of the novelist, possesses a potential for almost infinite refraction of meaning, a meaning both personal and social. It was the novelist's task to render, not to narrate, this affair. In the case of *The Good Soldier*, the Affair was based on two actual incidents: the man who parted with his ward with whom he was in love without a word, 'a very fine achievement' but also a 'manifestation of a national characteristic that is almost appalling'; and the case of the officer (Valentine Baker) who was accused of kissing a girl in a train.

The Good Soldier, Parade's End, and the early novels offer a microcosm of Edwardian society; they are entirely faithful to its tensions and internal contradictions. Unlike the novels of Wells, for example, they offer no simple programme for reform, no utopian visions; nevertheless, they provide a most powerful impressionistic criticism of society. An anonymous reviewer of *Some Do Not* remarked that 'in section' it presents, 'a complete view of English society before and during the war'; another reviewer noted how cleverly Ford had avoided 'H. G. Wells's long-winded explanations and sociological footnotes'; yet another reviewer noted that it did for the Edwardian Age what

Thackerary's *Vanity Fair* had done for the Victorian Age – it presented 'a picture of social life surpassed in poise, penetration and literary excellence only by Thackeray's'.[4] More recently a reviewer remarked that the opening scene of *Some Do Not* is the most brilliant evocation of a complete society in English fiction. Had the Marxist critic, Georg Lukács, looked at the fiction of Ford Madox Ford, he might have found it necessary to modify his thesis in *History and Class Consciousness* that the limits of middle-class consciousness are marked by its incapacity or unwillingness to come to terms with the category of *totality*.[5]

The story of *The Good Soldier* concerns the coming together of two couples, Captain Edward Ashburnham and his wife Leonora, and the narrator, John Dowell, a wealthy American, and his wife Florence. Ashburnham, who in a sense represents the inner decay of the feudal code of the English landed gentry and of the mystique of military service, is handsome, grave, generous, sentimental. The coldness of his wife and his sentimental nature involve him in a series of affairs: the servant girl he kisses in the train, referred to throughout as the Kilsyte case; the Duke's mistress who costs him £10,000; Maisie, a young officer's wife whose expenses Edward Ashburnham's own wife pays so that he may enjoy Maisie's company at the German Spa of Nauheim; Florence, the narrator's wife; and finally Ashburnham's ward, the young girl Nancy Rufford. Maisie, the only true 'heart case' among the characters at the Spa, dies from the shock of overhearing Ashburnham telling Florence that his wife had bought Maisie for him. Florence commits suicide when she discovers that Ashburnham loves his ward and that at any moment her own husband may hear of her earlier affair with another man. When the ward, Nancy, who has been packed off out of the way, sends a thoughtlessly gay telegram from Brindisi, Ashburnham slits his throat. Nancy goes mad. At the end of the novel the ruthless, purposeful Leonora has re-married, and the narrator John Dowell, who has spent so many years as the tame sick attendant to his deceitful promiscuous wife, Florence, now nurses the insane girl Nancy and tries to arrange and re-arrange his impressions of these events in order to discover in them some sort of meaning. He is left, remarks Mark Schorer, attempting to relate his new knowledge of this exposed reality to his long, untroubled faith in its appearance.

Ford Madox Ford's *The Good Soldier* (1915) renders the impotence of the old chivalric ideals, the incapacity of the gentlemanly code of honour, to survive in the modern world. Although its main action is essentially domestic and confined to a small group of characters belonging to the affluent, leisured class, the novel, by implication at least, embraces modern civilisation as a whole. The use of the obtuse, ineffectual American narrator, John Dowell, who watches and records Captain Ashburnham's tragic fate, fascinated by a civilisation that he only partly-comprehends and powerless to arrest its decline, imparts to the novel a Jamesian international perspective. The setting of much of the action in Europe, mainly at the small German Spa of Nauheim where the Dowells and the Ashburnhams first meet, prevents the novel from being narrowly insular, even though its chief characters are, in the words of the narrator, typically English, 'what in England it is the custom to call "quite good people" ', their outward lives models of good conduct, restrained emotion, and respect for codes of honour, while all beneath is violent disorder. Carefully selected details convey a vivid impression of the strict conventions that govern the relations of the English abroad, among themselves and with wealthy and aristocratic Europeans. Ford places his modern tragedy within a long historic context. It is during a visit to M—, the historic source of Lutheran Protestantism, that Edward Ashburnham's Catholic wife Leonora 'looks into the pit of hell', as she watches Edward touch Florence Dowell's hand and as she listens to her gay prattling about the moral liberation inaugurated by Luther's protest. Similarly the sections of the novel that record Edward's marriage to the sheltered Leonora in Ireland and all the details of life at the Irish country house of Branshaw Teleraugh are rich in social and religious implication. Moreover, the references to Captain Ashburnham's eight years' service in India, his affair with Maisie, the wife of a brother officer, and the final despatch of the young girl Nancy Rufford to Ceylon to join her tea-planter father, Colonel Rufford, serve to place 'A Tale of Passion' – the novel's subtitle – within an imperial context. More economically than either Kipling or Forster, Ford places the Empire in a total context of a dying world order. Finally, the immediate time-scale of the plot is as important as the wider historic perspectives or the sense of internationalism created by the geographical allusions. The sequence of repeated dates, 4th August, which includes Florence's birth on 4 August 1874, Maisie Maidan's death on 4 August 1904, Florence's overhearing Edward's conversation with Nancy on 4 August 1913, looks forward to the historic date, 4 August 1914, that brought the world of the good soldier and his society to an end. Few novelists have communicated the totality of the world situation with such economy. By contrast John Berger's *G* and Solzhenitsyn's *August 1914*, both a strange mixture of historical documentation and imaginative fiction, seem clumsy and tell us much less about the worlds they set out to depict.

Because the relationship between the narrator and the hero in *The Good Soldier* is a subtle one and because the narrator is directly involved in the events he pieces together, critical attention has tended to concentrate on these matters rather than on Ford's insight into the destructive forces at work in man and in society. Similarly, the problems raised by the novelist's intricate 'time-shifts', about which he wrote at considerable length in his critical writings, have distracted attention from the quality and range of his social criticism. Certainly the narrative technique, a form of prose impressionism analogous to imagism in poetry, is integral to the meaning of the novel as a whole, but it has often been made to seem an end in itself so intricate and beautifully organized is it. Ultimately it depends on two major elements: first, on the continuous play of irony arising from John Dowell's ignorance of the events as they occurred and his later knowledge acquired in the process of telling his 'rambling' story, as if he were in a 'country cottage, with a sympathetic soul opposite'; second, on the calculated shocks given to the reader, especially the rapid intensification of shock at the end, the *progression d'effet* on which Ford so prided himself.

The Good Soldier exhibits the tragedies, private and public, that ensue when the codes by which a society purports to live no longer correspond to actual behaviour. These codes relate to religious belief, sexual conduct, military honour, feudal responsibility, the handling of money. Of their nature they are largely unspoken, and it is a weakness of Ford's novels that his heroes should often be made to articulate the codes too explicitly. Part of John Dowell's problem in understanding the events he narrates arises from the fact that, as an American, he is an outsider and cannot be certain that he places the right interpretation on the laconic utterances, restrained gestures, silences, and subtle obliquities with which he is confronted and which exert a special fascination precisely because he is an outsider. Through him the reader himself is involved in the active process of sifting appearance and reality, of questioning the value of a civilisation based upon repression and polite disguise. He is also involved in doing justice to the contradictory facets of the hero's character: he comes to balance Edward Ashburnham's honourable behaviour to the young girl Nancy against his compulsive philandering; he also comes to experience the chill shock of Edward's suicide but also to recognise its tragic inevitability – to recognise the truth that the characters are not figures in a stately minuet but held within a prison or else enjoying the illusory freedom of partners in a cat's-cradle, or hapless shuttlecocks tossed backwards and forwards. After Ashburnham's death, the narrator of the story, reduced to the status of a male nurse to the demented girl Nancy Rufford, reflects in his muddled ironic fashion on the significance of all the events:

> And she repeated the word 'shuttlecocks' three times. I know what was passing in her mind, if she can be said to have a mind, for Leonora has told me that, once, the poor girl said she felt like a shuttlecock being tossed backwards and forwards between the violent personalities of Edward and his wife. Leonora, she said, was always trying to deliver her over to Edward, and Edward tacitly and silently forced her back again. And the odd thing was that Edward himself considered that those two women used *him* like a shuttlecock. Or, rather, he said that they sent him backwards and forwards like a

blooming parcel that someone didn't want to pay the postage on. And Leonora also imagined that Edward and Nancy picked her up and threw her down as suited their purely vagrant moods. So there you have the pretty picture. Mind, I am not preaching anything contrary to accepted morality. I am not advocating free love in this or any other case. Society must go on, I suppose, and society can only exist if the normal, if the virtuous, and the slightly deceitful flourish, and if the passionate, the headstrong, and the too-truthful are condemned to suicide and to madness. But I guess that I myself, in my fainter way, come into the category of the passionate, of the headstrong, and the too-truthful. For I can't conceal from myself the fact that I loved Edward Ashburnham – and that I love him because he was just myself. If I had had the courage and the virility and possibly also the physique of Edward Ashburnham I should, I fancy, have done much what he did. He seems to me like a large elder brother who took me out on several excursions and did many dashing things whilst I just watched him robbing the orchards, from a distance. And, you see, I am just as much of a sentimentalist as he was. . . . (*The Good Soldier*, pp. 217–18)

To call Dowell a moral eunuch, to exaggerate his limited sensibility, is to miss the point that in some respects Dowell is Ashburnham's double, as this passage makes clear. The reflective Prufock-like passivity of the narrator and the anguished activity of the hero reflect two major aspects of a civilization moving inexorably towards self-destruction. Ford makes the perfect rendering of his chosen affair the means of presenting the totality of the European situation immediately before the First World War.

The novels *Some Do Not* (1924), *No More Parades* (1925) and *A Man Could Stand Up* (1926) give a more extended sense of this totality, because they include not only the inexorable drift to destruction, the break-down of traditional codes of behaviour, but also a vivid portrayal of the collapse of civilised values in the War itself. Whether one considers *Last Post* (1928) as an integral part of the novels that make up *Parades End* must remain a matter of individual judgment.[6] The main structural principle on which the first three novels are based is ironic juxtaposition – of character, incident, and phrase. In *Some Do Not*, the juxtaposition of the successful opportunist and sly seducer Vincent Macmaster and the unsuccessful man of honour Christopher Tietjens serves to highlight the dramatic conflict between two rival philosophies of life, which may for the sake of convenience be called New Liberal and Old Tory. Yet the two men are friends, not enemies, drawn to one another by subtle ties, conscious and unconscious. Macmaster is destined to win an early knighthood (it comes from stealing one of Christopher's brilliant ideas), while Tietjens, alienated from his wife

Sylvia and desperately in love with the young suffragette Valentine Wannop, struggles to maintain his sanity and basic humanity in the trenches in France. Throughout *Parades End* Ford establishes the integral connection between public and private life, between political and sexual mores.

One of the most brilliant scenes in *Some Do Not* is a breakfast party attended by Macmaster, Tietjens, and Valentine Wannop. The well-bred guests preserve a façade of perfect propriety while Macmaster makes the first moves in his 'romantic' seduction of Mrs Duchemin and while 'Breakfast Duchemin', a clergyman subject to violent outbreaks of obscenity, interjects sexual innuendos in Latin and, ironically, breaks out with an eulogy on chastity.

> 'Chaste!' he shouted. 'Chaste you observe! What a world of suggestion in the word. . . .' He surveyed the opulent broadness of his tablecloth; it spread out before his eyes as if it had been a great expanse of meadow in which he could gallop, relaxing his limbs after long captivity. He shouted three obscene words and went on in his Oxford Movement voice: 'But chastity. . .' (*Some Do Not*, p. 127)

What had drawn Macmaster to the Reverend Duchemin is a shared interest in one of the Pre-Raphaelite poet-painters on whom Macmaster has written a monograph and many of whose works Duchemin possesses. The whole scene is an ironic exposure of a society based on repression: it reveals the gap between outward appearance and inward reality. Deftly Ford contrasts three approaches to sexuality: Duchemin's insane and dangerous clerical repression; Macmaster's disguising of his sexual opportunism beneath a cloak of romantic idealism; and Tietjens honest and civilised behaviour towards Valentine. The Pre-Raphaelite allusions (Ford's grandfather was the Pre-Raphaelite painter Ford Madox Brown and he wrote a book on him and on Rossetti) are not adventitious; they help to place the perverted sexuality in a larger social and cultural context.

The phrase that provides the title of the novel *Some Do Not* recurs as a *leit-motif* to mark the distinction between those who, like Dostoevsky's Ivan, regard all things as lawful, and those who live according to a code of honour. Although Vincent Macmaster quotes with relish the lines written by the subject of his monograph,

> The gods to each ascribe a differing lot:
> Some enter at the portal. Some do not!
> (*Some Do Not*, p. 34)

he is unrestrained by any honourable scruples in his quest for worldly fame and sexual conquest. Tietjens, though he falls in love with Valentine and is inhumanly treated by his sadistic and faithless wife Sylvia, exercises restraint. Both Valentine and he, aided it is true by the chance intervention of Valentine's drunken sailor brother who prevents any chance of their sleeping together before Tietjens returns to France, accept the moral principle that 'some do not'. Since the phrase is also used by a number of the minor characters, the driver of the knacker's van at the end of Part One, for example, it achieves a universalising thematic resonance in the novel.

Similarly the phrase 'No More Parades' recurs throughout the second novel in the *Parades End* sequence, not simply to point forward to the time when the war will be over, but to the coming into existence of a society that will no longer be ordered by traditional codes of behaviour. The central passage consists of Tietjens's ironic War Office anecdote and ensuing prophecy to a fellow officer, at the opening of *No More Parades*:

> 'At the beginning of the war,' Tietjens said, 'I had to look in on the War Office, and in a room I found a fellow. . . . What do you think he was doing . . . what the hell do you think he was doing? He was devising the ceremonial for the disbanding of a Kitchener battalion. You can't say we were not prepared in one matter at least. . . . Well, the end of the show was to be: the adjutant would stand the battalion at ease: the band would play *Land of Hope and Glory*, and then the adjutant would say: *There will be no more parades*. . . . Don't you see how symbolical it was: the band playing *Land of Hope and Glory*, and then the adjutant saying *There will be no more parades*? . . . For there won't. There won't, there damn well won't. . . . No more Hope, no more Glory, no more parades for you and me any more. Nor for the country. . . . Nor for the world, I dare say . . . None . . . Gone . . . Na poo, finny! No . . . more . . . parades!' (*No More Parades*, pp. 27–8)

With an envious and neurotic Captain as a companion, Christopher Tietjens performs amazing feats of intellectual organisation to retain his sanity and to carry out his duties, harassed alike by domestic and military persecution. Under fire, he composes a sonnet to given rhymes, compiles elaborate statistics, gets his replacement drafts ready in record time, wrestles with the problem of who is to inherit Groby while giving orders to Sergeant-Major Cowley, keeps the elaborate formality of the General's cook-house inspection, knowing that behind the ordered cleanliness lies a dirty apron stuffed in a cupboard, just as lies, deception and moral anarchy lie behind the polite world of London society that he has left behind, memories of which flood his mind as he conducts the General round the kitchens.

One of the most dramatic ways in which Tietjens's domestic affairs are linked with his mental sufferings in the trenches is through the parallel between Private '09 Morgan and himself. Morgan, like Tietjens, is estranged from his wife. In order to settle matters he applies for compassionate leave. Teitjens refuses the application, because he knows that Morgan will be beaten up by the wife's boxer lover, Red Evans. The rendering of Tietjens's inner thoughts, as he lowers the body of the dead '09 Morgan to the ground, is one of the greatest examples of the use of the stream of consciousness technique for capturing the complexity of human experience in the whole of English fiction. It possesses a Shakespearean fulness. By contrast the stream of consciousness in Joyce strikes one as needlessly scatalogical in emphasis, and in Virginia Woolf too purely aesthetic. In Ford's novel the swift alternations in Tietjens's mind between compassion for the dead man, tender memories of Valentine, fear of her pacifist disapproval, disgust at the dehumanising conditions of war, guilty responsibility for '09 Morgan's death, thoughts of home, build up a wonderful sense of the tensions of a whole society reflected in a single consciousness. The middle section of this long passage, however, specifically links the situation of the hero with that of the dead man.

> O God, how suddenly his bowels turned over! . . . Thinking of the girl. . . . The face below him grinned at the roof – the half face! The nose was there, half the mouth with the teeth showing in the firelight. . . . It was extraordinary how defined the peaked nose and the serrated teeth were in that mess. . . . The eye looked jauntily at the peak of the canvas hut-roof. . . . Gone with a grin. Singular the fellow should have spoken! After he was dead. He must have been dead when he spoke. It had been done with the last air automatically going out of the lungs. A reflex action, probably, in the dead. . . . If he, Tietjens, had given the fellow the leave he wanted he would be alive now! . . . Well, he was quite right not to have given the poor devil his leave. He was, anyhow, better where he was. And so was he, Tietjens. He had not had a single letter from home since he had been out this time! Not a single letter. Not even gossip. Not a bill. Some circulars of old furniture dealers. They never neglected him! They had got beyond the sentimental stage at home. Obviously so. . . . He wondered if his bowels would turn over again if he thought of the girl. (*No More Parades*, pp. 30–1)

Ford's introduction of Sylvia on to the battlefield is a further device for establishing the relation between the disorders of the private and the public life, carrying with it the suggestion that war is simply the logical extension of psychological and domestic anarchy. Improbable in some respects as Sylvia's visit to Army Headquarters may seem, it serves to dramatise the connection between the sexual and societal forces that harass Christopher Tietjens and drive him to the brink of insanity. The scene in which Christopher keeps up a laconic interchange with the affected lascivious adjutant Levin, while all the time wondering who the woman can be who is waiting in the General's car, is only one of the many scenes that render dramatically the sense of mind stretched to its limits by nervous tension as it struggles to preserve order and decency in the midst of chaos. Both novels, *No More Parades* and *A Man Could Stand Up*, establish that the true hell of war lies in the waiting; it arises from tense inactivity, not action. The high-pitched and long-sustained agonies of mind and spirit convey a more authentic impression of the horror of war and of the condition of man in an ailing and alien society than the open and discursive methods of most war novelists. That the agonies of mind are not restricted to the hero and his fellow sufferers in France may be seen from the opening of *A Man Could Stand Up*, where Ford portrays Valentine's tortured consciousness on Armistice Day. Acting as a temporary teacher in a school whose key-note is restraint, she is called to the phone to hear Sylvia's 'sibilating voice . . . spitting out spitefully' that Christopher had returned, that his mind was disordered, that he had no furniture, and that he was alone with no one to help him.

> Improbable-sounding pieces of information half-extinguished by the external sounds but uttered in a voice that seemed to mean to give pain by what it said.
>
> Nevertheless it was impossible not to take it gaily. The thing, out there, miles and miles away must have been signed – a few minutes ago. She imagined along an immense line sullen and disgruntled cannon sounding for a last time. (*A Man Could Stand Up*, p. 264)

Moreover, Valentine's experience of protracted waiting and her love for Christopher give her a sympathetic insight into the reality of war at the end of the novel:

> Ah, the dreadful thing about the whole war was that it had been – the suffering had been – mental rather than physical. And they had not thought of it. . . . He had been under fire. She had pictured him always as being in a Base, thinking. If he had been killed it would not have been so dreadful for him. But now he had come back with his obsessions and mental troubles. . . . And he needed his woman. And her mother was forcing him to abstain from his woman! That was what was terrible. He had suffered mental torture and now his pity was being worked on to make him abstain from the woman that could atone.
>
> Hitherto, she had thought of the War as physical suffering only: now she saw it only as mental torture. Immense miles and miles of anguish in darkened minds. That remained. Men might stand up on

> hills, but the mental torture could not be expelled. (*A Man Could Stand Up*, p. 452)

Ford, even more intensely than the War Poets, Isaac Rosenberg and Wilfred Owen, communicates the mental horror of war. And it is illuminating to compare Ford's presentation of Valentine as a schoolmistress with Lawrence's of Ursula at the beginning of *Women in Love*. Valentine's consciousness reflects in little the anguish of a whole civilisation in turmoil as she broods over her duties to her girls, while Ursula's reflects the more limited sexual and marital preoccupations of her creator. Neither novelist, of course, is to be judged by standards appropriate to purely realistic fiction. Yet it remains true, I think, that Ford's novels, for all their strange distortions of event, suspensions of time, and hallucinatory visual effects, offer a more penetrating and comprehensive criticism of contemporary society than do those of Lawrence. His characters are not only more deeply grounded in society – they work as well as talk; his characters also contain within their consciousnesses more of the totality of the European situation. And because Ford's stance towards his characters and their world – if not one of Flaubertian god-like remoteness – is more detached than Lawrence's, his criticism of society is more challenging and complex.

The English gentry, he suggests in a great variety of ways, have proved inadequate to their historic role in society; they have failed both as rulers and as custodians of culture. The code by which – in theory, at least – they regulate their lives is potentially a noble one. But it is too rigid; and those who try to live up to it like Edward Ashburnham and Christopher Tietjens are destroyed in the process. Moreover, the vicious, like Sylvia, and hypocritical, like Mrs Duchemin, employ the codes to shelter themselves and damage others. The last pages of *A Man Could Stand Up*, with their brilliant evocation of Armistice Day, when it becomes clear that Christopher and Valentine will break the code and live together at last, even though Sylvia is still alive and will not divorce Christopher, herald a new age in which codes will be made and remade by individuals in the light of their own consciences. It is an age that has finally rejected the stultifying effects of the old gentlemanly code of honour. An unsympathetic critic might complain that Ford reduces the whole question of the future of England to a matter of club law; General Campion, for example, thinks that it is the end of England when the two city gents break the club rule about talking about women at the bar. But such a complaint has very limited validity, since it ignores the ironic context in which such incidents take place. Ford will always be undervalued and misunderstood by both historians and sociologists, because his novels cannot be used as if they were historical documents masking as fiction, nor can any simple summaries of meaning be extracted from them. Ford created images of his time and these impressionistic images are embodied in the intricate imaginative organisation of his novels. Coleridge said of the art of poetry: it is untranslatable into any other words without sense of loss. The same might be said about Ford, the novelist, who carried the art of rendering to its highest point of perfection.

Three 'Condition of England' novels published during the present century offer interesting evidence about the relationship between artistic form and meaning, between the narrative techniques employed and the visions of society developed. These novels are Butler's *The Way of All Flesh* (1903), Wells's *Tono Bungay* (1909) and Forster's *Howards End* (1910) For all its ironic subversion of Victorian values, for all its potential dynamite, *The Way of All Flesh* presents a very muddled view of life: of the effects of heredity, of the slow processes leading to self-fulfilment, of the emancipation of the hero Pontifex from the shackles of custom and outmoded belief, of the relations between the liberated individual and social institutions. The muddle is reflected in every detail of the work, but nowhere more clearly than in the muddled narrative technique (often highly praised). Technically, the story is told by an impartial but indulgent bachelor-uncle figure, Overton; but, as has been frequently noted, it is impossible to distinguish between the world views of Ernest, Overton, and the author at the end of the novel. It is true that the novel has something of the inner dynamism and therapeutic function of the modern confessional novel, as Butler liberates himself, his hero, and his readers from the stuffiness of Victorianism. For Ernest, prison gives a truer insight into life than school or university, while for the heroes of later fiction similar illumination comes from solitary confinement in prisoner-of-war or concentration camp. Butler's hero is involved in a process of continuous discovery, and the logic of the novel demands a characteristically open-ended conclusion. But, in fact, Ernest's modern Odyssey is blocked off by his mocking all-wise creator who provided him with a comfortable salvation through money; it is also enclosed within the limiting framework of Overton's indulgent narrative. 'No-one' as G. D. H. Cole remarked, 'ever insisted more firmly than Butler on the Victorian virtue of having enough money to live on securely in a comfortable bourgeois way'.

Wells's novel *Tono Bungay* unlike Butler's novel, is truly confessional and open-ended. The story is presented as the gropings of a non-literary man, not as a 'constructed tale'. It has its appropriate 'social trajectory'. George, the engineer narrator, defines his main aim in the opening pages of the novel.

> I suppose what I'm really trying to render is nothing more nor less than Life – as one man has found it. I want to tell — *myself*, and my impressions of the thing as a whole, to say things I have come to feel intensely of the laws, traditions, usages, and ideas we call society,

> and how we poor individuals get driven and lured and stranded among these windy, perplexing shoals and channels. (Book 1, ch. 1, § 2)

The nautical images are proleptic. The book ends with a vision of George 'tearing into the great spaces of the future, through the channel created by the destroyer X 2 ', an ironic image, product of the narrator's acquired maturity – I have come to see myself from the outside, my country from the outside – without illusions'. Nevertheless, in spite of the gain in wisdom, life is still an on-going process; the novel is open-ended.

Howards End, compared with *The Way of All Flesh* and *Tono Bungay*, is a far more traditional 'Condition of England' novel. It has an artificially constructed plot. The plot, based on the symbolic union of the artistic Schlegels and the men of business, the Wilcoxes, embodies the main conflict of ideas. The novel moves forward to a prepared climax; and while the last scene looks forward to the future of England and implies that there are no final solutions, the novel has a certain finality and authority that arises from the well-made plot and Forster's stance as the omniscient author. Yet it is true, of course, that the author's persistent irony qualifies all positives – even the positives of harmony suggested through the symbolic union of Margaret Schlegel and Henry Wilcox.

A comparison of *Tono Bungay* and *Howards End* as 'Condition of England' novels reveals that their contrasting strengths arise from their respective forms. The confessional mode of *Tono Bungay* permits Wells to incorporate a large amount of incidental observation and analysis of society without seeming irrelevant or obtrusive, and without damaging the unity of texture. In *The Language of Fiction*, David Lodge remarks that 'the main vehicle of Wells's social analysis is not the story or the characters, but the descriptive commentary which, in most novels, we regard as the frame'. Apart from drawing attention to the intrinsic interest of Wells's commentary on the new techniques of advertising, the rise of the Edwardian plutocracy and many other aspects of the commentary, Lodge suggests that the organising principle of *Tono Bungay* lies not in the uncle's rise and fall, or in George's relation with women, but in 'the web of description and commentary by which all the proliferating events and characters of the story are placed in a comprehensive political, social, and historical perspective'. The organising principles of Forster's *Howards End*, on the other hand, are plot, character and image. I have already drawn attention elsewhere[7] to the way in which the images of the wisp of hay, the wych-elm bending over the house, the motor car, the Schlegel sword, the abyss, the rainbow bridge, serve through a process of 'repetition plus variation' to body forth Forster's vision of disintegration and potential harmony in England. I have also drawn attention to how obtrusive some of the passages of fine writing and essay-like commentary are. Incidental social commentary fits the discursive Wells type of novel; it often seems out of place in *Howards End* and in many of Lawrence's novels, too.

There is one further point worth noting about the form and spirit of *Tono Bungay* and Wells's early novels like *Kipps*, *Mr Polly* and *Ann Veronica*. In their directness and naivete, they brought a breath of fresh air into the stale atmosphere of cultural debate. Wells, the spokesman for the little man, appealed to a new generation of readers eager to find their place in society and to understand a rapidly changing world. In his novels, he successfully embodies both their aspirations and their painful confusions. He recorded the tensions created by a rapid increase in social mobility and had a deeper understanding of the positive side of this mobility than either Masterman in *From the Abyss* or Forster in the creation of Leonard Bast in *Howards End*. Wells's heroes look for happiness and salvation in self-improvement, Arthur Kipps for instance. In this respect the novelist is a latter-day Samuel Smiles. But they also look for it in freer sexual relations, as do George Ponderevo and Ann Veronica. And they look for it in conspicuous culture, that is, culture as a proof of having made one's way in the world and not culture as the harmonious development of all our faculties, which was Coleridge's and Matthew Arnold's ideal. His heroes also yearn for the simple life, not on the constructive Edward Carpenter model, but as a means of escape from the tensions and frustrations of society. As a result there is an unresolved conflict in Wells's early novels between the author's socialistic ambition to remodel society for the benefit of his little men and the desire of his heroes to create small reserved worlds of happiness for themselves outside society altogether. Mr Polly's retreat to the Potwell Inn is a plebian version of escape to the greenwoods.

Three images occupy an important place in many of the modern 'Condition of England' novels. These are the image of the city, the image of the country house, and the image of escape to the greenwoods. In *Country and City* (1973), Raymond Williams has charted the long historical traditions connected with two of these images; my own account is more narrowly focused and concentrates on a small selection of 'Condition of England' novels.

The image of the city as a prison or cancerous growth has become more pervasive in the twentieth century than the early image of the industrial city as an inferno. Dickens's vision of 'the restless and unheeding crowd' in chapter 32 of *Nicholas Nickleby* and his picture of the 'infection and contagion' propagated by the slum area Tom-All-Alone's in *Bleak House* have exerted a more powerful influence over later imaginations than his evocation of the blacking factory in *David Copperfield*, although the Dickensian image of the lonely city outcast worked powerfully on the imaginations of Dostoevsky and Gissing. There are two fairly obvious reasons why the images of the crowd and contagion prevailed. Partly as the result of the efforts of Shaftesbury and others, factory legislation gradually prevented the kind of conditions the novelist attacked in his account of the blacking factory. Secondly, the vast expansion of the great cities and the sheer increase in the number of cities meant that the city and all it stands for in the modern consciousness – destructive anonymity, 'jungle' or 'abyss', endless flux, extreme contrast between rich and poor, came to dominate. In the conversation between Margaret Schlegel and Henry Wilcox on the Embankment, in chapter 20 of *Howards End*, Margaret sums up her disquiet, as she sees evidence of change all around her.

> 'I hate this continual flux of London. It is an epitome of us at our worst – eternal formlessness; all the qualities, good, bad, and indifferent, streaming away – streaming, streaming for ever. That's why I dread it so.' (Penguin, p. 171)

Howards End is not only a powerful 'Condition of England' novel; it is also a novel about the modern city.

Throughout *Howards End*, Forster builds up a powerful contrast between the slow natural rhythms of the earth associated with Mrs Wilcox's house, Howards End, and the hectic pace of life in London, as more and more people are crammed onto its soil and the anonymous forces of modern capitalism transform the city into a gigantic emblem of human muddle. The novelist's description of the block of flats where Leonard and Jacky Bast perform their sterile *Waste Land* rituals of love and squalid domesticity has a moving representative quality.

> A block of flats, constructed with extreme cheapness, towered on either hand. Farther down the road two more blocks were being built, and beyond these an old house was being demolished to accommodate another pair. It was the kind of scene that may be observed all over London, whatever the locality – bricks and mortar rising and falling with the restlessness of the water in a fountain, as the city receives more and more men upon her soil. Camelia Road would soon stand out like a fortress, and command, for a little, an extensive view. Only for a little. Plans were out for the erection of flats in Magnolia Road also. And again a few years, and all the flats in either road might be pulled down, and new buildings, of a vastness at present unimaginable, might arise where they had fallen. (Penguin, pp. 45–6)

The process of rapid change is shown as affecting the wealthy and cultured Schlegels as well as the pathetic figures hovering over the 'abyss'. Once the lease of Margaret Schlegel's London house at Wickham Place has expired, she becomes aware for the first time of 'the architecture of hurry' and hears 'the language of hurry' in the 'clipped words' and 'formless sentences' of the Londoners around her. Henry Wilcox, alone of all the characters in the novel, appears unaffected by the inhuman aspects of the city and the impossibility of accommodating its monstrous impersonality within the human imagination. But then Wilcox, we are made to see, has learnt to live without the imagination and without personal relations; he is one of the makers of modernity. With his hands firmly 'on the ropes of life', he manipulates money and people to serve his blindly selfish ends. By contrast, the man of imagination feels only a desolating sense of alienation. A passage of rather too explicit commentary in chapter 13 sums up the novelist's struggle to comprehend the city.

> Certainly London fascinates. One visualizes it as a tract of quivering grey, intelligent without purpose, and excitable without love; as a spirit that has altered before it can be chronicled; as a heart that certainly beats, but with no pulsation of humanity. It lies beyond everything: Nature, with all her cruelty, comes nearer to us than do these crowds of men. A friend explains himself: the earth is explicable – from her we came, and we must return to her. But who can explain Westminster Bridge Road or Liverpool Street in the morning – the city inhaling – or the same thoroughfare in the evening – the city exhaling her exhausted air? We reach in desperation beyond the fog, beyond the very stars, the voids of the universe are ransacked to justify the monster, and stamped with a human face. (Penguin, pp. 102–3)

While the image of London in *Howards End* lacks the cosmic terror of the image of the Marabar Caves in *A Passage to India*, it nevertheless renders in a most disturbing manner all those forces in modern civilisation that defy the liberal imagination's power to create visions of order and harmony out of urban chaos.

The work of the French artist, Gustave Doré, illustrates the vital distinction that can be drawn between sociological reporting and the artist's vision. Doré, in collaboration with the London journalist Blanchard Jerrold, produced an illustrated book on London in 1872, aptly titled *London: A Pilgrimage*. Illustrations from it have been frequently reproduced in social histories and the work itself is now readily available in paperback. Two things strike us when we look at its pages: Doré's capacity to communicate the turbulent overcrowding of the streets, and his ability to render the spectral hopelessness of poverty, a gift that owed something to his admiration for the apocalyptic painter, John Martin.[8] We see the first most clearly in his picture of Ludgate Hill, the second in the famous 'Under the Arches'. Roughly at the same time that Doré and Jerrold were wandering through London forming images of the great city, the pioneers of sociological statistics, Charles Booth and Beatrice Webb, were collecting their valuable data about slum housing, overcrowding and urban poverty. Still earlier, in 1861, Henry Mayhew published his detailed accounts of urban life in *London Labour and London Poor*, using methods of interviewing that in some respects anticipated the use of the tape recorder today. His interview with a 'regular scavager' who had a very practical attitude to both human excrement and money is not only typical of his method but throws some light on the critical controversy about dust heaps, excrement and money in Dickens's *Our Mutual Friend*.

> 'Yes, I've heered on the Board of Health. They've put down some night-yards, and if they goes on putting down more, what's to become of the night-soil? I can't think what they're up to; but if they don't touch wages, it may be all right in the end on it'. (Selections from *London Labour and London Poor*, World's Classics, p. 161)

Thirty or forty years later Shaw put such a figure on the London stage in the form of the dustman, Mr Doolittle, in *Pygmalion*.

What is the essential difference between the sociologist's approach to society and the artist's, whether he be poet, novelist or painter? The sociologist asks himself 'what are the facts?' and proceeds to devise methods for establishing these in as objective a fashion as possible, placing his main reliance on statistics and the principle of quantification. The artist, on the other hand, asks himself 'what is the truth?' and seeks to create images that will communicate the total impact of the scene on his sensibilities and thus render its full human implications; facts and values are fused, as they are for all of us in the process of living, but in a permanent and memorable form. If we compare Doré's first sketches with his finished illustrations, we find that those of street scenes are altogether less crowded. They are probably more accurate as documentary records of the number of people and carriages actually there, but the scene works on the artist's imagination and what he finally produces is a unified image of the individual lost in the anonymous crush of a modern city.

As readers what we come to look for in the Edwardian novels about London is some unified image of the city and the society that produced it. Both *Tono Bungay* and *Howards End* retain their interest and vitality today because Wells and Forster penetrated below the outward appearance of things to the large-scale economic forces and human drives that were working to produce a new rhythm and pattern of life. Immensely powerful and original as their criticism undoubtedly was, it was only part of a much larger body of writing on the same subject that appeared at this time, which included fiction about the East End, such as Arthur Morrison's *Tales of Mean Streets* (1894). As a practical product of William Morris's and Ruskin's idealism, Ebenezer Howard offered a blueprint for the future in his *Garden Cities for Tomorrow*, and work was begun on creating such cities just outside London. Ford Madox Ford, in the little known *The Soul of London* (1905), *The Heart of the Country* (1906), and *The Spirit of the People* (1907), made striking comparisons between the new materialistic urban civilisation and the traditions of the past. Masterman, in a volume of essays on the city, in *From the Abyss* (1902), and in *The Condition of England* (1909) analysed the appalling conditions of life in London. In 'The English City', in 1904, he wrote:

> In England the cities are most monstrous, and black, and disorganized; and the aggregations which sprawl at the mouths of the rivers or amid the wastes of the manufacturing districts most effectually challenge the advocate of any life that is secure, and passionate, and serene.[9]

Masterman, as we have seen, read Wells's *Tono Bungay* before it was published in book form and was greatly impressed with the novelist's criticism of the dehumanising effects of the city on individuals and the health of the whole society.

The opening chapter of Book 2 of *Tono Bungay* illustrates how Wells's image of the city is bound up with his image of the country house. The latter is an old image, more deeply rooted in English poetry than in fiction. In Ben Jonson's 'To Penshurst' and Marvell's 'Appleton House', the country house becomes a symbol of the ideal life, a life of high civilisation, carried on in harmony with the rhythms of nature, unostentatious, dignified, and based on reciprocal rights and duties.[10] At the beginning of the eighteenth century, with the triumph of mercantile endeavour, the newly rich began to take over the great estates and noble houses, and to build new ones as conspicuous proof of their wealth and status. In the 'Epistle to Burlington', Pope satirises the tasteless splendours of Timon's Villa.

> At Timon's Villa let us pass a day
> Where all cry out, 'What sums are thrown away.'

Both in verse and prose, the country house very naturally became an image of harmonious culture, a condensed image of the right relationship between nature and art, agriculture and industry, aristocracy and the honest poor. Whereas the name of a Gothic Castle, 'Nightmare Abbey' came to epitomise romantic anarchy, the name of a house symbolised civilised order. For Jane Austen, Mansfield Park represents such an order, for James the house called Medley serves a similar function in *The Princess Casmassima*, while for many twentieth-century novelists, country houses serve as complex social symbols. In

Forster's novel, the question of who shall inherit the house Howards End can easily be made to suggest the larger question of who shall inherit England. Forster is certainly not the only modern novelist to use this motif. Ford Madox Ford's tetralogy turns on the question of who shall inherit the Yorkshire estate, Groby. And the cutting down of the Groby oak by the *nouveau riche* tenants symbolises the thoughtless attacks upon the older feudal culture by an aggressive commercial society. Evelyn Waugh, too, uses the country house inheritance motif in a somewhat similar fashion in *Unconditional Surrender*.[11]

To return to Wells after this slight digression, it is clear that in *Tono Bungay* he uses the country house Bladesover as an image to explain a whole slice of English social history. Bladesover represents the irreversible decay of the old aristocratic culture, the way of life of the English landed gentry. Its owner is infirm, the servants behind the baize doors perform a grotesque and meaningless mimicry of the speech and values of the dying aristocratic order. Other great houses in the neighbourhood have already been taken over: by the newly rich newspaper owner and by the Jewish financier, who owes obligations to no-one. The details suggest accurately enough two of the new classes in the Edwardian plutocracy to set up as members of the landed gentry. Ford Madox Ford's early novel *Mr Fleight* expresses a similar unease at the activities of rich Jewish financiers in Edwardian society. Wells's account of Bladesover at the beginning of *Tono Bungay* deftly combines two perspectives; it is seen through the 'young, receptive, wide-open eyes' of boyhood, and it is also seen retrospectively through the disenchanted eyes of George, now no longer a boy but a mature social observer. The two perspectives are fused in the narrative structure of the novel. While Bladesover is an image of decay, Forster's house in *Howards End*, with its protective wych-elm, its suggestion of the perfect union of masculine and feminine principle, is an image of harmonious growth. Unlike Penge, the decaying country house in *Maurice*, Howards End only awaits its rightful owner, who will know how to fuse the poetry and the prose of life, how to unite the monk and the beast in man, how to live a life in harmony with the rhythms of nature.

Wells's great achievement in the later stages of *Tono Bungay* is to offer an interpretation of the city in terms of the country house Bladesover. The key section comes at the beginning of Book 2 and it is obvious that Wells was proud of his achievement here, for through his narrator he indulges in a piece of justified self-praise: 'It was really a good piece of social comparative anatomy.' What is its essential feature? It is that the hierarchical order, once alive but now fossilised at Bladesover, has been superimposed upon London in a perverted form. Since this occurred, the great forces released by the industrial revolution, the blind forces of materialism and greed, threaten to destroy the last vestiges of the old order. There was once a unified culture in the seventeenth and eighteenth centuries, based on the great country house, with its library and art treasures. The London libraries and art galleries, Wells suggests, sprang from such a world of 'elegant leisure of the gentlemen of taste'.

> It is this idea of escaping parts from the seventeenth-century system of Bladesover, of proliferating and overgrowing elements from the Estates, that to this day seems to me the best explanation, not simply of London, but of all England. England is a country of great Renascence landed gentlefolk who have been unconsciously outgrown and overgrown. (Bk. 2, ch. 1, § 1)

Unlike both Forster and Lawrence, Wells does not yearn nostalgically for a lost feudal Eden; he does not develop a gospel of salvation based on a return to nature and instinctive emotions;[12] but he does think that the seventeenth century represented a stable, civilised order. In this, he is at one with Ford Madox Ford. In *A Man Could Stand Up*, Ford suggests that what keeps his hero going, up to his ears in mud among the dead and dying in the trenches, is an ideal picture of the seventeenth century as a time when a man could stand up on a hill, know that the land below him was his, and enjoy freedom of action and liberty of conscience. Long before Eliot suggested the same thing in *Four Quarters*, Ford used the parson poets and the small landed gentry of the seventeenth century as a cultural norm.

Ford acknowledges that the feudal ideal cannot survive in the changed conditions of the present century; yet he is fair to its continued attraction and its slightly illusory nature.

In *Lady Chatterley's Lover*, Lawrence brings the image of the city and the country house into close juxtaposition. The city is not London but the mining town of Tevershall, and its fumes drift over Sir Clifford's country house, Wragby. Connie asks herself the Wordsworthian question 'Ah God, what man has done to man?' when she observes with dismay the deadness of the mining community: 'dead, but dead. Half-corpses, all of them. . . . There was something uncanny and underground about it all. It was an underworld. And quite incalculable.' The Christian compassion for the poor that prevails in Mrs Gaskell's novels is totally absent; in its place we find only a mixture of contempt and shuddering fear. The image of a distinct 'underground' species, the Morlocks, which had appeared before the turn of the century in Wells's short science fiction novel *The Time Machine*, had by 1928 become a reality for Lawrence, or at least for his character, Connie. In the same year, in an essay called 'The State of Funk' he wrote more optimistically but still with apocalyptic fervour:

> Now England is on the brink of great changes, radical changes.

> Within the next fifty years the whole framework of our social life will be altered, will be greatly modified. The old world of our grandfathers is disappearing like thawing snow, and is as likely to cause a flood. What the world of our grandchildren will be, fifty years hence, we don't know. But in its social form it will be very different from our world of today. We've got to change. . . . Courage is the great word. Funk spells sheer disaster (*A Selection from Phoenix*, Penguin, pp. 366–7).

The gospel of tenderness preached in the gamekeeper's cottage, the importance of which has rightly been stressed by later critics who point out that the original title was to be 'Tenderness', appears to have no positive social consequences; it produces contempt not love; it increases the scorn shown by Connie for Sir Clifford, whom Lawrence rapidly transforms from conceited artist to evil industrialist, from a war-wounded man to a spiteful eunuch; and it increases the contempt for a machine-dominated society, for its slaves as well as its masters. There are two ways of summing up the political implications of Lawrence's *Lady Chatterley's Lover*, the one sympathetic, the other unsympathetic. The first is to say that it offers a vision of the redemption of man and society through returning to human tenderness and through reviving the bright flame of life by a more honest approach to sex. Using the four letter words, according to Frank Kermode,[13] 'was a way of emphasizing one of the themes of the novel, for our regarding them as shameful tends to prove the falsity of our attitude to sex. We evade the real thing or treat it either as a grey and dirty little secret, or as a joke, or a matter of hygiene.' The less sympathetic response to the novel is to say that it has no serious political value at all, because it fails to establish any real connection between its criticism of industrial deadness and the life-enhancing qualities attributed to the relationship of Connie and Mellors. In the first version of the novel, Lawrence did attempt a closer connection between Mellors and the Sheffield workers, but this dropped out in the later versions. In *Lady Chatterley's Lover*, as in *Women in Love* and *Kangaroo*, there is a yearning for human brotherhood certainly; but Lawrence seems unable to establish a bridge between individual tenderness and positive social values, as many passages describing Mellors' feelings illustrate.

> He loved the darkness and folded himself into it. It fitted the turgidity of his desire which, in spite of all, was like a riches; the stirring restlessness of his penis, the stirring fire in his loins! Oh, if only there were other men to be with, to fight that sparkling electric Thing outside there, to preserve the tenderness of life, the tenderness of women, and the natural riches of desire. If only there were men to fight side by side with! But the men were all outside there, glorying

in the Thing, triumphing or being trodden down in the rush of mechanized greed or of greedy mechanism. (Penguin, p. 125)

The tender love idyll in the gamekeeper's cottage leads not to a redeemed England, the promise of a New Jerusalem, but to the dubious hope enshrined in the last sentence of Mellors' letter to Connie at the end of the novel. 'John Thomas says good-night to Lady Jane, a little droopingly, but with a hopeful heart.' The promise of public and private redemption is to come through solipsism and innuendo. This marks a disastrous failure to live up to his own prescription contained in a private letter to E. M. Forster in 1915. 'I only want you to stick to the idea of a social revolution which shall throw down artificial barriers between men, and make life freer and fuller. Any big vision of life must contain a revolutionised society, and one must fulfil one's vision or perish.' Undoubtedly Lawrence thought of Forster and himself as guardians of the spirit of continuity, writing to him in 1924: 'To me you are the last Englishman. And I am the one after that.'

As a tailpiece, it is worth noting that there is another persistent theme in the Modern 'Condition of England' novel, a theme that mediates between the country house order and the destructive anarchy of the city. This is the theme of the greenwoods, the theme of voluntary exile. It is explored by three writers as unlike each other as Ford Madox Ford, Forster and Lawrence: all at some time in their fiction present this course as the way out for their characters. It is impossible to miss this theme in the delicate pastoralism of *Lady Chatterley's Lover*, with its explicit reminders of the escape of outlaws into the greenwoods, into Sherwood Forest, in fact. Escape into the greenwoods lies ahead for Maurice Hall and his working-class comrade Alex, in Forster's *Maurice*, a point made more clearly in the early version of the ending, while even in Ford's *Some Do Not*, the necessity of breaking social conventions and becoming in some sense a voluntary exile from society is clinched by Christopher Tietjens's quotation from the border ballad:

> And I must to the greenwood go,
> Alone: a banished man!

The modern novelist, however, allows him a mate and a prelapsarian joy in sex.

11 Utopian Fantasy

The dream of some ideal Republic has haunted the mind of Europe since the days of Plato and many writers have expressed their dreams in the form of literary utopias. The first and most famous is More's *Utopia*, written at the beginning of the sixteenth century. The actual word comes from the Greek *Topos*, meaning 'place'. More's prefix is ambiguous, since *u* could be thought to represent either *ou* ('no') or *eu* ('good), thus producing a play on 'no place' and 'good place'. Since then many writers have exploited the ironical potential embodied of the literary utopia, which is seldom wholly 'good'. Much of the enjoyment of reading such works arises from this ambivalence.[1]

Northrop Frye, with his usual genius for systematising, has pointed out that there are two social conceptions that can only be expressed in myths.[2] The first is the origin of society; the second is the end for which society exists. The myth that purports to explain its origin is the social contract, explicitly recognised as a myth in Coleridge's essay on the origins of government in the *Friend*;[3] the myth that purports to explain its aim is Utopia. The first, according to Frye, is a historical myth, while the second is a speculative myth. 'All Utopias', according to Arthur Koestler, 'are fed from the sources of mythology; the social engineer's blueprints are merely revised editions of the ancient text.'[4] In essence they are an expanded hypothesis; implicitly they say to us, 'only suppose that society were like this, what then?' No matter how fully the writer explores the human implications of his basic hypothesis, or how deeply he probes the emotions and inner conflicts of his characters, the work must always retain something of its abstract hypothetical origin. Consequently, its primary appeal is to the intellect. But, because this kind of fiction is a sub-genre of satire, both perhaps products of the myth of a Golden Age enshrined in the classical Saturnalia, it works through the emotions. Its aim is suasive, its methods at least in part rhetorical. Through a variety of devices the utopian writer shocks us into a new view of ourselves and society. By means of inventive fantasy, startlingly new perspectives, and calculated exaggeration, he forces us into a radical reassessment of the *status quo* and of the direction in which we are currently moving. The straight utopias, the 'plus' utopias as Zamyatin calls them,[5] offer an image of perfection that is not only a satire on the present but an incentive to reform the existing state of society so that it approximates more closely to this ideal. An example of such a 'plus' utopia is Morris's *News from Nowhere*, a powerful influence on the more idealistic strains of English socialism since it was first published in 1891 and now enjoying a new circulation among modern agrarian communes. The 'minus' utopias, works like Zamyatin's *We*, Huxley's *Brave New World* and Orwell's *Nineteen Eighty-Four*, offer us an image of what society may become if the present trends reach their logical conclusion. The plus utopia is a radiant promise; the minus utopia is a dire warning.

The dilemma that the writers of the Victorian Age inherited from the Romantics has been well defined by J. C. Garrett in his *Utopias in Literature since the Romantic Period*, 'whether to march breast forward into a future democracy of science and machinery or whether to turn back to the traditional hierarchical order of a simpler pre-industrial world'.[6] These two contradictory ideals appear in many of the Victorian utopias. With the triumph of industrialisation and science in the Victorian Age, it was natural for many writers to paint optimistic visions of the future. The best known is Winwood Reade's *The Martyrdom of Man*, published in 1873. However, the coming into existence of two new theories profoundly modified the central Victorian faith in progress. These were evolution and Marxism. The first inspired Bulwer Lytton to write the first evolutionary fantasy in *The Coming Race* (1871), a fantasy that demonstrated that, if society developed along the lines Victorians hoped, and were to be dominated by science, life would become unbearable. Evolutionary theory also plays some part in Butler's *Erewhon* (1872). The second of these theories, Marxism, inspired Edward Bellamy's tame vision of a classless society in *Looking Backward* and the more positive and vital vision of Morris's *News from Nowhere*, a vision that, in opposition to the repressive morality of the day, gives appropriate emphasis to sexual happiness. As George Levine remarks in an essay in *The Victorian City*,[7] 'by virtue of his capacity to accept the need for pleasure and a definition of pleasure that includes sexuality, Morris moves closer to a truly revolutionary way of seeing society'. Yet, for all the beauty, vitality and charm of Morris's decentralised medieval utopia, *News from Nowhere* is intellectually flawed. In rejecting industrialism, the author threw away the means by which the Marxist utopia could be maintained. His solution to nineteenth-century problems lay not in the workers taking over the means of production but in a voluntary return to a pre-industrial system. This would have been, given the population of Britain, to opt for mass deprivation, to accept a standard of living equal to that of one of the primitive Nilotic tribes. Morris was so enamoured with an illusory medieval ideal that he failed to recognise the logical consequences of his utopian dreams.

Despite its obvious logical and ideological flaws, however, *News from*

Nowhere is a very much better work than Butler's *Erewhon.* Its superiority arises from its greater vitality and its closer unity. Aldous Huxley commented that 'a book about the future can interest us only if its prophecies look as though they might conceivably come true'. Yet it is equally the case that a book about the future cannot interest us or continue to interest generations of readers unless it creates a unified imaginative world that obeys the laws of its own being and unless it creates a vitally human world. And we do not make it human by simply adding a love story, as both Wells and Butler seem to have thought. Much of our dissatisfaction with Butler's *Erewhon* arises from its imaginative confusion and its lack of genuine human interest.

The combination of different genres in *Erewhon*, the imaginary journey, utopian vision, and controversial essay, accounts for its lack of unity. Knowledge of its genesis throws some light on these mixed elements. Much of the work was written piecemeal and much was closely connected with Butler's other polemical works. As Butler's Preface to the Revised Edition makes clear (Harmondsworth, 1970, p. 33), parts were originally published as separate essays in the New Zealand paper, the *Press*, in 1863. He himself admitted that there was 'no central idea underlying *Erewhon*', adding that 'in *Erewhon* there was hardly any story, and little attempt to give life and individuality to the characters' (p. 36). What, then, we may ask, gives the book the interest and value it so obviously possesses?

First and foremost there is Butler's fertile comic invention. His invention of the Colleges of Unreason has a Swiftian brilliance.

> The main feature in their system is the prominence which they give to a study which I can only translate by the word 'hypothetics'. They argue thus that to teach a boy merely the nature of the things which exist in the world around him, and about which he will have to be conversant during his whole life, would be giving him but a narrow and shallow conception of the universe, which it is urged might contain all manner of things which are not now to be found therein. To open his eyes to these possibilities, and so to prepare him for all sorts of emergencies, is the object of the system of hypothetics. To imagine a set of utterly strange and impossible contingencies, and require the youths to give intelligent answers to the questions that arise therefrom, is reckoned the fittest conceivable way of preparing them for the actual conduct of their affairs in after life. (Penguin, pp. 185–6)

Equally Swiftian is his invention of the 'Musical Banks', an ingenious device for satirising the materialism and hypocrisy of Victorian religion. The success of this part of *Erewhon* does not depend solely on the originality of the idea however; it also depends on the author's subtle manipulation of different levels of meaning, so that the reader's mind is kept in constant activity, as it explores the multiple analogies between the musical banks and the church in Victorian England. Butler is 'the master of the oblique', as E. M. Forster pointed out in an essay called 'A Book that Influenced Me', in *Two Cheers for Democracy*.

The second quality that ensures the survival of *Erewhon* is its capacity to shock and surprise. The equation of embezzling with illness at the end of chapter 8 comes as a totally unexpected surprise and the puzzling reference to the 'straighteners' at first goes unexplained.

> 'He is a delightful man,' continued the interpreter, 'but has suffered terribly from' (here there came a long word which I could not quite catch, only it was much longer than kleptomania), 'and has but lately recovered from embezzling a large sum of money under singularly distressing circumstances; but he has quite got over it, and the straighteners say that he has made a really wonderful recovery; you are sure to like him.' (Penguin, p. 91)

The shock on the sensibilities of the narrator follows immediately in the opening paragraph of the next chapter.

> With the above words the good man left the room before I had time to express my astonishment at hearing such extraordinary language from the lips of one who seemed to be a reputable member of society. 'Embezzle a large sum of money under singularly distressing circumstances!' I exclaimed to myself, 'and ask *me* to go and stay with him!' (Penguin, p. 92)

Butler is perpetually cocking a snook at the characteristic forms of English hypocrisy, especially those relating to business ethics, the treatment of criminals and the quality of religious life. He takes a mischievous delight in reversing our expectations, turning the moral world upside down, and seems more interested in producing surprise than satiric illumination. The opening of chapter 10 on 'Current Opinions', the chapter in which he describes the current opinions in *Erewhon* on ill-health, criminality, and ill-luck, is a good example. We read with mounting surprise, attempting throughout to apply Erewhonian opinions to unacknowledged and undeclared attitudes in our own society. This the opening of the third paragraph explicitly encourages us to do:

> Foreign, indeed, as such ideas are to our own, traces of somewhat similar opinions can be found even in nineteenth-century England. If a person has an abscess, the medical man will say that it contains 'peccant' matter, and people say that they have a 'bad' arm or finger,

or that they are very 'bad' all over, when they only mean 'diseased'. (Penguin, p. 103)

Is this, we ask ourselves, the direction in which the earlier sections on ill-health, criminality and ill-luck have been pointing? Or is this paragraph on language a cunning digression, designed to disarm the reader, before launching a further assault on his stock notions? In reading Butler we are never quite certain. But, frequently, the unexpected turns and double ironies rebound on the author, producing not surprising illumination, but confusion.

The third quality that guarantees *Erewhon*'s survival is Butler's superb descriptive power, seen especially in the early chapters of the book. Even if the world Butler creates lacks imaginative unity, it does possess acute geographical realism. And this realism is our springboard into Butler's utopian realm. His capacity to use his close observation of the New Zealand countryside for utopian fantasy is related to his unique gift for mixing up the real and the imaginary to create shock, surprise and radically new perspectives on accepted social institutions. Yet, despite this element of fantasy so admired by E. M. Forster,[8] Butler is a mocking irritant rather than a positive or destructive force as a critic of Victorian society. Nevertheless, some kind of positive ideal does emerge from *Erewhon*, although it is not primarily for this that we read it. In the High Ydgrunites in chapter 17, Forster suggests, we come to what Butler thought desirable:

> Although a rebel, he was not a reformer. He believed in conventions, provided they are observed humanely. Grace and graciousness, good temper, good looks, good health and good sense; tolerance, intelligence, and willingness to abandon any moral standard at a pinch. This is what he admired.[9]

It is rather too tame an ideal for a critic of society. In fact, *The Way of All Flesh*, Butler's iconoclastic novel, is an altogether more radical and effective critique of Victorian society, since it strikes at the roots of Victorian hypocrisy through its exposure of Victorian ideas on sex, marriage, and the family. Yet Orwell was right to label Butler a 'Conservative' and to say that ultimately the moral of all his work was: 'Poverty is degrading; therefore, take care not to be poor.'[10]

In turning from Butler's utopia to those of H. G. Wells, we see a similar attempt to combine different genres within a single work: science fiction and utopian fantasy in *The Time Machine* (1895), fictional narrative and philosophical essay in *A Modern Utopia* (1905), where the adventures are projected on a screen and the philosophical discussions come from a commentator. How, we may ask, did Wells come to write scientific utopias? To begin with he was a scientist by training, and at first looked to scientific journalism as a way of making ends meet. Believing that he had the necessary qualifications for the job, he asked the blasphemous arch-amorist Frank Harris if he could review scientific works for the *Saturday Review*. 'Hell, Damn, Blast, Bloody, why don't you write funny stories about Science?' Wells did and proved an instant success. Ford Madox Ford relates the amused reaction of Edwardian readers to Wells's tale of the anarchist who was to steal a file of typhoid germs but stole a phial containing the bacillus of the colouration of the stern of the blue-behinded baboon. 'We were delighted', Ford remarks. 'We imagined ourselves – and still more our not so dear friends – going about, nervously hitching ourselves, with our back to cheval glasses.' According to Ford, not the most reliable witness perhaps, Wells read More's *Utopia* and came to the conclusion that the way to exert great influence over the new reading public was to write utopias 'to prophesy what the world would be like when the forces of Ignorance and Evil should have been forever overthrown'. If you could do that, Ford suggested to Wells, you would indeed 'become the General Officer Commanding the Forces of the Universe. You would shout to the world: "Humanity will Advance by the Right! Move to the Right in Fours. Form F–O–U–R–S! . . . RIGHT! . . . And Humanity would do it." '[11]

But Wells's vision of the future was not as naively optimistic as Ford's anecdote suggests, and the best of his early scientific stories, *The Time Machine*, presents a horrifying picture of the future evolution of mankind. Bernard Bergonzi, in *The Early H. G. Wells*, refers to it as 'an ironic myth'. A more appropriate term might be 'an ideological fable'. It is a curious mixture of naiveté and profound insight. The machine that enables the Time Traveller to travel into the year AD 802,701 is remarkably like a bicycle; the invention is a characteristic product of Wells's early childlike faith in the mechanical progress of science and well adapted to a popular audience's notions of science, but the vision of the future is far from childlike. Once the Traveller has arrived in the future the story develops at two related levels. At the superficial narrative level, it describes the Traveller's adventures with the beautiful but insubstantial race of people, the Eloi, and his emotional attachment to Weena, an Eloi girl whom he saves from drowning. At the deeper level, it records the Traveller's attempts to understand and interpret the society of the future in which he finds himself. His groping interpretations have obvious and terrifying implications. At first, before the Time Traveller has discovered the gruesome underground creatures, the Morlocks, he believes that the beautiful Eloi are decadent descendants of a race that had once achieved complete control of the environment and thereafter declined from lack of challenge and struggle. Next, he interprets the Eloi and Morlocks as Darwinian descendants of Capital and Labour, the Morlocks being the end-products of centuries of industrial slavery. But he then discovers that the Morlocks are vitally, not passively, servile. Finally, the Traveller comes to see the Morlocks as engineers and meat-eaters and the Eloi as their cattle, their human food. In the latter stages of the Traveller's discoveries, the descriptions of both races acquire a mythic terror that touches our deepest responses. The accounts combine the exciting precision of a good adventure story with the potent suggestion of dream landscape. This is one of the ways, as Zamyatin noted, by which Wells escapes from the static quality of most modern plus or minus utopias.

> Upon the hillside were some thirty or forty Morlocks, dazzled by the light and heat, and blundering hither and thither against each other in their bewilderment. At first I did not realise their blindness, and struck furiously at them with my bar, in a frenzy of fear, as they approached me, killing one and crippling several more. But when I had watched the gestures of one of them groping under the hawthorn against the red sky, and heard their moans, I was assured of their absolute helplessness and misery in the glare, and I struck no more.

It might appear from the account given that *The Time Machine* was a devastating attack on modern industrial society; but, actually, the story as a whole develops a vein of optimism, what Patrick Parrinder has described as a 'kind of hysterical exhilaration', as the Time Traveller goes off to discover yet new worlds. The same writer sums up very well the typical Wellsian ambiguity that is enshrined in all Wells's early stories.

> Wells's scientific romances alternate the ideas of hope and despair, mastery and slavery, release and submission, and in doing so they reflect the opposing images of predetermined life and utopian life which guide his social thought.[12]

What Wells lacked as a writer of utopian fantasy was an understanding of evil and an insight into the corruptions of political power.

Thirty-seven years separate Wells's *The Time Machine* (1895) and Aldous Huxley's *Brave New World* (1932). Wells's story was written to appeal to the products of the Education Act of 1870, the readers of the new popular penny newspapers; it was also conceived before the great advances in the biological sciences and in psychology. Thus the popular oversimplified treatment of science and the patronising tone arise in part from the nature of Wells's public. Huxley, on the other hand, addresses an altogether different class of reader. He expects a high level of education and sophistication; consequently, he feels free to employ a wide variety of narrative techniques and literary allusions. He counterpoints speeches and scenes for ironic effect in a highly sophisticated manner – a technique already tried in *Point Counter Point* (1928) – and he introduces scattered quotations from Shakespeare, the meaning of which depends on knowledge of their original context, in order to establish human norms in the abnormal world of the future. His theme is man's use of biology and psychology to achieve an ordered world. Inevitably it takes the form of a vision of the future. But, whereas Wells placed the action of *The Time Machine* in the year AD 802,701, Huxley places it in the foreseeable future AF 632, that is, 632 years after the birth of 'our Ford', Henry Ford, the founder, in some sense, of modern industrial society. The closeness makes the fantasy world more frightening, easier to apply to our own world (obviously there are some disadvantages in choosing too close a date, as Orwell did in *Nineteen Eighty-Four*). There is a further major difference between Wells and Huxley. Huxley's theme is not man's control over the physical world, but the much more radical and challenging one of man's control over human nature itself by the use of science. Wells lived in a world that worshipped mechanical inventions, Huxley in a world of biological discovery, psychological conditioning, and authoritarian ideologies. Thus, the major hypothesis of *Brave New World* is that a time may soon come when men will create a society in which the production of human beings will be scientifically planned, so that by artificial and selective breeding each man will fit in perfectly to his destined environment. With all the tensions between man and his environment removed, the result should be perfect harmony and happiness. It should be COMMUNITY, IDENTITY, STABILITY, the World State's motto, the words on the shield outside the CENTRAL LONDON HATCHERY AND CONDITIONING CENTRE. But is the outcome desirable? *Brave New World* suggests that it is not. It is one of the many anti-utopias that seek to demonstrate that certain kinds of order would destroy our essential humanity. Here is the paradox on which all utopias hinge. We long for a perfect world, but the worlds we dream of turn out to be enemies of our individual perfection.

Huxley's title, *Brave New World*, is ironic. And there is already an implicit irony in its original context in Shakespeare's *The Tempest*, for when Miranda cries out in rapturous happiness

> O wonder
> How many goodly creatures are there here;
> How beauteous mankind is! O brave new world
> That has such people in it

the faces she gazes at are the faces of the conspirators, the villains of the play.

Huxley expects his readers to be familiar with general scientific principles. But he constructs his work so that all the essential scientific information is released indirectly in the early chapters. Where Wells introduced the stupid Philby to ask questions about the Time Machine,

Huxley employs a conducted tour of the Hatchery and Conditioning Centre and a modified, ironic lecture technique. It is not necessary that the writer of Utopian fiction should give us a comprehensive description of every aspect of life in his fantasy world. What is essential is that he himself should have imagined it so intensely that it possesses inner coherence and therefore obeys the laws of its own being. Huxley succeeds triumphantly in creating a coherent, absolutely convincing world, a world in which we feel free to move around because we know the essential laws of its nature.

First, the reader enters the wintry, antiseptic atmosphere of the Fertilising Room at the Central London Hatchery, and listens to the Director explaining the process to a newly arrived troop of students.

> 'I shall begin at the beginning,' said the D.H.C., and the more zealous students recorded his intention in their notebooks: *Begin at the beginning*. 'These,' he waved his hand, 'are the incubators.' And opening an insulated door he showed them racks upon racks of numbered test-tubes. 'The week's supply of ova. Kept,' he explained, 'at blood heat; whereas the male gametes,' and here he opened another door, 'they have to be kept at thirty-five instead of thirty-seven. Full blood heat sterilizes'. (Penguin, p. 16)

The Director then goes on to explain the fertilising process: how if any egg remained unfertilised it was again immersed in free-swimming spermatozoa, and if necessary again; how the fertilised ova went back to the incubators, where the Alphas and Beta remained until definitely bottled, while the Gammas, Deltas, and Epsilons were brought out again after only thirty-six hours to undergo the Bokanovsky process.

> 'Bokanovsky's Process,' repeated the Director, and the students underlined the words in their little note-books. One egg, one embryo, one adult – normality. But a bokanovskified egg will bud, will proliferate, will divide. From eight to ninety-six buds, and every bud will grow into a perfectly formed embryo, and every embryo into a full-sized adult. Making ninety-six human beings grow where only one grew before. Progress. . . . But one of the students was fool enough to ask where the advantage lay. 'My good boy!' The Director wheeled sharply round on him. 'Can't you *see*? Can't you *see*?' He raised a hand; his expression was solemn. 'Bokanovsky's Process is one of the major instruments of social stability!'
>
> *Major instruments of social stability.*
>
> Standard men and women; in uniform batches. The whole of a small factory staffed with the products of a single bokanovskified egg. (Penguin, pp. 17–18)

Next, in *Brave New World*, the reader enters the NEOPAVLOVIAN CONDITIONING CENTRE. The secret there is hypnopaedia, the process of teaching, indoctrinating, and conditioning responses while people are asleep. The lesson that is in progress when the Director arrives with his class is 'Elementary Class Consciousness'. He asks the nurse to turn up the voice that is murmuring into the eighty identical cots so that his students may hear.

> 'Alpha children wear grey. They work much harder than we do, because they are so frightfully clever. I'm really awfully glad I'm a Beta, because I don't work so hard. And then we are much better than the Gammas and Deltas. Gammas are stupid. They all wear green, and Delta children wear khaki. Oh no, I *don't* want to play with Delta children. And Epsilons are still worse. They're too stupid to be able. . . . (Penguin, p. 33)

As the Director explains to his listeners, hypnopaedia is 'the greatest moralizing and socializing force of all time'.

Once the preliminary explanations have been dramatised in this fashion in the opening two chapters, Huxley bounces his readers straight into his world of the future and we begin to discover in detail what the people are like, how they act, what they believe in, and how they enjoy themselves. Although it is certainly a fantasy world it is remarkably self-consistent. We soon come to learn how everything works and therefore to suspend all disbelief. But the ominous thing is that it constantly reminds us of the worst features of our own society. Sex has become separated from love, procreation, and marriage, and has become pointless. Literature has degenerated into mere emotional engineering, in other words, advertising and propaganda. Religion has become meaningless mumbo jumbo, emotional rituals for achieving group solidarity. Soma has replaced alcohol as the source of joyful oblivion but, unlike alcohol, it is non-addictive and produces no hangovers. Sport has become completely mechanised, its main purpose being to maximise consumption. Huxley, by carrying twentieth-century trends to their logical conclusion and by clever parodies of modern social rituals, makes us feel the pressing relevance of *Brave New World*.

A typical example is the description of the Solidarity Service. Here Huxley parodies some of the rituals of the Christian church and introduces incongruous elements (erotic dancing and nursery rhymes) to suggest that religion is either a sublimation of sex or a return to childishness.

> Round they went, a circular procession of dancers, each with hands on the hips of the dancer preceding, round and round, shouting in unison, stamping to the rhythm of the music with their feet, beating

it, beating it out with hands on the buttocks in front; twelve pairs of hands beating as one; as one, twelve buttocks slabbily resounding. Twelve as one, twelve as one. 'I hear him, I hear him coming.' The music quickened; faster beat the feet, faster, faster fell the rhythmic hands. And all at once a great synthetic bass boomed out the words which announced the approaching atonement and final consummation of solidarity, the coming of the Twelve-in-One, the incarnation of the Greater Being. 'Orgy-porgy,' is sang, while the tom-toms continued to beat their feverish tattoo:

> Orgy-porgy, Ford and fun,
> Kiss the girls and make them One.
> Boys at one with girls at peace;
> Orgy-porgy gives release.

'Orgy-porgy', the dancers caught up the liturgical refrain, 'Orgy-porgy, Ford and Fun, kiss the girls. . . .' And as they sang, the lights began slowly to fade – to fade and at the same time to grow warmer, richer, redder, until at last they were dancing in the crimson twilight of an Embryo Store. (Penguin, pp. 73–4)

By such parodies Huxley could have allowed the world he creates in this novel to make its own implicit criticism of itself. But utopian fiction and satire are two closely connected literary forms. And most satirists have felt the need to create some kind of formal detached critical perspective. If everyone were happy in *Brave New World* because bred and conditioned to be happy, how could anyone be critical of this world? That was the technical problem Huxley faced as a writer. He solves it by a couple of ingenious cheats. He imagines that there are some 'misfits' who haven't quite turned out as they should have. Something went wrong with Bernard Marx's blood surrogate and Helmholtz Watson has discovered that poetry offers a truth higher than emotional engineering. As a result these two are more critical of the system than anyone else and provide the necessary critical viewpoint. The second cheat is that Huxley imagines that within the world state, but quite uninfluenced by it, is a Savage Reservation where people live the old primitive life involving love, childbirth, dirt and ignorance. This invention produces two critical perspectives: one arises from the ironic juxtaposition of two such contrasted worlds, and the other develops when John the Savage leaves the Savage Reservation and visits the Brave New World, when the reader begins to see the scientifically ordered society through John's innocent incredulous eyes. The Savage becomes a norm of sanity, not so much because he has been brought up in a non-test-tube, non-psychologically conditioned environment, but because his one book has been Shakespeare's plays. And that is really cheat number three. But it works reasonably well, especially for the reader who can recognise his quotations from Shakespeare's bitterest and most tragic plays, *Troilus and Cressida*, *Othello* and *King Lear*. John soon becomes sick of civilisation and hangs himself. And that's what many readers feel like doing at the end of this grimly pessimistic anti-Utopia.

Why? Because neither of the alternatives that Huxley offers us is acceptable. No one, except the inhabitants of totalitarian countries or the underprivileged in the undeveloped countries of Asia and Africa, would be prepared to buy happiness and social solidarity at the price of losing all individuality. And no one would be prepared to return to the filth and ignorance of a pre-scientific primitive life. If these are the only choices then John's suicide seems the only answer. This bleak pessimism, this clever paradox, was very typical of Huxley's views when *Brave New World* was first published in 1932.

But when he wrote a Preface for the book in 1946 he said that he now thought that he had been wrong to offer only an absurd choice between two impossible worlds. The Preface holds out a hope to mankind. It talks about the peaceful use of nuclear energy and contains pious platitudes about the need for de-centralisation and the use of science to extend, not to limit, man's freedom. There is little of the old satiric rage and indignation. And it was really that that made Huxley a powerful critic of society.

What in the end does Huxley's criticism in *Brave New World* amount to? First and foremost, it warns us that in our present society man is ceasing to exist as an end in himself. This is the danger that was foreseen by Coleridge and the nineteenth-century critics of society. They saw that industry, which holds out the promise of infinite wealth, in fact tends to reduce man to a cog in a machine; that science, which promises to explain the universe, explains little and becomes applied science, concerned with means not ends; that the utilitarian philosophy, based on the principle of the greatest happiness for the greatest number, turns into Gradgrind's worship of fact and the destruction of those very qualities that constitute our full humanity; that economic planning which should improve the quality of life tends to reduce man to a mere statistical unit.

This whole conflict between the individual as an end in himself and as insignificant part of a social plan is finally dramatised in the confrontation between the Controller of the World State, Mustapha Mond, and John the Savage, a confrontation reminiscent of Dostoevsky's Fable of the Grand Inquisitor and Christ. John rejects Mond's world:

> 'But I don't want comfort. I want God, I want poetry, I want real danger, I want freedom, I want goodness. I want sin.'
> 'In fact,' said Mustapha Mond, 'you're claiming the right to be unhappy.'

> 'All right then,' said the Savage defiantly, 'I'm claiming the right to be unhappy.' (Penguin, p. 187)

In addition to making this one great major criticism of the tendency of our planned industrial societies to dehumanise and create totalitarian order, *Brave New World* also criticises the misapplication of scientific discovery, the misuse of religion and mass emotion, and the reduction of literature to state propaganda.

One of its chief weaknesses, as even its author came to see, was that it had too little to say about the nature of power; about the psychology of power and the means now available for securing and retaining power. In this respect, Orwell's *Nineteen Eighty-Four* is a much more impressive book, as we shall see in the next chapter. However, we need to remember that by the time Orwell wrote his anti-utopia, after the Second World War, he had had the advantage of studying the European dictators and their propaganda machines. Yet even if *Brave New World* had been written much later than 1932, one suspects that it would still not have had much to say about the cult of power. Although Huxley failed to foresee many of the instruments of slavery that Orwell incorporated into *Nineteen Eighty-Four*, his satire in *Brave New World* is remarkably comprehensive. Despite its pessimistic message, it is a high spirited work, continuously entertaining, deeply serious and with enough emotional complexity to make it a successful piece of fiction as well as a powerful criticism of society.

Oddly enough Huxley's satire might never have been written if a Russian scientist had not visited England during the First World War, discovered that Wells had created a new form of fiction, and gone on to write his own daring anti-utopia. That Russian was Yevgeny Zamyatin. So daring was the criticism of totalitarian order in his book, *We*, that it was never published in Russia and its author died in exile. 'For me as a writer', he wrote to Stalin, 'to be deprived of the opportunity to write is a sentence of death: matters have reached a point where I am unable to exercise my profession because creative writing is unthinkable if one is obliged to work in an atmosphere of systematic persecution that grows worse every year.' (Penguin, p. 12)

We is set in the future, a thousand years after the creation of The One State. The action opens 110 days before the completion of the Integral, which will soar into universal space on its mission to integrate the creatures of the other planets. It begins with an extract from the *State Gazette*.

> There lies before you the subjugation of unknown creatures to the beneficent yoke of reason – creatures inhabiting other planets, perhaps still in the savage state of freedom. Should they fail to understand that we are bringing them a mathematically infallible hap-

piness, it will be our duty to compel them to be happy. But, before resorting to weapons, we shall try words. (Penguin, p. 19)

The opening thus not only sets up the basic opposition between the enforced rational order and the savage state of freedom; it also announces the theme, common to most anti-utopias, of compelling people to be happy.

The story is related in the form of extracts from the diary of the builder of the Integral; he is one of the mathematicians of The One State and is known as D–503. Traditionally, the diary form records the intimate 'I'; here it records the collective 'we'. 'I shall merely attempt to record what I see, what I think – to be most exact, what *we* think (*we*, precisely, and let this *We* serve as the title of the entries I am making).' Obviously this is a society that has realised Bakunin's wish: 'I do not want to be I, I want to be "We".' As one entry follows another, the general characteristics of The One State become clear. Essentially it is a mathematical utopia. There are no people in the state, only numbers. They live in an insulated world of ordered angles, planes and surfaces, entirely removed from wild irregularities that lie beyond the Green Wall. As the diarist explains, every aspect of life is ordered and regimented through the Tables of Hourly Commandments, we 'constantly live in full sight of all, constantly bathed in light and surrounded by our glass walls'. Only on Sexual Days are the blinds lowered, but first the number must attend the appropriate office, specify the desired opposite number, and obtain a certificate. The transaction is completed by tearing off the counterfoil from the other number's pink coupon. It is an amusing irony that D–503's regret for his past happiness with the angular, sadistic female number E–330 should be marked by the sight of 'the pink coupons, like rose petals fallen and trampled on . . . each bore a drop of myself, molten, brimming over. And this was all that remained.'

The One State is ruled over by The Benefactor. He exercises his control through the Guardians, who maintain order by hovering overhead with their hanging proboscises of spying tubes at moments of crisis.

It is so gratifying to feel somebody's vigilant eye upon one, lovingly guarding one from the least . . . erring step. It may sound somewhat sentimental, but that same analogy again comes to my mind – that of the *guardian angels*, whom the ancients used to dream about. (Penguin, pp. 75–6)

At first, D-503 is an ordinary obedient servant of the state, but as the result of a rudimentary love tangle, when he is torn between the rounded, pink, complaisant O–90 and the mocking E–330, whom he meets surreptitiously at the House of Antiquity, he discovers he has a soul. He thus becomes critical of all that he had previously accepted. Although E–330 tries to involve him in a plot to subvert the launching of the Integral on its purposed mission, he is restored to docile obedience after an interview with the Benefactor (such an interview is an essential structural element in most anti-utopias), and as the result of undergoing the newly discovered operation for the removal of the imagination, fantasiectomy. The Benefactor expounds the doctrine, first explored by Dostoevsky through the Grand Inquisitor and later by Huxley through Mustapha Mond, that freedom produces misery not happiness.

> Let's talk everything over to the end. I ask you: what have men, from their swaddling-clothes days, been praying for? . . . Why, to have someone tell them, once and for all, just what happiness is – and then weld them to this happiness with chains. (Penguin, p. 204)

Once D–503 has undergone fantasiectomy he sits at the same table as the Benefactor and watches, without emotion, the torture of E–330 under the Gas Bell Jar. Although there are still rumblings of insurrection in The One State and the savage world threatens to break through the insulating Green Wall, the reconverted diarist ends on a note of optimism, terrible in its implications within the novel's ironic framework: 'And I hope that we will conquer. More than that: I am certain that we shall. For rationality must conquer.' (Penguin, p. 221)

We was never published in Russia, but it was translated into English in 1924. Huxley read it and so too did Orwell years later. The vision of a world state in which man was enslaved by technology provided the germ for Huxley's *Brave New World*, while what Orwell described as Zamyatin's 'intuitive grasp of the irrational side of totalitarianism – human sacrifice, cruelty as an end in itself, the worship of a Leader who is credited with divine attributes',[13] together with all the details relating to daily regimentation and thought control, undoubtedly inspired Orwell's own *Nineteen Eight-Four.* It is a curious fact of literary history that it was a Russian who saw the true originality of Wells's science fiction and helped to bring into being the two great anti-utopias of this century: Huxley's *Brave New World* and Orwell's *Nineteen Eighty-Four.*

12 The Cult of Power and the Power of Culture

This second chapter on modern utopias looks at the work of a number of writers who have been concerned with the struggle between the cult of power and the power of culture. By the cult of power, I mean the worship of authoritarian rule that found its chief expression in Nazi Germany under Hitler; by the power of culture I mean that faith in the liberal values of reason, justice, mercy, and brotherhood that are imperfectly enshrined in our political institutions but are more perfectly embodied in some of the great literary and artistic works of the past. The writers with whom I shall mainly be concerned are Rex Warner, George Orwell, and Shirley Hazzard.

Rex Warner is an unfairly neglected author today. Born in 1905, he was an Oxford friend of W. H. Auden, Cecil Day Lewis and Stephen Spender in the 1920's; and, like many of his generation, he was strongly drawn towards Marxism. Over the years he has established a reputation for himself as a poet, novelist, essayist and translator. Three of his works are of special interest as criticisms of society: the two allegorical novels, *The Professor: A Forecast* (1938) and *The Aerodrome: A Love Story* (1941); and a book of essays called *The Cult of Power* (1946). Much of Warner's inspiration as a writer has come from his contemplation of the problem of power in the modern world.

The main theme of *The Professor* is the failure of the idealistic democrat to recognise the force of the totalitarian idea and his consequent refusal to take practical steps to avert the triumph of Fascism in a small, unnamed European state. Written in 1938, the novel's relevancc to Germany's threatened annexation of Austria and Czechoslavakia in that year is obvious. But, by casting the novel in the form of allegory, Warner succeeds in universalising his political theme. His message in 1938 was not: this is what will happen in Austria and Czechoslavakia; but, this is what may happen in any democratic country where liberals are not prepared to fight for their ideas. The central character, the Professor, who becomes Chancellor of the state, can hardly be regarded as a fair representative of the democratic ideal, however. He is too unworldly, too naive, too utterly unpractised in the political arts to represent any system of political values at all. Nevertheless, the novel does create a striking impression of what can happen when one of the chief custodians of culture is faced with the cult of power, as it is embodied in Colonel Grimm, the Chief of Police, who takes over the radio station and invites foreign troops to march in to help him maintain law and order. In the first half of the story, a gross convert from scholarship to totalitarian politics, Julius Vander, states the nature of the conflict to the Professor in the simplest terms: 'You offer them a world to love; we give them a tangible minority to hate.' Various characters in the novel, including the Professor's own son, who asks his father to arm the workers, urge the Professor to oppose the threats to freedom with force, but he retains his faith in words and abstract ideals. Throughout, he is buoyed up by his love for Clara, his mistress, only to find that she has all the time been secretly helping the fascist powers. Finally, he is shot in the back while attempting to escape from prison. *The Professor*, in intention if not wholly in imaginative effect, is a disturbing political allegory. Read today the novel acquires a new level of significance in relation to the incapacity of universities to defend themselves from extremist politics. Even if the Professor cannot adequately represent the typical strengths as well as the inner weaknesses of liberal democracy, he does represent the impotence of the free academic mind when faced with violence and unreason, its impotence when confronted by hatred, the lust for power, and unscrupulous discriminatory policies.

Warner's presentation of the cult of power is even more allegorical in *The Aerodrome*. In this book, two forms of life are contrasted. The village, which stands for ordinary life in the West, is characterised by lust, muddle and unreflective enjoyment. Life at the Aerodrome, which suggests life under totalitarian rule, is characterised by ruthless efficiency, amorality and blind obedience to the leader. The hero of the novel leaves the village to become the favourite of the Commander of the Aerodrome, who can be regarded as symbolising the leader of a fascist state. Finally, the young man rejects the standards of the Aerodrome and returns to the village. But neither Aerodrome nor Village represents a valid way of life. When the Commander is killed in an air crash, Warner underlines the symbolic implication of the whole novel: 'The new order, resting as it did on the desperate will of one man, had been broken and the old order could never be restored.'

The theme of 'the desperate will of one man' links together most of the essays in Warner's *Cult of Power*. In the title essay, he suggests that 'at the root of the whole cult of power and violence, including fascism, is the philosophy of the moral anarchist, of the individual asserting himself against general standards that seem too weak to be able to restrain them'. In the book as a whole, he approaches the cult of power from three different angles: firstly, through a discussion of the relationship between Lawrence's insistence on blood, sex and maleness, and the creed of fascism, a creed that undoubtedly Lawrence would have disowned had he lived to see its evil fruits; secondly, through the distinction between the Shakespearean tragic hero and the cult of power by the totalitarian leader, where Warner points out that the tragic hero exists in a moral universe that re-establishes itself after the assaults upon it by such a figure as Macbeth, while the modern leader can so change the moral standards of society that it may never assert itself or restore traditional values. And, thirdly, he explores the origins of European moral anarchism in an essay called 'Dostoievsky and the Collapse of Liberalism'. The general argument of this essay is of crucial importance to any understanding of the ideological background of utopian fiction.

In his novels, Dostoevsky seems to suggest that there are three stages in the growth of individualism and atheism. The first stage is marked by the emergence of the emancipated rationalist, European in his sympathies and affinities, someone already more than half an atheist, such a man as Stepan Trofimovitch in *The Possessed.* In the second stage emerges the more thorough-going rationalist, who denies the existence of God and is confident in man's powers to build the temple of humanity on earth. Both these classes may be called liberal humanists. In the last stage emerges the wholly destructive individualist, who believes that the worship of humanity as well as the worship of God is an irrational prejudice, since humanity consists mainly of fools and weaklings. Therefore the people must be ruled over by a strong man who will become their only law. The individual leader, having reached this stage in which he finds that he is all powerful, now discovers that all that is left is violent self-assertion. He finally comes to the realisation of the pointlessness of everything.

In three of his novels Dostoevsky explores the cult of power, in *Crime and Punishment* through Raskolnikov's claim to throw off all moral restraints, in *The Possessed* through a group of moral nihilists, and in *The Brothers Karamazov* through Ivan's attempt to carry out the idea that 'all things are lawful'. Only Ivan of all Dostoevsky's characters, however, has the necessary stature to embody the universal conflict between revolutionary self-assertion and the moral order of society; he alone of Dostoevsky's characters has the capacity to imagine the great allegory about freedom and political power that is contained in the poem about Christ and the Grand Inquisitor.

In the fifth book of *The Brothers Karamazov* there is a long conversation between Ivan and his brother Alyosha, a saintly young man who has been educated in a monastery. During its course Ivan explains why he rejects God and his divine harmony. The grounds of his rejection are purely humanitarian. He cannot accept a God who permits senseless and fiendish cruelty to animals and children. 'People talk sometimes of bestial cruelty,' he points out to Alyosha, 'but that's a great injustice and insult to the beasts, a beast can never be so cruel as a man, so artistically cruel.' Turning to the argument that without suffering man-would not have known good and evil, he asks indignantly why he should know that diabolical good and evil when it costs too much. The whole world of knowledge is not worth one child's suffering. What Ivan demands is justice: 'And not justice in some remote infinite time and space, but here on earth, and that I could see myself.' He must therefore renounce altogether the higher harmony that assimilates suffering and 'most respectfully return Him the ticket'. In explanation, he tells Alyosha the prose poem he has written of how Christ came down to earth again, how he was brought before the Grand Inquisitor, and how he was once again sentenced to death. The core of this political allegory lies in the Grand Inquisitor's speech to Christ. The Inquisitor tells Christ that he was wrong to resist the Devil's three temptations in the wilderness. In refusing them he refused to take man's freedom away. He thus imposed an impossible burden of responsibility on man. All man's unhappiness has come from his inability to choose between good and evil. He does not want freedom. What he most desires is food, security and happiness. And he will only worship the power that brings him these things. The Grand Inquisitor therefore points out that Christ should have followed the Devil's suggestion; he should have ruled through miracle, mystery and authority. The Inquisitor's church satisfies mankind because it gives them bread instead of freedom and because it compels men to be good by power and authority. This is the only force men respect. The relevance of this political allegory to recent history is clear, especially its connection with the modern leader principle. The leader in a totalitarian state takes away the freedom of the people in return for the promise of security and material welfare, although his motives are certainly not as saintly as the Grand Inquisitor's. As Irving Howe has remarked, 'ultimately the anti-utopian novel keeps returning to the choice posed by Dostoevsky's legend of the Grand Inquisitor in *The Brothers Karamazov*: the misery of the human being who must bear his burden of independence against the contentment of the human creature at rest in his obedience'.[1]

If we compare Dostoevsky's *The Brothers Karamazov* and Orwell's *Nineteen Eighty-Four* however, it is clear that their analysis of the cult of power is very different. For Dostoevsky it is a perverted humanitarianism; for Orwell, on the other hand, the object of power is power. In the second stage of Winston Smith's process of integration, O'Brien instructs him in the reality of power.

> 'We are the priests of power,' he said. 'God is power. But at present power is only a word so far as you are concerned. It is time for you to gather some idea of what power means. The first thing you must realize is that power is collective. The individual only has power in so far as he ceases to be an individual. You know the Party slogan: "Freedom is Slavery". Has it ever occurred to you that it is rever-

> sible? Slavery is freedom. Alone – free – the human being is always defeated. It must be so, because every human being is doomed to die, which is the greatest of all failures. But if he can make complete, utter submission, if he can escape from his identity, if he can merge himself in the Party so that he *is* the Party, then he is all-powerful and immortal. (Penguin, p. 212)

Thereafter O'Brien goes on to emphasise that it is control over the mind as well as the body. Ultimately he sums up the idea that the object of power is power in a single brutal image. 'If you want a picture of the future, imagine a boot stamping on a human face – for ever.' If we ask ourselves which is the better image of the reality of power, Dostoevsky's fable of the Grand Inquisitor or Orwell's, the answer must be that each is to some extent a characteristic product of an individual temperament and of a particular moment in history, Dostoevsky's of his religious, messianic temperament and distrust of nineteenth-century Russian nihilism, Orwell's of his secular, masochistic insight into the typical manifestations of hate and power in the modern world. Similar images recur throughout Orwell's writings, for example the brutal unexpected, 'smashing people's faces in with a spanner', in the early novel *Coming up For Air*.

The formative influences that shaped Orwell's final political vision in *Animal Farm* and *Nineteen Eighty-Four* were extremely varied and extended over much of his life. The child is father of the man. What sort of a child was Eric Blair, the child born of British parents in India in 1903, who became George Orwell, one of England's most controversial writers, according to one critic, 'the greatest satirist since Swift'? Someone who knew him when they played together as children but did not discover that Eric Blair was George Orwell until a year after his death, recalls an incident that took place in the spring or summer of 1915.

> We were playing French cricket in the roughish field-part of the garden, by the clump of elm trees. . . . In the farmer's adjoining field, on the other side of the boundary fence, a boy, rather bigger than my brother . . . was standing on his head. This was a feat we had never observed before, and we found it intriguing; so one of us, polite but curious, asked him 'Why are you standing on your head?' To which he replied: 'You are noticed more if you stand on your head than if you are right way up.' [2]

In later life, Orwell did not always find it necessary to stand on his head to attract attention. But he had a natural love of paradox as well as of truth; and he belongs to a long line of English eccentrics, all enormously gifted, but all frequently misunderstood.

Orwell's favourite reading in that summer of 1915 was Wells's *A Modern Utopia.* For years afterwards Wells remained one of his favourite authors. It's not difficult to see how Wells influenced Orwell. Like Wells, Orwell used two kinds of fiction to criticise his society: novels about the present and the immediate past, for example, *Keep the Aspidistra Flying* and *Coming Up for Air*; and visions of the future, *Animal Farm* and *Nineteen Eighty-Four.* In Wells, the two kinds are represented by *Tono Bungay* and *The Time Machine.* In an essay on Wells, written in 1941, Orwell recalled:

> Back in the nineteen-hundreds it was a wonderful experience for a boy to discover H. G. Wells. There you were, in a world of pedants, clergymen and golfers, with your future employers exhorting you to 'get on or get out', your parents systematically warping your sexual life, and your dull-witted schoolmasters sniggering over their Latin tags; and here was this wonderful man who could tell you about the inhabitants of the planets and the bottom of the sea, and who *knew* that the future was not going to be what respectable people imagined.[3]

We even find a sniggering schoolmaster in Orwell's own novel *Coming Up for Air*, and Orwell, like Wells, showed that 'the future was not going to be what respectable people imagined'.

Two problems dominated Orwell's thought as a novelist and journalist. These were: first, the nature of political power – what makes men crave for power? how do they exert it? how do they maintain it? And second, the difficulties involved in communicating political truth. In fact, the 'Introduction' to *Animal Farm* was to have been a long essay on 'The Freedom of the Press', but it was never printed with the book, and has only recently been discovered.[4]

All the main events in Orwell's life helped to shape his political vision. It is clear from his novel *Burmese Days*, and the two short pieces 'A Hanging' and 'Shooting an Elephant', that his experience as a young officer in the Indian Imperial Police, in Burma, opened his eyes to the evils of imperialism. Having seen 'the dirty work of empire at close quarters', he resigned and came home. His experience as a dish-washer in Paris in 1928–9 and of near starvation in England gave him first-hand knowledge of the evils of poverty. A passage about people's attitude to beggars, in his book *Down and Out in Paris and London*, vibrates with irony, compassion and subdued indignation.

> Beggars do not work, it is said; but then, what is *work*? A navvy works by swinging a pick. An accountant works by adding up figures. A beggar works by standing out of doors in all weathers and getting varicose veins, bronchitis etc. It is a trade like any other;

> quite useless, of course – but, then, many reputable trades are quite useless. And as a social type the beggar compares well with scores of others. He is honest compared with the sellers of most patent medicines, high-minded compared with a Sunday newspaper proprietor, amiable compared with a hire-purchase tout.[5]

His scorn, in the last sentence, is directed at some of the same objects as Wells's so many years earlier through the meteoric career of the inventor of the patent medicine in *Tono Bungay*.

Orwell's experience of fighting in the Spanish Civil War in 1936–7 produced complete political disenchantment.[6] Like many left-wing intellectuals of his generation, he regarded the fight against General Franco as a crusade; but he soon became sickened when he saw how the Communists exploited events to liquidate their political enemies. Moreover, he soon saw that the political parties and newspapers were deliberately distorting the truth. From this experience, and later from his work for the BBC and the Ministry of Information during the Second World War, he came to understand the power of a mighty propaganda machine. In addition to his observations of Nazi and Russian propaganda, this experience gave him all his imagination needed to produce the frightening world of *Nineteen Eighty-Four*. It also intensified his determination not to be taken in by left-wing or right-wing propaganda in England. It made him clear-sighted. It reinforced his native honesty and integrity. But it made him touchy, hypersensitive, almost paranoic at times. And it is not surprising that he made as many enemies as friends among English socialists. But it was this quality of incorruptible honesty that led his contemporaries to see him as a modern saint. Writing in the *New Statesman* on his death, V. S. Pritchett crystalised this view:

> George Orwell was the wintry conscience of a generation which in the thirties had heard the call of the rasher assumptions of political faith. He was a kind of saint and, in that character, more likely in politics to chastise his own side than the enemy.[7]

The image of Orwell as a modern saint has remained, even if his halo has slipped a little, as we become more critical with the passage of time.

Much of Orwell's best political writing is in his essays. One of the best-known is 'Politics and the English Language'.[8] Here he exemplifies the truth that good English is simple English. More importantly, he demonstrates how thought corrupts language and language thought. 'In our time,' he remarks, 'political speech and writing are largely the defence of the indefensible.' One of the examples he gives is the way the word 'pacification' is used to describe the process by which 'defenceless villages are bombarded from the air, the inhabitants driven out into the countryside, the cattle machine-gunned, the huts set on fire with incendiary bullets'.[9] In this essay we can see the seeds of 'doublethink' and Newspeak, which he invented in *Nineteen Eighty-Four*.

Other essays, such as the essays on Boys' Weeklies and those on the sports and pastimes of the English working-class, establish Orwell as a pioneer in analysing popular culture. This is the field that Richard Hoggart and Raymond Williams have made their own, and both have paid tribute to Orwell's originality.[10] What Orwell was doing in this part of his work was offering the power of culture as an antidote to the cult of power. Not Matthew Arnold's idea of culture, based on the classics and the virtues of sweetness and light, but a genuine, democratic culture, based on the life and customs of the people.

But there is something very odd and unsatisfactory about Orwell's analysis. At one moment his norm is the moneyed, gentlemanly culture of pre-1914 England; at another, it is working-class culture. At different times he tried to identify with each, but failed, and felt himself an Outsider. He never quite knew whether his father's post as a 4th Class Opium Officer established him as a gentleman or not; and, as an ugly, ungainly scholarship boy at Eton, he felt ill at ease among England's future rulers. Yet his gentlemanly education and accent made it impossible for him to identify closely with the English working class. So his sympathies oscillated between the patricians and the proles, Orwell's name for the honest working-class in *Nineteen Eighty-Four*. And because he saw both mainly from the outside, his analysis suffers.

The two books by which Orwell is best known today are *Animal Farm* and *Nineteen Eighty-Four*. When they first appeared they were political dynamite. Today, they have become tame schoolbooks, except in the iron-curtain countries, where pirated copies are read avidly by the party leaders, and the people prevented from reading them. Because they were political dynamite, Orwell had great difficulty in finding publishers. *Animal Farm* was turned down by four. In 1944 and 1945, the prevailing orthodoxy in England was public admiration of Soviet Russia. One publisher said it would be 'highly ill-advised to publish at the present time', and made the absurd suggestion that it would be less offensive to Russia 'if the predominant caste in the fable were not pigs'. T. S. Eliot, who read it for Faber & Faber, thought it a 'piece of distinguished writing', and that it achieved something 'very few authors have achieved since Gulliver'. But, even so, he advised his firm not to publish. No wonder Orwell was stirred to write an angry Preface on the silent censorship imposed, not by the state, but the publishers. In it, he observed shrewdly:

> The sinister fact about literary censorship in England is that it is largely voluntary. Unpopular ideas can be silenced, and inconvenient facts kept dark, without the need for any official ban.[11]

But Orwell was wise not to include this angry Preface when finally he found a willing publisher in Frederick Warburg. The Preface would have left a nasty taste in the mouth and spoilt the reader's appetite for the superb animal fable that followed. It would also have tended to limit the allegory to Russia, whereas in fact the allegory is universal in its application. Orwell himself said of *Animal Farm*: 'It was the first book in which I tried, with full consciousness of what I was doing, to fuse political purpose and artistic purpose in a whole.' [12]

George Woodcock, Orwell's most understanding and sympathetic critic has said:

> Orwell succeeded admirably, and produced a book so clear in intent and writing that the critic is usually non-plussed as to what to say about it; all is so magnificently there, and the only thing that really needs to be done is to place this crystalline little book in its proper setting. [13]

The clarity may be misleading, since some of its deepest meanings relate to the community of suffering rather than to the fallacies of the Soviet myth and the implications of the beast fable are sometimes as ambiguous as Swift's handling of Houyhnhnms and Yahoos in the fourth book of *Gulliver's Travels*.

There is certainly great artistry in *Animal Farm*. Orwell creates an enclosed, self-consistent world, with no sign of strain or effort. There is a perfect balance of 'tenderness and terror'. He incorporates references to the main stages in the Russian Revolution and clever parodies of Trotsky's style of argument, without in any way overloading the work. It possesses symmetry of form; neat ironic reversals of political values, as in the change of the slogan ALL ANIMALS ARE EQUAL to read ALL ANIMALS ARE EQUAL BUT SOME ANIMALS ARE MORE EQUAL THAN OTHERS, which achieves the status of 'one of those permanent statements about the gap between pretence and actuality'. And it contains subdued horror at the end.

> The creatures outside looked from pig to man, and from man to pig, and from pig to man again; but already it was impossible to say which was which. (Penguin, p. 120)

Animal Farm, then, is well-nigh perfect artistically; but because of its form, the beast fable, which is always to some extent reductive, and, with English writers, whimsical into the bargain, it simplifies the political issues and fails to move us as deeply or as directly as *Nineteen Eighty-Four*. *Animal Farm* reduces the role of the proletariat to that of dumb suffering, as represented by Boxer, the noble but stupid horse, and softens its otherwise unpalatable meanings by such coy and sentimental touches as Mollie's vanity and weakness when tempted by lumps of sugar and coloured ribbons. *Nineteen Eighty-Four* is less perfect artistically, but it is more intellectually challenging and moves us at deeper levels of our nature. It occupies that curious middle-ground between utopian fantasy and fully-fledged novel. It has been criticised for failing to be either, but in fact it gathers much of its extraordinary power from assimilating the characteristic strengths of each: Utopian fantasy and novel.

Orwell's reading of two books, both of which he reviewed before writing *Nineteen Eighty-Four*, contributed much to the basic conception of this work. One was James Burnham's *The Managerial Revolution*. This outlined, with apparent approval, the coming into existence of a new elite, an elite that would rule over a great slave class. But it gave no account of why men crave for such power. The other was Zamyatin's *We*. Orwell had read the French version of this great anti-utopian book, lost it for a time, and then had his interest revived when he was asked to review a new English translation. As we have already seen in the previous chapter,[14] all the essential features of *Nineteen Eighty-Four* are to be found in Zamyatin's *We*. The similarities are remarkable. Nevertheless *Nineteen Eighty-Four* is still a highly original work.[15]

As a writer, Orwell owes allegiance to two traditions, the realist and the symbolist.[16] The two fuse in *Nineteen Eighty-Four*. His invented utopian world is symbolic, but it has an obvious relationship to the actual world: to the three power blocks that emerged at the end of the Second World War; to the vast increase in central authority; to the growing importance of the mass media in creating a race of servile automata; to the organisation of the war-time BBC and the Ministry of Information; to the immediate post-war conditions, characterised by food shortages, grubby canteens, unappetising food, drab uniformity, government controls, and the whole spirit of exhausted, world-weary pessimism. In creating his shabby utopian world, Orwell draws on that acute sensitivity to taste and smell most evident in his essay 'Such, Such Were the Joys. . .', where he recaptures the sour smell of the bath towels and the taste of school food with wonderful accuracy. *Nineteen Eighty-Four* allows him greater scope as an early description makes clear:

> In the low-ceilinged canteen, deep underground, the lunch queue jerked slowly forward. The room was already very full and deafeningly noisy. From the grille at the counter the steam of stew came pouring forth, with a sour metallic smell which did not quite overcome the fumes of Victory Gin. On the far side of the room there was a small bar, a mere hole in the wall, where gin could be brought at ten cents the large nip.
>
> 'Just the man I was looking for,' said a voice at Winston's back.
>
> He turned round. It was his friend Syme, who worked in the

> Research Department. Perhaps 'friend' was not exactly the right word. You did not have friends nowadays, you had comrades: but there were some comrades whose society was pleasanter than that of others. Syme was a philologist, a specialist in Newspeak. Indeed, he was one of the enormous team of experts now engaged in compiling the Eleventh Edition of the Newspeak Dictionary. He was a tiny creature, smaller than Winston, with dark hair and large, protuberant eyes, at once mournful and derisive, which seemed to search your face closely while he was speaking to you.
>
> 'I wanted to ask you whether you'd got any razor blades,' he said.
>
> 'Not one!' said Winston with a sort of guilty haste. 'I've tried all over the place. They don't exist any longer.'
>
> Everyone kept asking you for razor blades. Actually he had two unused ones which he was hoarding up. There had been a famine of them for months past. At any given moment there was some necessary article which the Party shops were unable to supply. Sometimes it was buttons, sometimes it was darning wool, sometimes it was shoelaces; at present it was razor blades. You could only get hold of them, if at all, by scrounging more or less furtively on the 'free' market.
>
> 'I've been using the same blade for six weeks,' he added untruthfully. (Penguin, p. 42)

One of Orwell's great achievements in the book as a whole is to raise realistic details to the level of powerful symbolism. They come to represent the evil produced by the cult of power. The realist and symbolist elements thus re-inforce each other.

There are two interacting centres of interest in *Nineteen Eighty-Four*. There is the interest that centres on all the machinery of power and domination, machinery which is close enough to what already exists to act as a terrible warning to us. I mean, of course, the Thought Police, the Ministry of Truth that dispenses lies, the re-writing of history for political purposes. And there is the more personal interest that centres on the theme of escape and betrayal. Orwell's development of this theme perhaps lacks the nightmarish quality of Kafka's; but, even so, the story of Winston Smith's betrayal is subtle and horrifying. And this, in a way, is surprising, since Winston and Julia are more like simplified cartoon figures than real people. It is through the situations in which they are placed and through an intricate pattern of imagery that Orwell develops this theme of escape and betrayal.

The image of 'the place where there is no darkness' develops a grim irony. At first, Winston associates it with escape to a better world, the 'golden world' of his dreams, only to find at the end that the 'place where there is no darkness' is the constantly lit torture chamber. The image of the paperweight symbolises a world of beauty that transcends political power, time and death; it links past and present; it symbolises private joy.

> The paperweight was the room he was in, and the coral was Julia's life and his own, fixed in a sort of eternity at the heart of the crystal. (Penguin, p. 120)

This world is shattered when the Thought Police break in and smash the paperweight.

> Someone had picked up the glass paperweight from the table and smashed it to pieces on the hearth-stone.
>
> The fragment of coral, a tiny crinkle of pink like a sugar rosebud from a cake, rolled across the mat. How small, thought Winston, how small it always was! (Penguin, p. 177).

Related to this internal world of private happiness, which proves to be so vulnerable, are two other images: the image of the skull and the image of the protecting arm. Again and again in the novel, Winston and Julia take comfort in the idea that Big Brother and the Thought Police 'can't get inside you'. And this internal safety is specifically linked to the image of the glass paperweight. But Winston comes to learn that, even if 'reality is inside your skull', the wielders of power can invade this sanctuary. Thus we are betrayed by what we most trust, the mind. And we betray each other in our attempt to save ourselves. This is the final turn of the screw. To add yet further emotional horror to the theme of escape and betrayal, the image of a protecting arm, which is first associated with Winston's mother, next with Julia, is finally transferred to the protective but betraying arm of Winston's torturer, O'Brien, in the torture chamber. In the midst of the chamber, Winston finds himself 'abruptly . . . sitting up with O'Brien's arm round his shoulders' (Penguin, p. 201). In his fear of being eaten by the rats he makes the ultimate human betrayal. He cries out:

> 'Do it to Julia! Do it to Julia! Not me! Julia! I don't care what you do to her. Tear her face off, strip her to the bones. Not me! Julia! Not me!' (Penguin, p. 230)

He has betrayed the sanctity of a human person. He has lost all self-respect. These are the necessary pre-conditions for total loving surrender to the Leader. The book ends with the two grim sentences: 'He had won the victory over himself. He loved Big Brother.'

In *Animal Farm* and *Nineteen Eighty-Four* we have two further examples of the connection between political meaning and literary artistry. The beast fable in *Animal Farm* renders further political commentary unnecessary. 'If it does not speak for itself', Orwell said 'it is a failure.' In the case of *Nineteen Eighty-Four* the whole intricate pattern of symbols, made up of the place where there is no darkness, the glass paperweight, the human skull and the protective arm, gives to Orwell's indictment of the totalitarian system a complexity and subtlety that makes it a great work of art as well as powerful criticism of society.

The most important elements in Orwell's critique are first, his recognition that power can invade the inner citadel of man's integrity; second, that the object of power is *power*, pursued for its own sake; third, that the past, and therefore the whole of our cultural heritage and system of humane values, can be rewritten or annulled in the interests of a ruling ideology; and fourth, that language, the very organ of truth itself, can be refashioned to become the instrument of political power, in the form of Newspeak. These last two, the importance of the past and the importance of language, link Orwell to one of his great predecessors in the fight against tyranny. In an essay championing the Spanish in their fight against the French in 1809, Coleridge wrote:

> But the history of the past is the birth-right of every present generation, and to falsify its records either positively by interpolation or virtually by omission, is a species of public robbery, which it is the duty of every honest man to expose on detection.[17]

The duty becomes more difficult daily. With Orwell's Winston Smith, we know that if the ruling power can 'thrust its hand into the past and say of this or that event, it never happened' – that, surely 'is more terrifying than mere torture and death', yet the very distortions of the past make honest exposure more difficult. If Orwell's concern with the history of the past links him with Coleridge, his concern with language and the insidious evil bred by bureaucratic institutions links him with a later writer, Shirley Hazzard.

In *People in Glass Houses* (Harmondsworth, 1967), Shirley Hazzard has written a penetrating criticism of the current debasement of language and the destructive contradictions of institutional life.[18] Just as Orwell drew on his experience of war-time propaganda to create Newspeak, Thought-crime, and Double-think, so Shirley Hazzard has drawn on her ten years experience of working for the United Nations to create her picture of the insane and destructive power of institutional life. The result is a less horrifying book than *Nineteen Eighty-Four*. It is less coherently constructed, consisting as it does of loosely related sections that originally appeared separately in the *New Yorker*. But, in some respects, it touches us more closely. It does so because most of us have suffered at first hand from the insane logic of large institutions and because the irony on which *People in Glass Houses* turns is more easily accommodated to our immediate experience. The main irony is the idea that the great international agencies for saving the undeveloped peoples of the world not only succeed in destroying them but involve the agents of good in a self-destroying process. The book comes as a fitting climax to a long line of utopias and anti-utopias, since it takes as its subject the actual institution set up by the nations of the world after the Second World War for realising the utopian dreams of centuries, and it shows how the attempt to bring the power of culture to people is everywhere frustrated by the cult of power. Reason and language, potentially the great liberating forces for mankind, become the means by which men distort reality for the purpose of obtaining power. That it is often petty power that they seek magnifies rather than diminishes the impact of Shirley Hazzard's satire. The opening paragraphs establish the link between the misuse of language and the perversions of power.

> 'The aim of the Organization,' Mr Bekkus dictated, leaning back in his chair and casting up his eyes to the perforations of the sound-proof ceiling; 'The *aim* of the Organization,' he repeated with emphasis, as though he were directing a firing-squad – and then, 'the *long-range* aim,' narrowing his eyes to this more distant target, 'is to fully utilize the resources of the staff and hopefully by the end of the fiscal year to have laid stress –'
>
> Mr Bekkus frequently misused the word 'hopefully'. He also made a point of saying 'locate' instead of 'find', 'utilize' instead of 'use', and never lost an opportunity to indicate or communicate; and would slip in a 'basically' when he felt unsure of his ground. (Penguin, p. 9)

While the second paragraph might seem to suggest that the satire is to be directed at modern verbal solecisms, the first paragraph, with its military metaphors and inappropriate violence, prepares us for the more serious theme of the book, the manner in which the palace of culture is transformed into a centre of ambition and power, a new tower of babel, in which language becomes the chief means for evading reality and wielding petty rule.

In the first chapter, called 'Nothing in Excess', we meet one of the victims of the system, the good classical scholar Algie Wyatt, a man of varied talents, already destined by Mr Bekkus for compulsory retirement, although he does not yet know it. As an individualist, Algie cannot subordinate his strongly developed personality and sense of values to the uniform anonymous image of the Organization. 'To Algie it seemed that he was constantly being asked to take leave of those senses of honour, proportion, and the ridiculous that he had carefully nurtured and refined throughout his life.' He finds relief from the boredom and absurdity of his job in his love of apt quotation and in his hobby of collecting contradictions in terms, such contradictions as 'military intelligence' and 'competent authorities'. A slightly younger colleague, Olaf Jaspersen, tries to persuade him to appeal against his compulsory retirement, remembers Algie's love of apt quotation, and suggests that the Greek inscription 'Nothing in Excess' would be a fitting motto to put in the main lobby of the Organization.

> Algie finished another codfish cake and drank his wine, but when he replied Jaspersen was startled by the energy in his voice.
>
> 'Nothing in excess,' Algie repeated. 'But one has to understand the meaning of excess. Why should it be taken, as it seems to be these days, to refer simply to self-indulgence, or violence – or enjoyment? Wasn't it intended, don't you think, to refer to all excesses – excess of pettiness, of timorousness, of officiousness, of sententiousness, of censoriousness? Excess of stinginess or rancour? Excess of bores?' Algie went back to his vegetables for a while, and Jaspersen was again surprised when he continued. 'At the other end of that temple, there was a second inscription – "Know Thyself". Didn't mean – d'you think – that we should be mesmerized by every pettifogging detail of our composition. Meant we should understand ourselves in order to be free.' Algie laid down his knife and fork and pushed away his plate. He handed back to Jaspersen the Procedure of Appeal. 'No thanks old boy, really. Fact is, I'm not suited to it here, and from that point of view these chaps are right. You tell me to get inside their minds – but if I did that I might never find my way out again.' (Penguin, pp. 25–6)

Algie retires with the intention of using his lump sum to buy a small house somewhere along the Mediterranean, but dies the following year. His former colleagues move up the promotion ladder. 'Mr Bekkus has received *his* promotion, though over some objections. He is still combing the Organization, with little success, for unutilized sources of ability and imagination. He continues to dictate letters in his characteristic style, and his baby is now verbalizing fluently along much the same lines.' Only the girl Lidia misses Algie's sane presence. In his last letter to her, written a few days before he died,

> he reported the discovery of several new contradictions in terms and mentioned, among other things, that Piero della Francesca died on the same day that Columbus discovered America, and that there is in Mexico a rat poison called The Last Supper. Such information is hard to come by these days; now that Algie was gone, Lidia could not readily think of another source. (Penguin, p. 32)

There is no place for the ironic intelligence in institutional life.

A number of the chapters extend the view beyond the glass house itself to encompass the lives of the people that the Organization sets out to help. One of the most telling of these is the one called 'The Meeting'. It gains its peculiar power through a double set of contrasts. In the first place there is the contrast between the bored bureaucratic atmosphere of the report meeting, presided over by Rodriguez-O'Hearn, a civilized Chilean with musical ambitions, and the lively pictures of human poverty and hardship that flash upon the screen. The other contrast is between the two experts, Edrich and Flinders, who make their reports to the meeting. Edrich, a smooth professional who has mastered the jargon of the Organization, has been on a three-year assignment as a Civil Coordination expert in the Eastern Mediterranean. Flinders, a shy, inexperienced but honest forester and agricultural conservationist has been teaching people to plant trees. When Edrich confidently shows a film of the region he has visited, Flinders is immediately struck by its similarity to his own. But their solutions to each region's problems is as different as their methods of reporting. Edrich describes the deplorable condition of the area when he arrived, reminds his listeners in the gobbledygook that they understand that 'the objects of the Civil Coordination Programme is to tap the dynamics of social change in terms of local aspirations for progress', and shows pictures of the people engaged in violent activity, chopping down trees, bridging streams, until 'a little blockhouse of raw brick was laboriously constructed among the whitewashed domes and in no time at all bore the legend "Administrative Building" in three languages'. Flinders is embarrassed by Edrich's professionalism but appalled at the thought of the improvements that were 'being inflicted on those static industries that had for centuries repeated themselves in the graceful jars about the well'. Deftly the author assimilates the projection technique into the satire itself. 'What of the laughing child,' Flinders wonders, 'that somewhere on the machine spun back to his former deplorable condition – and the flocks of chickens now laying their eggs in electrified coops all through the night?' All Flinders can offer the report meeting is a speech beginning 'In classical times' and referring to erosion, and a few slides. The last slide shows two young men in djellabahs scrambling aboard a truck to hand down young trees to the peasants below – 'on the hillside above the road, dozens of small craters had already been turned in the fresh earth'. A voice in dark says '*They* look happy, at any rate', and a technician remarks laconically, 'I guess that's all.' The lights go on, the futile meeting is over, the members disperse in different directions, Flinders regretting that he had not troubled to make a proper film or learnt to 'address the meeting in its own language – that language of ends and trends, of agenda and addenda', but he is still unaware that his services will no longer be required. Only the Chairman, Rodriguez-O'Hearn, and his Indian secretary, Miss Shamsee are left. Ironically Rodriguez-O'Hearn recalls his ambition to be a conductor of an orchestra and is reassured by Miss Shamsee that that is what he is in a manner of speaking.

> 'No, no,' he said, but tipped his chair down again. 'Such mistakes we make,' he said.
>
> When the girl went out he looked through his In-tray. He then wrote a note asking Addison to bring Flinders to see him the following day, signed several recommendations for new experts, and began to read a report, making notes in the margin. When his secretary next came in, however, with an armful of files, she found him looking out of the window.
>
> 'Miss Shamsee,' he said gravely, 'I'm afraid we have suffered much erosion since classical times.'
>
> She was used to him, and merely put the files in his In-tray. She saw, as she did so, that on the edge of his blotter he had drawn a small tree. (Penguin, p. 56–7)

In 'The Meeting' it is unnecessary for the author to move outside the Glasshouse to satirize the Organization's activities abroad. The flickering images on the screen tell their own story with a peculiar poignancy, juxtaposed as they are between slices of vacuous sociological jargon and unreal commentary. But, in some of the chapters, we move outside the Headquarters of the Organization. In 'Swoboda's Tragedy', there is a touching vignette of Miss Shamsee's unrequited love affair with a married geophysicist in Milan, while in 'A Sense of a Mission' the reader visits Rhodes at a moment of supposed crisis. Clelia Kingslake, a middle aged Canadian spinster, is sent by H.Q. to the island on an assignment, 'the instrument of a great cause', she is made to feel. Through her experience we are given a representative picture of the shortsightedness, the fatuous self-justification, and self-importance of the Organization's officers abroad. The chapter offers an ironic exposure of their exclusive concern with their own comfort and status, and the unreal atmosphere they create to justify their presence on the island and the special privileges they enjoy. The episode ends with the local representative, a regional variant on Mr Bekkus, dictating to Miss Kingslake.

> 'Can't talk all day. I've got a job to do.' He tipped his chair back and locked his hands behind his head. He looked expansive – not only in the physical sense, for his face assumed a contented anticipatory smile.
>
> 'Letter. For today's pouch.'
>
> Miss Kingslake poised her pencil.
>
> 'One flimsy.'
>
> 'Just one.' She made a note.

> 'White.' Grilli gazed upward, his eyes – half-closed in the act of composition – rotating over the motionless ceiling fan. His lips moved once or twice before he actually spoke.
>
> 'Dearest Mom,' he began. (p. 149)

In a sense all Shirley Hazzard's characters are displaced persons, and none so displaced as the Organization's officers, whether they come from all the countries of the world to work in the glass tower of Babel in New York or whether they serve as specialists abroad.

An image that recurs throughout the episodes that go to make up *People in Glass Houses* is of the lost and defeated faces that look out of the windows of the great central building of the Organization. They are the faces of men like the Japanese, Nagashima, or the Greek, Pylos, who have left their homelands to serve a noble humanitarian cause, a shining utopian dream, but who have become dehumanised by the institution they serve and are in danger of maiming the peoples they are dedicated to help. Those who gaze out of their windows dreaming of a saner private world left behind are unaware of their common predicament:

> Girolamo Pastore had been standing by the window. In fact, his window was directly below Nagashima's and, had the human eye been capable of distinguishing forms thirty storeys up, the two would have been on view in identical attitudes, one a few inches above the other and quite unaware of the proximity. (Penguin p. 120–1)

Every detail of the daily lives in the Organization serves to suggest its inhuman, cosmopolitan, hierarchical structure. Everyone is clearly graded. The main *aim* – to use Mr Bekkus's favourite phrase – of almost everyone is personal promotion. Those who genuinely want to serve humanity, like Algie Wyatt or Asmole-Brown, soon find themselves edged out. Nothing has real existence unless it can be filed, docketed and given an impressive label. An experienced manipulator like the tiny angular secretary, Miss Sadie Graine, can make or break men, but even she meets her match in the Greek official Pylos. Yet, throughout all the petty struggles for power, it is not personal motives that occupy the foreground but the irresistible moulding power of the Organization.

What gives *People in Glass Houses* its special power is Shirley Hazzard's perception that the debasement of language and the dehumanising of man are but different aspects of a single process, a perception that we first encounter in a fully articulated form in Coleridge. Language becomes the chief instrument of power, self-delusion, and unreality. The impressive titles invented for the various departments, together with their capitalised abbreviations, bestow an august and anonymous authority upon them. The author makes great satiric play with this side of the United Nations Organization. She is also adept in showing the various gradations in the breakdown of communication. In an organization in which English is a second language for many, even polite gestures can produce ludicrous results as may be seen in the conversation in the lift between the Japanese Nagashima and the Cambridge educated Olaf Jaspersen.

> Striking a personal note, Jaspersen enquired, 'Your daughter at college now?'
> 'He's at the university, yes.'
> 'I thought –'
> 'Yes, yes. Just the one son.'
> 'What's he studying?'
> 'Humanities.' Nagashima nodded, smiling.
> 'Only the one play?' asked Jaspersen, who thought he had said 'Eumenides'.
> Nagashima beamed. 'Yes. Yes.' The elevator stopped at the Organization Clinic and, with a polite farewell, Nagashima got out. (Penguin, p. 122–3)

Verbal confusions operate at more serious levels also so that there is no hope of subtle communication between individuals. When the Chief hears that Olaf has been talking to Nagashima about his daughter he overwhelms him with congratulatory cliches about the Organization 'shaping the personal lives of our own people', merging 'their cultures through their personal relations'. 'We hear a lot about the Two Cultures, but I say it's the Hundred Cultures we have to deal with.' A web of abstractions comes between the officials and reality. These not only serve to distance them from facts but create a comforting sense of technological mastery. A man without food or a family with no house mean nothing until they have been reduced to abstract phrases or statistics. Nothing illustrates so poignantly the gap between individual need and the cumbersome machinery brought into operation to deal with that need as the last incident in the whole book. Glendenning, one of the officials at H.Q., comes across a letter asking for assistance in education from a resident in a village on the upper reaches of the Limpopo River. 'Below the carefully formed signature, there appeared the world "Help".' Glendenning's reply epitomises the death of Humane Reason at the hand of the Official Word.

> Dear Sir,
> Your letter of 6 March addressed to the Director-General has been passed to me for reply. I regret to inform you that, in accordance with the legislation governing our existing aid programmes, applications for study grants cannot be considered by this

> Organization unless forwarded through the appropriate ministry of the government concerned.
>
> Alternatively, may I direct your attention to the manual Paths to Learning,' issued by the Research and Amplification of the Natural Sciences, Arts and Culture Commission, an agency affiliated with this Organization, which lists fellowships and scholarships available under numerous international programmes. A copy of the most recent edition of this manual (RANSAC 306/Ed.4) may be consulted in your local library.
>
> With good wishes for the fulfilment of your aspirations, I am
>
> Yours sincerely (pp. 159–60)

Like the author of *Catch-22*, Shirley Hazzard makes us aware of the relationship between the structures of language and the structures of power. By focusing on the greatest practical attempt to realise Utopia, she exposes the dangers inherent in man's noblest dreams, without recourse to fantasy or future projections, unlike Huxley and Orwell.

The questions we are forced to ask ourselves at this stage and for which there seem no obvious or consoling answers are: Firstly, has language no inbuilt strength to resist the manipulative control of technocrats and politicians? Secondly, has culture no power to offer an alternative to organised slavery, organised slavery however skilfully disguised? Thirdly, do we now live, as many would have us believe, in a post-cultural period in which values must be individually not socially derived, a period in which the main aim is individual pleasure, not social harmony? Fourthly, is such a post-cultural period the new Barbarism? Or, is it the beginning of a new civilisation, an age of pleasure, tenderness, tolerance, and respect for individual difference, an age which will in time breed its own critics of society, or if not society, at least critics of the quality of human life?

All the writers considered in this chapter show in their various ways how easily the power of culture may be used to serve the cult of power, but paradoxically their works are living examples of the power of creative language to withstand the tyranny of technocrats and the specious appeals of scientists, sociologists and powerhungry utopians.

13 Science Fiction

In the course of an interesting three-part debate on Science Fiction between C. S. Lewis, Brian Aldiss, and Kingsley Amis,[1] Brian Aldiss remarked that it was characteristic of the English to want to categorise everything. Whether this is true or not, no attempt will be made here to classify this immensely popular fiction into discrete categories according to literary form, imaginative technology or planetary geography. In essence, Science Fiction expresses man's highly ambivalent attitude to science, as a benefaction and as a curse. Even in the early days of scientific development, the perils of misuse were as apparent to some as its benefits. Swift, in the third book of *Gulliver's Travels*, holds up to ridicule the ingenious perverters of knowledge and recalls his readers to the prime function of scientific knowledge, which is to provide more amply for man's basic needs, to make two blades of grass grow where only one grew before.

Interesting as an anticipation of later responses by literary men, Swift's vision was to some extent limited by the restricted science of his own day, as were the much earlier visions of the second century Greek writer Lucian, Bacon in the *New Atlantis*, and Cyrano de Bergerac in *Voyage dans la Lune* (1650). But, by the second half of the nineteenth century, science had made great advances and it was therefore natural for such early practitioners of Science Fiction as Jules Verne and H. G. Wells to create fantasy worlds that were either optimistic visions of the future or logical extensions of the actual achievements of contemporary science and technology. Jules Verne was primarily an entertainer; Wells was both entertainer and serious social prophet. As we have already, seen, *The Time Machine* develops a more profound image of the effect of science on society than any contained in realistic or socialistically oriented novels. It does so for a variety of reasons. It permits a wider scope for the writer's speculative imagination; it provides a convenient outlet for largely sub-conscious hunches about the biological and social evolution of man in an industrial society; and it creates a startlingly new perspective from which to view the present state of the world. But, because it was written primarily to entertain, it does not escape triviality, and because it has to satisfy readers looking for romance as well as science, it has to include a mawkish love story.

Though he knew much about sex, Wells knew little of love; though later science fiction writers often know a great deal about science, they do not always know enough about life.

In many ways, it is surprising that it has taken so long for Science Fiction to establish itself as a distinct literary genre. We might say that it has been struggling for status throughout the century and has never been able to throw off its disreputable connection with boys' adventure stories and horror comics. The pronouncements made by the advocates oscillate between the extremes of cautious defence and arrogant championing. For example, in 1961, Kingsley Amis, in his Editor's Introduction to *Spectrum*, a Science Fiction anthology, put forward rather extravagant claims for Science Fiction only to retract them:

> It will be seen that we are not putting forward exaggerated claims for the quality of modern science fiction. It in no way, as yet, approaches the best work done in the long cultivated and efficiently fertilized fields of conventional fiction . . . perhaps a dozen contemporary practitioners seem to have attained the status of the sound minor writer.

If the situation is still the same nearly twenty years later, we might ask ourselves: why should we bother with sound minor writers when there are already so many exciting major writers working within the traditional literary forms?

In answer, I might say that the situation has probably improved, that there are several writers who are something better than 'sound minor writers', and that, in any case, Science Fiction is the one kind of fiction that is widely read today, both among the intelligentsia and also among the newspaper and magazine reading public. That part of it, therefore, that is concerned with criticising society, deserves to be taken seriously in a book like the present one concerned with a broad spectrum of images of society.

In a review of a volume called *Hell's Cartographers*, James Blish, a distinguished writer of Science Fiction himself, quotes a passage from Brian Aldiss which suggests that Science Fiction writers are the poor man's highbrows:

> We are an entirely new sort of popular writer, the poor man's highbrows. We wrote against the grain and were accepted against it. . . . We had faith in what we were doing; individualists though we were, it transpired that the faith virtually created a movement. (*TLS* 23 May, 1975)

Here, perhaps, Aldiss is confusing the trades union or monopolist activities of Science Fiction writers with their activities as serious artists. Like the writers of detective fiction, the writers of Science Fiction have found that it pays to band together and form clubs. But to do that does not necessarily constitute a literary movement nor establish the actual literary status of the form.

From the point of view of a casual, rather than a devoted reader, it is the variety of Science Fiction that impresses and bewilders. I do not think of a movement. What I think of are individual writers and individual books. It is with these that I shall be concerned in this chapter. But first, so that we know what kind of fiction is under discussion, we might remind ourselves of Kingsley Amis's definition of Science Fiction:

> Science fiction is that class of prose narrative treating of a situation that could not arise in the world we know, but which is hypothesised on the basis of some innovation in science or technology, or pseudo-science or pseudo-technology, whether human or extra-terrestrial in origin (*New Maps of Hell*, p. 18).

Its closest neighbour, as Amis remarks, is fantasy, but while Science Fiction

> maintains a respect for fact or presumptive fact, fantasy makes a point of flouting these; for a furniture of robots, space-ships, techniques, and equations it substitutes elves, broomsticks, occult powers, and incantations' (p. 22).

It will be convenient to begin with a fifty-four page short story by Frederick Pohl, called 'The Midas Plague', published in *Spectrum* in 1961 (edited by Kingsley Amis and Robert Conquest). Now this little story illustrates very well that some mid-century Science Fiction often takes up a single idea contained in one of the early scientific utopias or distopias and extends it a few stages further. The idea Pohl takes up is Huxley's idea that consumption will become a social necessity in a highly mechanised, planned industrial society. In *Brave New World*, it will be recalled, even sport had to be assimilated into the mechanical consumer pattern.

In Frederick Pohl's 'The Midas Plague', the newly married couple, Morey Fry and his wife Cherry, soon run into trouble, because they cannot consume their appropriate ration of social goodies: food, drink, baths, and so on. Ultimately, the solution is for the robot servants to consume what their master and mistress are unable to consume. The donnée of the story is good. It is full of ironic potential. And the title is apt. For Midas, we remember, everything he touched turned to gold. In the title the 'gift' becomes a 'plague'. The story suggests that one can have too much of a good thing, too many of the luxuries of life, so that their overwhelming plenitude causes maximum anxiety instead of maximum pleasure. What chiefly distinguishes this Science Fiction short story from Huxley's *Brave New World* (1932) or Orwell's *1984*, is its almost total lack of literary quality. It lacks originality of invention. Its appeal is to readers with impoverished imaginations, familiar with the stereotypes of cinema and TV screen, but unable to enter a completely new world that obeys the laws of its own being. The robot butler, Henry, for instance, is a not very ingenious variant on the cinema prototype. And the social decor and scientific details are so adapted to minds fed on women's magazines and scientific comics that they never come alive in any interesting or challenging way. In this respect I differ from Kingsley Amis, who praises the inventive detail and says that 'The Midas Plague' not only 'informs us that the results of overproduction may be fantastic, hilarious, or desperate', but also comments on the 'revolution in manners which human beings will swallow', for example, it now becomes good manners to let the other man pick up the bill in a restaurant, as it helps his consumer credit tally. Certainly, this is momentarily funny, but ultimately trivial. What 'The Midas Plague' lacks, and what much Science Fiction so often lacks, is telling detail, and telling detail is the characteristic product of a finely creative mind.

In Ray Bradbury's *Fahrenheit 451*, the ex-Professor, Faber, offers Montag a definition of quality in terms of telling detail. 'What does the word quality mean?' he asks. And answers:

> To me it means texture. This book has *pores*. It has features. This book can go under the microscope. You'd find life under the glass, streaming past in infinite profusion. The more pores, the more truthfully recorded details of life per square inch you can get on a sheet of paper, the more 'literary' you are. That's *my* definition, anyway. *Telling detail.* Fresh detail. The good writers touch life often. The mediocre ones run a quick hand over her. The bad ones rape her and leave her for the flies (Corgi p. 82).

Although this definition of literary quality is obviously more relevant to fiction in the realistic or naturalistic mode, it is also applicable, with suitable modification, to Science Fiction.

All three of the main works that I propose to discuss have literary quality. The three works are, in order of publication, Ray Bradbury's *Fahrenheit 451* (1954), Anthony Burgess's *A Clockwork Orange* (1962) and Kurt Vonnegut's *Slaughterhouse-Five* (1970). They are very different in scope and technique and therefore serve to some extent to illustrate the variety of the kind: that is, Science Fiction that develops a criticism of society. All three seem to posit a background of global war and universal violence. And all present a society in which high culture is no longer operative, in any vital way.

Fahrenheit 451 takes its place in a long line of works concerned with the survival of language and the written word, since it not only presents a future in which there is constant war or threat of war but one where there is no legitimate place for books. The infamous burning of the books in Nazi Germany provides the historical model for Bradbury's fictional projection. On this model, he imagines a future society in which reading and the possession of books are anti-social activities and therefore must be eradicated.

The curious title is based on the scientific notion that Fahrenheit 451 is 'the temperature at which book-paper catches fire and burns', and the first paragraph of the book describes the special pleasure of seeing things burn. 'It was a special pleasure to see things eaten, to see things blackened and changed.' Since the meaning of the whole book centres on the character called Montag, it is necessary to establish his function as a fireman and to introduce explanations for his abnormality, his deviation from accepted behaviour. Bradbury introduces his first bit of verbal play in explaining Montag's function in this future society. He is a fireman. Whereas, in our society, a fireman extinguishes fires, in Bradbury's a fireman extinguishes books. He destroys them with fire. A far less successful fictional invention is the character, Clarisse McClellan, the seventeen-year-old social misfit, who likes 'to smell things and look at things, and sometimes stay up all night, walking, and watching the sun rise'. In many ways a sentimental device to represent the natural values and interpersonal relationships that have been lost, she also serves as an effective contrast to Montag's wife, Mildred, who is completely adapted to a life of drug-taking and passive consumption of 'sound thro' little seashells, thimble radios in the ears, and T.V., or rather wall entertainment'. Bradbury himself wrote:

> In writing the short novel *Fahrenheit 451* I thought I was describing a world that might evolve in four or five decades. But only a few weeks ago, in Beverly Hills one night, a husband and wife passed me, walking their dog. I stood staring after them absolutely stunned. The woman held in one hand a small cigarette package-sized radio, its antenna quivering. From this sprang tiny copper wires which ended in a dainty cone plugged in her right ear. There she was, oblivious to man and dog, listening to far winds and whispers and soap opera cries, sleepwalking, helped up and down curbs by a husband who might just as well not have been there.

When Mildred takes an overdose, Bradbury describes the two machines that restore her to normality. The operator of one could look into the soul of the person, as the machine pumped out all the poisons accumulated with the years. The other machine 'pumped all the blood from the body and replaced it with fresh blood and serum'. The invention is an extrapolation from present psychiatric and medical practice to reinforce the notion that human beings have ceased to be regarded as individual personalities and have been reduced to the level of things or controllable processes. This is one of the fairly peripheral bits of social documentation. Less peripheral is the detail that relates to the wall TV, especially the contrast between the mindless mush that Mildred and her neighbours enjoy, and the effect on them of two passages from Matthew Arnold's *Dover Beach.* The women cannot help being moved by Arnold's lines, but one of them, Mrs Bowles, condemns poetry and Montag roundly:

> I've always said, poetry and tears, poetry and suicide and crying and awful feelings, poetry and sickness; *all* that mush! Now I've had it proved to me. You're nasty, Mr Montag, you're *nasty.*

The trouble with Montag, of course, is that he has discovered the value of books. He keeps some hidden away behind the ventilator grille. And the reader realises that it is only a matter of time before he is discovered. Bradbury develops a certain amount of suspense and drama through Mildred's fears, through the poker-face duels between Montag and the fire chief Beatty, and through the ominous sounds outside Montag's door. One of the most effective minor climaxes in *Fahrenheit 451* occurs when the firemen are called out and Montag finds, to his horror, that the address they have been sent to to destroy books is his own.

It must be admitted that Bradbury is more successful in creating the horror of mechanised anti-culture than in evoking the positive and continuing power of literature and civilisation. The burning scenes have intense power and the pursuit of Montag by the Mechanical Hound, especially in the last section of the book, is in the best tradition of Gothic pursuit; mysterious, but relentless. By comparison, the evocation of culture is either laboured or sentimental. It is laboured, because Bradbury cannot rely on his readers picking up his allusions. He therefore has to explain laboriously; for instance, the fact that Ridley was one of the Oxford martyrs of 1555 who was burnt at the cross as a martyr to truth. In case the relevance of the words spoken by the woman burnt up by the Mechanical Hound is missed, Bradbury supplies an explanatory recapitulation a few pages later:

> They said nothing on their way back to the firehouse. Nobody looked at anyone else. Montag sat in the front seat with Beatty and Black. They did not even smoke their pipes. They sat there looking out of the front of the great salamander as they turned a corner and went silently on.
>
> 'Master Ridley,' said Montag at last.
>
> 'What?' said Beatty.
>
> 'She said, "Master Ridley." She said some crazy thing when we

came in the door. "Play the man," she said, "Master Ridley." Something, something, something.'

'We shall this day light such a candle, by God's grace, in England, as I trust shall never be put out,' said Beatty. Stoneman glanced over at the Captain, as did Montag, startled.

Beatty rubbed his chin. 'A man named Latimer said that to a man named Nicholas Ridley, as they were being burnt alive at Oxford, for heresy, on October 16, 1555.'

The idea of culture is embarrassingly false in the interview with Faber, who then becomes Montag's better self, through the minute transistor that he carries around with him and which acts as his mechanical conscience. It is painfully folksy in the whole section relating to Montag's meeting with Granger and his greenwoods exiles, each of whom has memorised a great book or part of a book. The theme here is the independence of culture from physical objects, but the notion of a revived oral culture is not developed very far in this piece of pre-McLuhan fiction. Most painful of all are Granger's recollections of his artist grandfather's philosophy of individualism. Putting Christmas-cracker sentiments into the mouths of a now dead grandfather does not make them any less trite.

The image of fire undergoes a double transformation in the last part of the book. What had been the destroyer of culture before becomes the centre of civilised life, as Granger and his exiles gather round the camp fire. Finally, the fire that has destroyed nations in the international conflict is seen as a Phoenix. Bradbury provides a characteristically popular explanation through Granger.

> There was a silly damn bird called a Phoenix back before Christ; every few hundred years he built a pyre and burned himself up (Corgi, p. 158).

A writer who has to explain all his allusions and symbols for the benefit of lowbrow readers is at a considerable disadvantage. But a writer who resorts to condescending explanations like this one probably repels both highbrow and lowbrow readers alike.

When in doubt how to end, there is nothing like putting in a Biblical passage to achieve spurious prophetic power. With the evidence of widespread destruction everywhere, the reader is reminded that there is a time to break down and a time time to build up, and Montag recalls a passage from the Bible:

> And on either side of the river was there a tree of life, which bore twelve manner of fruits, and yielded her fruit every month; And the leaves of the tree were for healing of the nations.

Books create diversity and harmony, that is the final message of *Fahrenheit 451*. It is an intensely serious work of popular Science Fiction but it is flawed by sentimentality and meretricious appeals to high culture.

Anthony Burgess's *A Clockwork Orange* differs from most of the works already considered in this book in focusing on a sub-group with its own culture, and not on society as a whole. In the late 1950s and early 1960s, there was an alarming outbreak of violence among teenagers everywhere in the world. The violence was often directed against the helpless and the aged but also against the obvious representatives of old-fashioned culture, for instance, writers and straight musicians. Much of it was motiveless. It was violence and destruction for its own sake. A favourite occupation, then and now, was slashing the upholstery in railway carriages. The recalling of these details makes it clear that *A Clockwork Orange* is an extrapolation from the conduct of a sub-group in contemporary society. Burgess extends the scope of his work to include not only the theme of senseless violence but a number of other important subjects as well. These are the idea of free will, the right to make a free choice between good and evil, a topic of special importance to Burgess as a lapsed Catholic. The right to choose, even the right to choose unhappiness, it will be recalled, occupied a vital place in the ending of Huxley's *Brave New World*, when John the Savage demanded the right to be unhappy. Another important theme in Burgess's *A Clockwork Orange* is the related issue of criminal cure through aversion therapy. As the Minister for the Interior explains, Alex is to be used as a 'trailbearer'.

> He's young, bold, vicious. Brodsky will deal with him tomorrow and you can sit in and watch Brodsky. It works all right, don't worry about that. This vicious young hoodlum will be transformed without recognition.

The ending of the book throws doubt on the Minister's confidence. The Minister, in a congratulatory interview with Alex, pronounces him cured, reassures him that the Government has dealt with his old enemy, the liberal writer, F. Alexander, and promises him a bright future. Alex signs off as cured, but the last paragraph of the book reveals clearly enough that the subconscious connection between music and violence is as strong as ever. As Alex listens to good old Ludwig Van's Ninth, he reflects,

> Oh, it was gorgeosity and yum yum yum. When it came to the Scherzo I could riddy myself very clear running and running on like very light and mysterious nogas, carving the whole litso of the creeching world with my cut-throat britva. And there was the slow

movement and the lovely last singing movement still to come. I was cured all right.

From directing violence at individual people and objects, Alex now directs it at the face of the whole world. In the light of his betrayal by his mates, his harsh handling in prison, and his therapy treatment, it is hardly surprising. Burgess obviously brings two criticisms against such therapy treatment which is already widely used in our present society to 'cure' alcoholics, sexual deviants, and criminals: one, that it is immoral, because it tries to take away free will; two, that it is ineffective, because irrational connections may survive conditioned brainwashing. The main spokesman for the moral question is a conspicuously unsympathetic character. While it is true that we only see and smell the Prison Chaplain through Alex's distorting senses, we are meant to think of him as a moralist who has been corrupted by the institution he serves, so that though he says that 'very hard ethical questions are involved', he is more concerned in apologising for his part in the scheme of things than in justifying moral conditioning on moral grounds.

For a work of fiction about a sub-group to succeed, it is essential for a writer to establish the rules and conventions that govern the behaviour of its members. In this respect, *A Clockwork Orange* is a great success. And its success does not depend entirely on Burgess's linguistic ingenuity in creating a new language for the sub-group, although this is indeed his main device. It also depends on references and allusions to values recognised by the group and to conventions of behaviour. Alex has mastered some of the main techniques of the leader principle. You lead by directing the hatred of others towards the defenceless. Alex also recalls his droogs (his mates) to correct behaviour. He reproves Dim for his gluttony and vulgarity, for being a 'filthy drooling mannerless bastard'. And since Alex accepts the basic axioms of the leader principle, an offence against the group is an offence against the leader. Alex comments (p. 26), 'It was me really Dim had done wrong to.' The attentive reader will notice that what irked Alex most was Dim's insensitivity to music, an unpardonable flaw in his make-up from Alex's point of view.

In considering Burgess's use of a special language in *A Clockwork Orange*, it is more important to note its function than to trace its origin in Polish and Russian. One function, as we have noted, is to create an impression of a cohesive sub-group, with its own distinctive sub-culture. Another is to suggest that the creation of a set of special terms is part of the self-justifying process adopted by a dissenting sub-group. An essential element in justifying the persecution of others is the invention of terms to reduce the humanity of the persecuted, so that they become objects of hatred and contempt, things to be destroyed, not individuals with their own distinctive forms of thought and behaviour. Coleridge, in his insistence on the distinction between persons and things and in his objection to the use of such terms as 'hands' for men and women working in factories, was the earliest writer to recognise the connection between language and the exercise of political power. A further function of the special language in *A Clockwork Orange* is to add linguistic modes and tones that operate on the reader in a variety of ways. The language demands concentration as a pre-requisite for entry into Burgess's fictional world. Its inventive playfulness gives the combined satisfaction of learning a new language and solving a series of riddles. And the riddle element is often of supreme importance in literary works, as may be seen in *Catch-22.* Frequently the language serves to distance the horror and to reduce the physical immediacy of the most brutal scenes. One of the reasons why the film caused a public outcry and the book did not, when it was first published, was that the film could not discover a visual equivalent to the cerebral quality of the language. In Burgess's stylised descriptions of violence, the language reduces the stark emotional horror by keeping the mind at work translating the unfamiliar words. A good example is the bit of gang warfare, when Alex and his droogs carve up Billyboy and his five droogs, round by the Municipal Power Plant. The writing is fanciful, even exotic at the beginning, with the allusion to the moon as 'the old Luna':

> So there we were dratsing away in the dark, the old Luna with men on it just coming up, the stars stabbing away as it might be knives anxious to join in the dratsing. With my britva I managed to slit right down the front of one of Billyboy's droog's platties, very very neat and not even touching the plott under the cloth. Then in the dratsing this droog of Billyboy's suddenly found himself all opened up like a peapod, with his belly bare and his poor old yarbles showing, and then he got very very razdraz, waving and screaming and losing his guard and letting in old Dim with his chain snaking whisssssshhhhhhhhh, so that old Dim chained him right in the glazzies, and this droog of Billyboy's went tottering off and howling his heart out. We were doing very horrorshow, and soon we had Billyboy's number-one down underfoot, blinded with old Dim's chain and crawling and howling about like an animal, but with one fair boot on the gulliver he was out and out and out. (Penguin, pp. 16–7)

The science fiction element in *A Clockwork Orange* is largely restricted to the aversion therapy. But, in that it is an extrapolation from our known world and a projection into the future, it is closely related to the other works under discussion. As a work that offers a criticism of society it compels us to look afresh at the problems of violence, psychological treatment in prison, and social indoctrination. By attempting too much, it does not escape confusion. And Burgess's personal pre-occupation with two subjects, free-will and music, are not entirely assimilated into the imaginative whole. But of the author's intelligence and literary sensibility we are never in doubt. He is clearly an altogether more accomplished writer than Ray Bradbury and appears to be writing for a more sophisticated public.

The same is true of Kurt Vonnegut, author of *Slaughterhouse Five.* Like Heller's *Catch-22, Slaughterhouse-Five* is a work that needs to be read several times. For anyone unacquainted with Vonnegut's other works the most puzzling element is, in fact, the science-fiction one, that is Billy Pilgrim's experience on the planet Tralfamadore. The end of the long title page establishes the connection with Vonnegut's other works in which Tralfamadore provides the necessary perspective from which to view the unhappiness and misery on earth with equanimity. The end of the title page runs 'This is a novel/Somewhat in the Telegraphic Schizophrenic/Manner of Tales/of the Planet Tralfamadore,/Where the Flying Saucers/Come From./Peace.'

The main thrust of *Slaughterhouse-Five* is against the insanity of war, and, in this respect, it closely parallels *Catch-22.* But the scale is smaller. It focuses on the fire-bombing of the beautiful city of Dresden by the Americans towards the end of the war. Billy, a prisoner-of-war, escapes, while hundreds of thousands die. Billeted in an underground slaughterhouse and sharing his billet with frozen meat, he looks out to see a whole city reduced to ashes.

If the arena of war is smaller than in *Catch-22*, the perspective of destruction is wider. It encompasses the destruction of the Universe itself:

> 'How – how does the Universe end?' said Billy.
>
> 'We blow it up, experimenting with new fuels for our flying saucers. A Tralfamadorian test pilot presses a starter button, and the whole Universe disappears.' So it goes.
>
> 'If you know this,' said Billy, 'isn't there some way you can prevent it? Can't you keep the pilot from *pressing* the button?'
>
> 'He has *always* pressed it, and he always *will.* We *always* let him and we always *will* let him. The moment is *structured* that way.' (p. 101)

Slaughterhouse-Five is a work based on three major elements: time travel, the idea of eternity, and the idea of a structured universe. Only the first, time travel, is common in Science Fiction.

Billy is free to move in time and space. The brief sections, sometimes only a paragraph long, range from this earth to Tralfamadore, where Billy, is displayed naked in a zoo with Montana Wildhack, a beautiful movie star. They describe Billy's life as a soldier in World War II, his experiences as a prisoner-of-war, his relations with other soldiers and other prisoners-of-war, his subsequent career as a successful optometrist who marries the daughter of an even more successful optometrist, his relations with his daughter, the details of a plane crash of which he is the sole survivor. They also describe his discovery that his science fiction idol, the writer Kilgore Trout, who lives just round the corner, is a mere nobody, a man who has to bully and wheedle the boys who work for him on his paper-round. The main purpose of the swift transitions from one incident to another is twofold. It is Vonnegut's method of establishing a philosophical principle that Billy learns from the Tralfamadorians: that happiness lies in concentrating on the intensely significant moments of life. And, negatively, the fragmentary narration is his method of revealing the connection between the absurdity of peace and the absurdity of war. Billy's life with Valencia, his career as an optometrist, is as devoid of meaning as the organised destruction of Dresden.

The concepts of eternity and a structured universe provide a source of consolation and equanimity. Most of us have rather odd notions about eternity, sometimes thinking of it as the ultimate hope and sometimes as the ultimate horror, an enternity of suffering, such as Faustus envisaged in Marlowe's tragic play. From his visit to Tralfamadore, Billy acquires an idea of eternity that transcends the limitations of human temporal vision. From the same source, he acquires his insight into a structured universe. Far from creating a sense of a deterministic universe, with the concomitant effect of human impotence, the idea of the structured universe and the structured moment make life bearable for Billy, and ultimately for Kurt Vonnegut's readers. There is a tenderness and compassion in Vonnegut's vision that is typical of the liberal humanist. When we come to the end of *Slaughterhouse-Five* we feel that he has succeeded in transforming a vision of random contingency 'So it goes' into structured order 'So it goes'.

> If what Billy Pilgrim learned from the Tralfamadorians is true, that we will all live forever, no matter how dead we may sometimes seem to be, I am not overjoyed. Still – if I am going to spend eternity visiting this moment and that, I'm grateful that so many of those moments are nice (pp. 182–3).

Slaughterhouse-Five, like most works of Science Fiction, cannot stand up to intense critical scrutiny. Vonnegut never entirely resolves the contrast between the insane suffering brought about by war and man's brief moments of happiness. The pseudo-philosophic framework is too gimcrack to serve its intended purpose when viewed analytically, but it provides a satisfying sense of aesthetic order.

In an article called 'The Social Content of Science', Oscar Shaftel concludes that some of the 'vitality' and 'respect' that Science Fiction has earned from an increasing number of serious people is due to its 'social content'.[2] This may well be true. But, so far, its criticism of society has lacked the human incisiveness that we have found in the best novelists and in the best writers of anti-utopias. Another critic, H. L. Gold, writing in *Galaxy Science Fiction*, claims that 'few things reveal so sharply as Science Fiction the wishes, hopes, fears, inner stresses and tensions of an era, or define its limitations with such exactness'. Exactness? My own view is that Science Fiction is often imprecise as definer and image maker, but I would certainly agree that it reveals the wishes, hopes, fears, inner stresses, and tensions of an era. It may be that the function of Science Fiction has so far been to act as a popular safety-valve for unconscious anti-social instincts rather than as a deeply responsible criticism of society and that in time it may take over more of the roles of the traditional novel and philosophic essay.

14 Protest and Anti-War Literature

In a century that has already witnessed the ravages of two World Wars, it is not surprising that much of the best protest literature has been about war. Other issues have certainly created their own literature of protest. In America there is a growing body of fine fiction protesting against the treatment of the Negro, while in South Africa and elsewhere the theme of racial discrimination has come to occupy an important place in literature. Attacks upon sex discrimination have become more common in almost all countries. Overlapping these definable kinds are two other forms, the one with a long tradition, the other an expression of a new mode of consciousness. The first, often Marxist in orientation, is a generalised protest against the social and political system, as in Edward Upward's *In The Thirties*. The other is the literature of the absurd, which is always, implicitly if not explicitly, a protest against the situation in which man finds himself in the universe.

Joseph Heller's *Catch-22* is a novel that deliberately sets out to show that we live in an absurd universe. In the world that Heller creates we feel a stranger and yet at home. We feel lost because, as Camus remarks in *The Myth of Sisyphus*, 'in a universe that is suddenly deprived of illusions and of light, man feels a stranger'. But we also feel at home, because unreason seems to rule so much of our ordinary everyday lives. The comic formula 'Catch-22' sums up man's position in an absurd universe, and the novel shows that it applies to every aspect of life: to war, to love, to business, even to religion.

If you are an American flier in wartime you find yourself caught up by this formula. The conversation between the hero, Yossarian, and Doc Daneeka illustrates man's predicament within the war machine. Yossarian asks the doctor:

> 'Is Orr crazy?'
> 'He sure is,' Doc Daneeka said.
> 'Can you ground him?'
> 'I sure can. But first he has to ask me to. That's part of the rule.'
> 'Then why doesn't he ask you to?'
> 'Because he's crazy,' Doc Daneeka said. 'He has to be crazy to keep flying combat missions after all the close calls he's had. Sure, I

can ground Orr. But first he has to ask me to.'

'That's all he has to do to be grounded?'

'That's all. Let him ask me.'

'And then you can ground him?' Yossarian asked.

'No. Then I can't ground him.'

'You mean there's a catch?'

'Sure there's a catch,' Doc Daneeka replied. 'Catch-22. Anyone who wants to get out of combat duty isn't really crazy'. (Corgi, p. 54)

Here, as Burr Dodd has noted, the formula acts as a 'logically illogical smokescreen to bemuse and befuddle subordinates, who must in fact do whatever their superiors demand'.[1] That puts the matter neatly as far as it applies to this kind of situation. But the point is that 'Catch-22' applies to many different levels of life. Reduced to essentials and as it applies to them all, the formula states that something can only happen if a certain condition is fulfilled but then the very fulfilling of that condition prevents it from ever happening. In war a man cannot plead that he is crazy to escape flying further combat missions. In love he can never marry the person he wishes to, as Yossarian discovers on leave in Rome when Luciana says she won't marry him because he is crazy:

His heart cracked, and he fell in love. He wondered if she would marry him.

'*Tu sei pazzo*,' she told him with a pleasant laugh.

'Why am I crazy?' he asked.

'*Perchè non posso sposare.*'

'Why can't you get married?'

'Because I am not a virgin,' she answered.

'What has that got to do with it?'

'Who will marry me? No one wants a girl who is not a virgin.'

'I will. I'll marry you.'

'*Ma non posso sposarti.*'

'Why can't you marry me?'

'*Perchè sei pazzo.*'

'Why am I crazy?'

'*Perchè vuoi sposarmi.*'

Yossarian wrinkled his forehead with quizzical amusement.

'You won't marry me because I'm crazy, and you say I'm crazy because I want to marry you? Is that right?'

'Si.'

'Tu sei pazz'!' he told her loudly (Corgi, p. 172).

But the formula extends beyond love and war. Through Milo Minderbinder it touches the roots of capitalist enterprise. It reveals that behind the compulsive acquisitiveness of capitalism lies a completely amoral destructive force, blind in its operation and totally unconcerned with human consequences. At the highest level it seems to apply to God's laws as well as man's; or, rather, men project their own irrationality on God. For example, Colonel Cathcart shouts at the Chaplain, 'I'm not going to set those damned prayer meetings up just to make things worse than they are'. Yossarian asks Lieutenant Scheisskopf's wife indignantly how one can revere 'a supreme Being who finds it necessary to include such phenomena as phlegm and tooth decay in His divine system of creation? What in the world was running through that warped, evil, scatalogical mind of His when He robbed old people of the power to control their bowel movements?' (p. 194). An old Italian farmer whose son has been killed in the war asks Yossarian when he dies to 'talk to the man upstairs',

> Tell Him it ain't right for people to die when they're young. I mean it. Tell Him if they got to die at all, they got to die when they're old. I want you to tell him that. I don't think He knows it ain't right, because He's supposed to be good and it's been going on for a long, long time. Okay?' (Corgi, p. 201)

As may be seen from such passages, Heller invents dialogue rich in humour and pathos in order to fit the serious religious and philosophical implications of 'Catch-22' into his comic novel. To the extent that the verbal formula is worked out mainly through the predicament of a group of fliers in the Second World War, *Catch-22* is a war novel; but to the extent that Heller shows it operating throughout the whole of Western capitalist society, mainly through Milo Minderbinder's activities, it is a novel of social protest; and to the extent that Heller shows it operating throughout the universe, through the basic structure of the human mind, through the mind of God himself, the novel becomes a metaphysical novel, a novel of the absurd, to be linked with the work of Sartre and Camus.

Catch-22 is not simply a novel about the futility of the Second World War. The author himself has said, 'I wrote it during the Korean War and aimed it for the one after that. The Cold War is what I was truly talking about, not the world war.' Yet even this statement drastically limits a work that transcends the conventional fictional categories. Certainly, at first sight, it appears to be just another war novel. From the time of the First World War there have been hundreds written, some of the best of which are Remarque's *All Quiet on the Western Front* (1929), Frederick Manning's *Her Privates We* (1930), and Norman Mailer's *The Naked and the Dead* (1948). Most of the novels in this genre have two things in common: they seek to show the bloodshed and misery caused by war, and they seek to demonstrate its futility. Mailer's novel forms a useful contrast to *Catch-22*. Apart from the use of the cinema flashback technique, which takes the reader from the war to civilian life and back to the war again to establish that American society is in fact a disguised form of authoritarian army, *The Naked and Dead*, centres on war and is fairly conventional in technique. Even as a war novel, Mailer's work ultimately fails because his sympathies become too deeply engaged with his masterful 'baddies', General Cummings and Sergeant Croft, and he can do nothing with his radical 'goodies'. Nothing similar happens in *Catch-22* because of its unique intellectual and literary structure.

Catch-22 is not an anti-war novel like *All Quiet on the Western Front* or *The Naked and the Dead*, but a comprehensive indictment of modern society. It achieves its amazing breadth – without loss of unity – through the application of the same comic formula to every aspect of life. This riddle links the humour and the tragedy. In *The Scope of Anthropology*, Lévi-Strauss has shown how pervasive the riddle element is in the structure of the human mind, in folk lore, and in great literature. Through its comic formula or riddle, Heller's novel expresses the apparently inescapable human predicament. We are caught. Although we enjoy an illusion of freedom, as soon as we reach out to grasp it, we become more firmly enslaved. To opt out of the irrational is to be labelled crazy with Yossarian: to accept the irrational power structure is to be labelled sane with the maniac Colonel Cathcart, who constantly increases the number of combat missions. In chapter 1, when Yossarian has temporarily found refuge in hospital, he says, 'this is the only sane ward in the whole world'. And, of course, he is right.

In the novel as a whole, Heller carefully manipulates patterns of language and logic to lay bare two opposite structures of behaviour and belief. On the one hand there is the system of irrational conformity represented by the unthinking generals. On the other hand there is the system of rational revolt typified by the rebels Yossarian and Orr. Each group regards the other as insane. A single word may reveal the contrasting structures. An example occurs when Yossarian is talking to the Chaplain about one of the officers, Dunbar, and praises him as 'A true prince. One of the finest, least dedicated men in the whole world' (p. 20). We expect the phrase 'one of the finest, *most* dedicated men', but find instead '*least* dedicated'. Here we have an example of Heller's skill in manipulating language to reveal the opposed structures of irrational conformity and rational revolt. If someone speaks of Dunbar as one of the finest, *most* dedicated men, he unconsciously indicates his irrational conformity, his unthinking adherence to the idea that it is princely to dedicate oneself to an institution geared for wholesale destruction. By using the word 'least' Yossarian indicates his conscious rational revolt against the whole system. Although we cannot miss the humour of much of the dialogue, we may perhaps miss its deeper significance unless we grasp this basic idea of the two contrasted structures of thought. Take the following exchange between Yossarian and Clevinger, for example.

> 'They're trying to kill me,' Yossarian told him calmly.
> 'No one's trying to kill you,' Clevinger cried.
> 'Then why are they shooting at me?' Yossarian asked.
> 'They're shooting at *everyone*,' Clevinger answered.
> 'And what difference does that make?' (pp. 23–4)

Here once again Heller renders two structures of thought to expose the illogicality of the commonly accepted view: that it is illogical to complain that anyone is killing you, because in war the enemy is trying to kill everyone. What is really illogical is the belief that a multiplication of cases alters the structure of the individual case. Similar examples recur at the beginning of the novel. The reader thus becomes soon alerted to the idea that two standards of rationality are being contrasted: what seems rational to those who accept war and authoritarian institutions; and what seems rational to those who reject them. The latter are people like Yossarian and Orr, who place self-preservation, integrity, and personal sanity first; or the Chaplain, who feels himself haunted by what he calls 'immoral logic' at every turn. Heller realised that one of the most effective ways of juxtaposing these two value systems would be by distorting the logical patterns of his sentences. Much of the novel's deepest meaning and much of its best comedy arises from the lively play with logic and language.

Another source of humour and profound significance is Heller's original handling of time. At first the time shifts are confusing, but the very difficulty in working things out keeps the reader alert and actively involved in exploring the insane world of *Catch-22*, which is in fact the world of all of us. There is much that he needs to notice about the time scheme.[2] The first two things that we observe are that no simple chronological progression takes place and that every event as it is related seems equally present. Heller relates each event as if it were happening at that moment, even though it gradually becomes clear that some of the events occurred before and some after Yossarian's hospitalisation described at the beginning of the novel. They are recounted as happening in the present, because all are equally present in Yossarian's mind. What we have then is psychological time, not clock-time.

The references to the combat missions and Yossarian's various escapes into hospital establish a framework of clock-time. Without these, we would have little sense of the order in which the main events actually occurred. One of Colonel Cathcart's maniac oddities is to increase the number of combat missions that a man has to fly before he can return home. These missions gradually increase, rising to 55 when Yossarian appeals to Major Major, and to 80 near the end of the book. The references to the number of missions have several functions: firstly, they establish the actual chronological order of events; secondly, they serve to create the psychological development of the central character Yossarian; thirdly they epitomise the insanity of the war machine.

The novel's structure may be divided into three fairly equal sections. At the beginning of the book, we meet Yossarian in hospital. He has pretended to have a liver complaint when the missions have been raised to 45. The cheerful Texan drives him from his safe refuge, and he resumes his duty, only to find that the missions have now been raised to 50 – this fact is announced by Doc Daneeka at the end of chapter 2.

> 'Fifty missions,' Doc Daneeka told him, shaking his head. 'The colonel wants fifty missions.'
> 'But I've only got forty-four!'
> Doc Daneeka was unmoved. He was a sad, birdlike man with the spatulate face and scrubbed, tapering features of a well-groomed rat.
> 'Fifty missions,' he repeated, still shaking his head. 'The colonel wants fifty missions.' (p. 28)

It soon becomes clear to us, as we read the first three or four chapters, that a great deal of the important action has already taken place. There are unexplained references to characters and to places (Avignon, Ferrara) and to actual flying actions, for example, the 'Great Big Siege' of Bologna. A typical passage alluding to mysterious details in the characters' lives occurs in the middle of the second chapter. There Heller briefly mentions Havermayer, his peanut brittle, and his habit of shooting tiny field-mice every night. Heller mentions, but does not explain, Clevinger's absence from the tent he shared with McWatt, he mentions Nately's absence in Rome with his sleepy whore. His general method, in the first main section of the novel, which extends to chapter 16, is to introduce the reader gradually to most of the main characters, and to fill in the details of the events that led to Yossarian's escape into hospital in the first chapter. But the filling in is not through simple flashbacks or orderly narrative, but through a complex interweaving of past and present.

When Yossarian returns to Pianosa, after his night in Rome with Luciana, he finds that the missions have been raised to 40 (at the end of chapter 16). He promptly rushes to hospital (at the beginning of chapter 17).

> Ten days after he changed his mind and came out, the colonel raised the missions to forty-five and Yossarian ran right back in, determined to remain in the hospital forever rather than fly one mission more than the six missions more he had just flown. (p. 179)

We are once more back at the starting point, the situation where we first met Yossarian in the first chapter. The first main section of the book is complete.

The second section is also framed by hospital scenes. After a brief allusion to Yossarian's very first hospitalisation at Lowery Field, when he malingered, much of the action in this second part of the novel is concerned with present events. The missions are raised to 60. Dobbs plans to kill Colonel Cathcart. But even though the main emphasis is on the present, past events are certainly of crucial importance. These scenes concentrate on the events at Avignon, the moaning at the briefing sessions when the Colonel orders that Danby should be taken out and shot, Snowden's death, and the details of Yossarian naked in a tree. Since Avignon took place *before* Bologna, this means that events have now gone even further back in time than at the end of the first main section. At the end of that section, it was the details of Bologna we were given. At the end of the second main section of the novel, Yossarian once again returns to hospital. He has been wounded as the result of Aarfy's inefficient navigation. Once again a confusion of identities is repeated. At last Yossarian persuades Major Sanderson, the psychiatrist, that he is mad in one of the funniest debunkings of psychological jargon in modern fiction.

> 'This fish you dream about. Let's talk about that. It's always the same fish, isn't it?'
>
> 'I don't know,' Yossarian replied. 'I have trouble recognizing fish.'
>
> 'What does the fish remind you of?'
>
> 'Other fish.'
>
> 'And what do other fish remind you of?'
>
> 'Other fish.'
>
> Major Sanderson sat back disappointedly. 'Do you like fish?'
>
> 'Not especially.'
>
> 'Just why do you think you have such a morbid aversion to fish?' asked Major Sanderson triumphantly. . . .
>
> 'I suppose I have an ambivalent attitude toward it.'
>
> Major Sanderson sprang up with joy when he heard the words 'ambivalent attitude'. 'You do understand!' he exclaimed, wringing his hands together ecstatically. 'Oh, you can't imagine how lonely it's been for me, talking day after day to patients who haven't the slightest knowledge of psychiatry, trying to cure people who have no real interest in me, or my work! It's given me such a terrible feeling of inadequacy.' A shadow of anxiety crossed his face. 'I can't seem to shake it.' (pp. 314–15)

But Yossarian's efforts are all to no effect, and he finds himself returned to combat missions.

In the third main section of the novel the action speeds up, more of it takes place in the present, and the horrors increase in intensity. The brief summary by Jan Soloman establishes this clearly:

> The chief officers become even more self-seeking and incompetent. Lt. Scheisskopf . . . becomes a General, and takes over Special Services from General Dreedle [actually Peckham] at the moment when Special Services takes over the control of combat. More of Yossarian's fellows die, and their deaths are more bizarre. McWatt buzzes the raft and cuts Kid Sampson in half. Even Orr, shot down again, is missing. As the missions sky-rocket to 80, the chaplain is arrested and questioned about Washington Irving in a scene that repeats the earlier mad trial of Clevinger. Dunbar 'is disappeared', and finally Nately dies, his whore becoming a ubiquitous assassin threatening Yossarian.[3]

By the time the narrative reaches the third section, enough of the past has been revealed for Heller to press forward to the nightmare scenes in Rome, to the news of Orr's arrival in neutral Sweden, and Yossarian's decision to opt out of the system and join him. The frequent circling back of the narrative to the crucial episode of Snowden's death in the plane provides the ultimate justification for Yossarian's decision to desert.

There is one further characteristic of the time scheme that needs to be observed if the reader is to understand the full force of Heller's criticism of contemporary society. It is this. There are in fact two time sequences, one that relates to Yossarian's conflicts with authority and the other that relates to Milo Minderbinder's sensational successes in the world of big business. These Heller deliberately confuses. It is impossible to reconcile the introduction of Milo Minderbinder in chapter 7, ambitious to form his syndicate, with the fact that he has already performed many of his most infamous exploits. We are led to believe that Milo's plunge into the cotton market caused the bombing of the squadron and yet the bombing of the squadron had taken place before the opening of the novel, when Milo had not yet embarked on his infamous career. In general, the impossibility of reconciling the Yossarian and the Milo Minderbinder time-schemes simply heightens the sense of the absurd. But it also serves a more important purpose. At significant moments in the novel, their paths cross. Consequently, the reader is made more aware of the contrast between Yossarian's unsuccessful rebellion against authority and Minderbinder's unprincipled successes. The most effective of these juxtapositions occurs in the fullest account of Snowden's death. At the moment of Yossarian's deepest agony, we are reminded of Minderbinder's cheerful successes. The morphine tablets have disappeared. They had been replaced by a cleanly lettered note that said, 'What is good for M & M Enterprises is good for the country. Milo Minderbinder' (p. 460), an ironic allusion to the triumph of the business ethic in capitalist society and a direct echo of Woodrow Wilson's slogan 'What's good for General Motors must be good for America.'

From all this it is clear that Heller has arranged his time-scheme with deliberate care, but this does not mean that Heller expected the average reader to follow these schemes in all their complexity. The primary function of the scrambled time scheme is to remove all sense of rational purpose from Heller's fictional world. And surely this is the essential point we all grasp. After all most novelists write to be read, not to be analysed in patient detail by literary critics. Heller justifies Yossarian's decision to opt out on two grounds. The first is:

> 'Now I'm going to fight a little to save myself. The country's not in danger any more, but I am.'
>
> 'The war's not over yet. The Germans are driving toward Antwerp.'
>
> 'The Germans will be beaten in a few months. And Japan will be beaten a few months after that. If I were to give up my life now, it wouldn't be for my country. It would be for Cathcart and Korn. So I'm turning my bombsight in for the duration. From now on I'm thinking only of me.' (p. 470)

This passage has seemed to some readers to mark a disastrous weakening and confusion of purpose. The whole logic of the novel seems to require that Heller will have the courage to say that the Second World War was a fraud, that its declared issues – to destroy totalitarianism, to destroy Fascism, to defend freedom – were a sham, 'all bullshit', to use the idiom of the novel. Earlier in the novel, it has been made abundantly clear that the enemy is everywhere: it is certainly not just Germany or Japan. When Ford Madox Ford said in the First World War 'we'll beat the buggers yet', he was not referring to the Germans but to the Generals on both sides. The fact that Milo Minderbinder owes no allegiance to either side, but serves both, suggests that the enemies of individual liberty are to be found in the American capitalist society and the war machine, just as much as in the German and Japanese totalitarian orders. Had Heller gone on to suggest that the ideology of the Second World War, for all its apparent idealism and nobility, was as bogus as the ideology of Colonel Cathcart and the Generals, he would have avoided inconsistency. But, as a writer aiming at popular success, he could not afford to give American readers such a slap in the face. So he softens and consequently falsifies the end, which is a great pity as the Eternal City section is intensely moving and has the universality of Dante, or Dostoevsky, or, in recent times, Solzhenitsyn's *The First Circle*.

In the first place, it was probably a mistake to mention Germany and Japan at all at this stage of the novel. This locates the moral dilemma in a specific context, thus limiting its relevance and awakening strong emotional passions and prejudices which have to be taken care of. Heller is thus faced with the task of justifying Yossarian's decision to opt out in terms that will win over readers who have suddenly been reminded of the great causes and heroic sacrifices associated with the Second World War. He makes Yossarian defend his action on the grounds that he has already flown 'seventy goddam missions' in fighting to save his country and that now the war is over his services are no longer required. This is all nonsense. In the earlier part of the book he has evaded missions, shown no patriotism, and his decision to opt out has nothing to do with the imminent end of the war, but is the final expression of his rational revolt against an irrational system. Most of the great books that blow the top off our heads by exposing the horror and futility of life wisely avoid localising the issues, for example, *Gulliver's Travels*, Camus's *The Plague*, or Voltaire's *Candide*. This sudden localising of the issue by Heller is not only an artistic blemish, it represents a lack of moral courage. And it produces a confusion of purpose at the critical place in the novel.

Heller's other method of enlisting our sympathies for Yossarian's decision to opt out of the system is much more successful. Here Heller shows great skill in arousing our maximum sympathy for Yossarian when we finally discover what happened in the plane with the dying flier Snowden. The information is released just before Yossarian's decision to opt out and is the fifth and fullest account of Snowden's death. Questions of war policy are utterly irrevelant here. We respond through participating in Yossarian's new vision of man, as he remembers gazing down despondently at the grim secret of the dying Snowden. We are won over by the intense rendering of consciousness:

> 'I'm cold,' Snowden whimpered, 'I'm cold.'
>
> 'There, there,' Yossarian mumbled mechanically in a voice too low to be heard. 'There, there.'
>
> Yossarian was cold, too, and shivering uncontrollably. He felt goose pimples clacking all over him as he gazed down despondently at the grim secret Snowden had spilled all over the messy floor. It was easy to read the message in his entrails. Man was matter, that was Snowden's secret. Drop him out of a window and he'll fall. Set fire to him and he'll burn. Bury him and he'll rot, like other kinds of garbage. The spirit gone, man is garbage. That was Snowden's secret. Ripeness was all.
>
> 'I'm cold,' Snowden said. 'I'm cold.'

'There, there,' said Yossarian. 'There, there.' He pulled the rip cord of Snowden's parachute and covered his body with the white nylon sheets.
'I'm cold.'
'There, there.' (p. 464)

With its Shakespearean allusion to the tragic world of *King Lear*, this is an assertion of a tough-minded modern humanism. If man is matter, then self-preservation becomes the ultimate goal. For the reader, Yossarian seems doubly justified. His compassion for his dying fellow man transcends all other moral questions. His insight into man's nature vindicates his decision to join Orr in neutral Sweden. It is not true, as Carl Oglesby argues,[4] that 'in the end, very like Camus, Heller has tried to buy time for himself and his culture, snarled with lunacy and injustice as it is, by wrapping up everything in a tissue of cynicism and privileged impotence'. What *Catch-22* communicates, with a mixture of crazy exhilaration and tragic intensity, is the possibility for the individual of rational revolt against irrational power structures.

At this stage in the argument it should be clear that *Catch-22* achieves much of its powerful effect through Heller's skilful manipulation of time and deliberate dislocations of language and logic. But striking as these innovations are, they depend for their success on Heller's talent for creating a wide range of absurd characters. Absurd situations require absurd characters. For all their odd, unpredictable behaviour, however, they must appear to obey the insane laws that govern the world of the novel. And they must be capable of sustaining the inspired lunacy of the dialogue. This they do magnificently well, as may be seen from the climax of comic negatives in Clevinger's trial before the bloated colonel: 'Clevinger took a deep breath. "I always didn't say you couldn't punish me, sir" ' (p. 88). What we have in the novel is a large cast of eccentrics, each cherishing a dream: for Doc Daneeka it is a lucrative practice, for the generals it is military glory, while for Orr and Yossarian it is escape from the absurd situations in which they find themselves. A mere name dooms Major Major to a role that he is unwilling to sustain. Undoubtedly some grouping takes place in the reader's mind, but it is a mistake to divide the characters into the masters of the system and its victims, because in some sense everyone is a victim of the system. Yet we are clearly intended to distinguish between the unwilling victims (Orr and Yossarian) and the willing dupes (General Dreedle and Colonel Cathcart).

Yossarian is the only psychologically dynamic character in the novel, but was played as a gibbering psychotic in the film, thus destroying all credibility in his inner resilience, his capacity for development, and the battle of wits by which he beats the system. The other characters are largely static; they have enormous comic vitality but do not change.

The narrative strategy of the novel ensures that we share Yossarian's experience by entering into the full horror of his situation and by finally endorsing his moral choice. The other characters, while having a vital eccentric life of their own, are carefully subordinated to Yossarian. They are not only static but represent varying attitudes towards war and authority that are also reflected in the hero and may be felt often as projections of his state of mind.

The Chaplain and Orr occupy a special place in the scheme of the novel. The Chaplain stands outside the system. He can thus develop the metaphysical implications of the novel and act as a useful spokesman and sympathetic listener. Where most of the other characters are enclosed in little worlds of their own imaginative creation, the Chaplain reaches out to others and reminds the reader of the existence of love and sympathetic imagination. Orr represents the little man, inconspicuous, devious, long-sighted, practical, persevering, capable of achieving success at impossible odds. 'He didn't *wash* ashore in Sweden. He *rowed* there! He *rowed* there' (p. 473). Thus encouraged, Yossarian is ready to follow Orr's example. Yossarian's decision is more a testimony to man's foolhardy and indomitable spirit than an endorsement of escapism and neutrality.

Catch-22 is a gimmicky, bawdy novel that owes much of its popular success to its attack upon authority, its deliberate shock tactics, and its moments of inspired farce. Yet it stands up to rigorous analysis and only yields its full meaning when the intricacies of the time scheme and the inversions of language and logic have been grasped. It offers a model proof that the secret of truth-telling lies in form-making. Change the form – as the film showed – and you distort the truth. Heller found just the right form; and his novel, like the comic novels of Peacock a century earlier, demonstrates the power of the comic spirit to generate a profound criticism of society.

Conclusion

Despite the vigorous attacks made on the Word by the prophets of the counter-culture and the insidious erosions made by the mass media, there can be little doubt that the writer will retain his function as interpreter and critic of his society. Even within the high-decibel culture there will be occasional oases of quiet where his words will be heard and his images will do their silent work. The demands that serious literature makes on the mind are an implicit challenge to the undemanding appeals of enveloping sound. The writer sets up rhythms of expectation and response that require active personal engagement. These rhythms, which are products of the solitary contemplative mind, are inimical to the regular pulsations of electronic sound. In this conflict between the unifying rhythms of mass culture and the personal rhythms of the individual conscience, we have the latest demonstration of the truth that the serious writer, no matter how deeply he may be involved in contemporary issues, must be able to detach himself sufficiently to achieve a personal voice and to offer society a new image of itself.

Yeats, for many years, was actively engaged in Irish politics, yet his greatest poetry completely transcends local contemporary issues. In 'The Second Coming', he presents an image of society returning to darkness and anarchy.

> Turning and turning in the widening gyre
> The falcon cannot hear the falconer;
> Things fall apart; the centre cannot hold;
> Mere anarchy is loosed upon the world,
> The blood-dimmed tide is loosed, and everywhere
> The ceremony of innocence is drowned;
> The best lack all conviction, while the worst
> Are full of passionate intensity.
>
> Surely some revelation is at hand;
> Surely the Second Coming is at hand.
> The Second Coming! Hardly are those words out
> When a vast image out of *Spiritus Mundi*
> Troubles my sight: somewhere in the sands of the desert

> A shape with lion body and the head of a man,
> A gaze blank and pitiless as the sun,
> Is moving its slow thighs, while all about it
> Reel shadows of the indignant desert birds.
> The darkness drops again; but now I know
> That twenty centuries of stony sleep
> Were vexed to nightmare, by a rocking cradle,
> And what rough beast, its hour come round at last,
> Slouches towards Bethlehem to be born?

Drawing on Christian tradition, on Vico's theories of cyclical history, and on the rich resources of the collective unconscious, Yeats has created a definitive image of modern anarchy. For concentrated power it is unmatched by anything in fiction or discursive prose. In view of Yeats's achievement and that of such poets as Shelley and Blake in criticising their societies through great universalising images, it may seem surprising that more has not been said about the poet's role. Some concentration seemed desirable in exploring so wide a theme as the subject of this book; therefore little has been said about the function of poetry and drama in criticising society. But one has only to recall Shaw's plays and the poetry of the left-wing poets of the 1930's to recognise the part played by the dramatists and poets in offering images critical of the social world.

The Marxist or the structuralist critic will not find in this study the kind of simplifying principle he champions. No attempt has been made to interpret the works discussed by exclusive reference to changes in the means of production or to matters relating to class and consciousness or by means of regarding the 'surface of a work as a kind of mystification of its structure',[1] although such approaches have been used where relevant, especially in the chapter on the Victorian 'Condition of England' novel. Moreover, despite my admiration of Lucien Goldmann's genetic structuralism, of his recognition that even in the greatest works the literary structures are as much a product of society as of the individual creative mind, I can detect no simple interpretative models for the various literary texts I have examined. After examining a wide variety of writing, I am forced to the conclusion that there are only highly complex interactions between the social and the personal in the great writers of the last two centuries; there are no simple submerged or half-discerned structures just awaiting the perceptive and inventive eye of the structuralist critic.

This book has an informing principle. It is derived from the facts of literary experience rather than from any ideological standpoint. The principle that underlies this whole study is that literature only releases its full meanings when the mind surrenders itself to the work in all its bewildering complexity, that the work must never be treated as if it were equivalent to either a historical document or to life itself. T. S. Eliot comes very close to defining the dialectic of surrender and detachment required from the reader or critic, in a letter to Stephen Spender in May 1935. 'You don't,' he said, 'really criticize any author to whom you have never surrendered yourself. . . . Even just the bewildering minute counts; you have to give yourself up, and then recover yourself, and the third moment is having something to say, before you have wholly forgotten both surrender and recovery. Of course the self recovered is never the same as the self before it was given.'[2] This book is written in the belief that such a dialectical engagement is preferable to the certainties of dogmatic or ideological criticism.

Finally, it remains to suggest that as readers we have a special responsibility in resisting the current erosions of language and humane values. George Orwell, Joseph Heller and Shirley Hazzard all demonstrate in their different ways that the manipulators of power are also the perverters of the Word, that one of the means by which they achieve power is through the debasement of language. To the extent that we acquiesce in that perversion we become accomplices in our own enslavement. The special value of the great tradition of writing that, starting with Coleridge, insists that language is the true index of cultural health is that it raises to full consciousness the myths, metaphors, and images that sustain society and invites us to question their continuing life and validity.

Notes

Notes to chapter 1

1 *Culture and Anarchy*, edited with an introduction by J. Dover Wilson (Cambridge, 1960), pp. 48–9.
2 *Mary Barton*, edited with an introduction by Stephen Gill (Harmondsworth, 1970), Introduction, pp. 24–5.

Notes to chapter 2

1 William F. Kennedy, *Humanist versus Economist: the Economic Thought of Samuel Taylor Coleridge*, University of California, Publications in Economics 17 (Berkeley, 1958).
2 D. L. Munby, *The Idea of a Secular Society* (Oxford, 1963), p. 43.
3 *Political Tracts of Wordsworth, Coleridge and Shelley*, edited by R. J. White (Cambridge, 1953), pp. 102–4.
4 See below, ch. 9.
5 'Coleridge and Politics', *S. T. Coleridge: Writers and their Background*, edited by R. L. Brett (London, 1971), p. 261.
6 Roger Kojecky gives a full account of the Moot and its importance in the development of Eliot's ideas in *T. S. Eliot's Social Criticism* (London, 1971), pp. 163–97.

Notes to chapter 3

1 *Mill on Bentham and Coleridge*, with an introduction by F. R. Leavis (London, 1959) p. 1; all subsequent references are to this edition.
2 *Mill's Essays on Literature and Society*, edited with an introduction by J. B. Schneewind (New York, 1965), p. 28.
3 Coleridge attributed this view to Bacon in *The Statesman's Manual* (1816); actually he took it from Sir James Steuart's *Inquiry into the Principles of Oeconomy* (1767).
4 Entry for 12 September, 1831, *Table Talk*.

5 'All the different philosophical systems of political justice, all the theories on the rightful Origin of Government, are reducible in the end to three classes correspondent to the three different points of view, in which the Human Mind itself may be contemplated.' Section the First, Essay 1, *The Friend*, edited by Barbara E. Rooke, vol. 4 of *The Collected Works of Samuel Taylor Coleridge* (Princeton and London, 1969), I, 166.
6 See the discussion of Mill's poetic theory in M. H. Abrams *The Mirror and the Lamp: Romantic Theory and the Critical Theory* (London, 1953).
7 Schneewind, *op. cit.* p. 122.
8 Noel Annan, 'John Stuart Mill', *The English Mind*, edited by Hugh Sykes Davies and George Watson (Cambridge, 1964), p. 235.

Notes to chapter 4

1 This is the conclusion reached by two modern studies: Howard Mills, *Peacock: his Circle and his Age* (Cambridge, 1969) and Carl Dawson *Thomas Love Peacock*, Profiles in Literature Series (London, 1968). Two other valuable accounts are J. I. M. Stewart, *Thomas Love Peacock*, Writers and their Work Series (London, 1963), and 'Peacock' in Ian Jack, *English Literature, 1815–1832* (Oxford, 1963). The Halliford Edition, edited by H. F. B. Brett-Smith and C. E. Jones (London, 1924–34) contains almost everything Peacock wrote, while *The Novels of Thomas Love Peacock*, edited with introductions and notes by David Garnett, 2 vols (London, 1963), is the best modern edition, and is cited hereafter.
2 The gloomy setting, the misanthropic character of Mr Glowry, and the melancholy servants are all closely based on Godwin's novel; see my 'Godwin's *Mandeville* and Peacock's *Nightmare Abbey*', *Review of English Studies*, n.s. 21 (1970), 331–6.
3 Ronald Mason, 'Notes for an Estimate of Peacock', *Horizon*, April, 1944.

Notes to chapter 5

1 Sheila M. Smith, 'Willenhall and Wodgate: Disraeli's Use of Blue Book Evidence', *Review of English Studies*, n.s. 13 (1962), 370.
2 *The Friend*, edited Barbara E. Rooke, vol. 4 of *The Collected Works of Samuel Taylor Coleridge* (Princeton and London, 1969), I, 190.
3 Quoted by Alfred Cobban, *Edmund Burke and the Revolt Against the Eighteenth Century*, second edition (London, 1960), p. 219; see also Geoffrey Carnall, *Robert Southey and His Age* (Oxford, 1960), who points out that Southey was not as pessimistic as Macaulay suggested in his hostile review of the *Colloquies* in the *Edinburgh Review*, pp. 180–1.
4 *Thomas Carlyle: Selected Writings*, edited with an introduction by Alan Shelston (Harmondsworth, 1971), hereafter cited.

5 *Dickens and Carlyle: The Question of Influence* (London, 1973), p. 150; see also conclusion of Michael Goldberg, *Carlyle and Dickens* (Athens Georgia, 1972). 'That part of Dickens' thinking that was consciously regulated, the main line of his social criticism, was directly influenced by Carlyle' (p. 227).
6 Mark Roberts, 'Carlyle and the Rhetoric of Unreason', *Essays in Criticism*, 18 (October, 1968), 397–419.
7 For this view, see *The Early Chartists*, edited Dorothy Thompson (London, 1971). Another historian, E. P. Thompson in *The Making of the English Working Classes* (Harmondsworth, pp. 781–2), establishes that even twenty years earlier towns and even villages hummed with the energy of the autodidact and that from 1830 onwards a more clearly defined class consciousness, in the customary Marxist sense, was maturing, in which working people were aware of continuing both old and new battles on their own. Like Dr Wearmouth, the historian of Methodism, Thompson, a Marxist historian, points to the genius for organisation that the working class early demonstrated.
8 Carlyle was regarded as a Sage by his contemporaries and is treated as such by John Holloway in *The Victorian Sage*.
9 See Eric Trudgill, 'Prostitution and Paterfamilias', in *The Victorian City: Images and Realities*, edited H. J. Dyos and Michael Woolf, 2 vols (London, 1973), pp. 693–705. Having quoted the shocked reaction of a German visitor, Trudgill writes 'How was it, wondered foreigners, that the British paterfamilias with his cult of domesticity, with his determination to avoid anything in public discourse that might bring a blush to the cheek of modesty, could yet allow the streets and places of public amusement to be infested with open harlotry?' He shows how the paterfamilias had to abandon the false Victorian sexual and domestic ideals before the trade in prostitution could be curbed.

Notes to chapter 6

1 In *Culture and Society 1780–1950*, Raymond Williams uses the term 'Industrial Novels' and argues that the novels 'illustrate clearly enough not only the common criticism of industrialism, which the tradition was establishing, but also the general structure of feeling which was equally determining,' (Harmondsworth, 1961), p. 119.
2 John Lucas gives an interesting account of Mrs Gaskell's strengths and weaknesses in 'Mrs Gaskell and Brotherhood', *Tradition and Tolerance in Nineteenth-Century Fiction: Critical Essays on Some English and American Novels*, edited by David Howard, John Lucas and John Goode (London, 1966), pp. 141–205.
3 F. R. Leavis, *The Great Tradition* (Harmondsworth, 1962), p. 250.
4 The reference to the antithesis between the wisdom of the Head and the Heart here, and Dickens's attempt to suggest the need for a synthesis in *Hard Times*, implicitly establish a link with the English Romantic poets, especially with Coleridge, who frequently uses the same antithesis in his prose writings.

5 '*Hard Times*: A History and a Criticism', *Dickens and the Twentieth Century*, edited by John Gross and Gabriel Pearson (London, 1962), p. 168.
6 The Norton Critical Edition of *Hard Times*, edited by George Ford and Sylvère Monod (New York, 1966) reproduces Dickens's article 'On Strike' (pp. 286–99), together with much other relevant contemporary material that has been drawn on in the present discussion.
7 William Oddie, *Dickens and Carlyle, The Question of Influence* (London, 1972), pp. 49–50.
8 *The Social Novel in England 1830–1850, Dickens, Disraeli, Mrs Gaskell, Kingsley*, translated with a Foreword by Martin Fido (London, 1973), p. 293.

Notes to chapter 7

1 Lionel Trilling, *The Liberal Imagination: Essays on Literature and Society* (Harmondsworth, 1970, pp. 69–101. Trilling sees James's novel as 'an incomparable representation of the spiritual circumstances of our civilization'.
2 Louise Bogan, 'James on a Revolutionary Theme', *Literary Opinion in America*, edited by M. D. Zabel, 2 vols, Harper, Torchbook edition (New York, 1962), I, 351–6.
3 Stephen Spender, *The Destructive Element: A Study of Modern Writers and Beliefs* (London, 1935), p. 45.

Notes to chapter 8

1 William Ashton's frequently reprinted *The Functions and Disorders of the Reproductive Organs* (1857), typifies the Victorian attitude. 'As a general rule, a modest woman seldom desires any sexual gratification for herself. She submits to her husband, not only to please him; and, but for the desire for maternity, would rather be relieved from his attentions.' Quoted in Steven Marcus, *The Other Victorians: A Study of Sexuality and Pornography in Mid-Nineteenth-Century England* (London, 1966), p. 31.
2 See ch. 10, 'White Slavery', in Constance Rover, *Love, Morals and the Feminists* (London, 1970), pp. 89–91.
3 '*Albergo Empedocle' and Other Writings by E. M. Forster*, edited, with introduction and notes by George H. Thomson (New York, 1971), pp. 135–6. Forster first read the paper to the Working Men's College Old Students' Club on 1 December 1906; it was subsequently published in the College *Journal*.
4 Steven Marcus, *The Other Victorians*, pp. 274–5.
5 Lytton Strachey, *Eminent Victorians*, Harmondsworth, 1948, p. 152.
6 *The Girl of the Period and Other Essays* (Leipzig, 1844), pp. 15–16. Elizabeth Lynn (1822–98), the daughter of a clergyman and granddaughter of Dr Samuel Goodenough, Bishop of Carlyle, came to London in 1845 and rapidly established herself as a successful journalist and novelist, enjoying the

patronage of the aging W. S. Landor. Although she was attracted to young women and not men, she married the wood-engraver and chartist agitator William James Linton in 1858; but the marriage was unhappy and Linton emigrated to America in 1866, leaving his wife to carry on her career as a writer.

7 *The Bodley Head Ford Madox Ford* (London, 1963), III, 88–9.

8 In 'Fictional Feminists in The Bostonians and The Odd Women', Nan Bauer Maglin gives useful information about the feminist movements in England and America and remarks that despite the two novelists' hostility to feminism 'both novels convey a sense of the excitement, the passion and the power of the feminist movement in the late 1880's'; *Images of Women in Fiction, Feminine Perspectives*, edited by Susan Koppelman Cornillon (Ohio, 1973), pp. 216–36.

Notes to chapter 9

1 See chapters 18–23 in *The Victorian City: Images and Realities*, edited by H. J. Dyos and Michael Woolf, 2 vols (London, 1973); and also Alexander Welsh, *The City of Dickens* (Oxford, 1971),

2 For further discussion of Mrs Lynn Linton, see above p.108 and F. B. Smith *Radical Artisan: William James Linton 1812–97* (Manchester, 1973), ch. 6.

3 *D. H. Lawrence Selected Literary Criticism*, edited by Anthony Beal (London, 1955), p. 18.

4 *The Standard Edition of the Complete Psychological Works of Sigmund Freud* (London, 1961), XXI, 122.

5 John Lester, in *Journey Through Despair: 1880–1914 Transformation in British Literary Culture* (Princeton, 1968), stresses the movement towards some form of existentialism, while Samuel Hynes in the *Edwardian Turn of Mind* (Princeton and London, 1968), charts the great diversity of Edwardian literature against the background of the age with exemplary detachment.

6 Richard Ellmann traces the assimilation of nineteenth-century religious terms into a secular context in 'The Two Faces of Edward', in *Edwardians and Late Victorians*, edited by R. Ellmann, English Institute Essays, 1959 (New York, 1960).

7 For further details, see my *E. M. Forster: The Personal Voice* (London, 1975), p. 6 and pp. 32–4, 54–6, 223–4.

8 Just as Forster's account of G. Lowes Dickinson's happiness at Cambridge, in chapter 7 of his *Life* of his friend, throws light on Forster's suppressed homosexuality and search for 'comradeship', so too Dickinson's choice of this passage from *My Days and Dreams* is determined by his own discovery of his homosexuality at Cambridge; cf. E. M. Forster, *Goldsworthy Lowes Dickinson* (London, 1934), p. 35 G. L. Dickinson's 'Edward Carpenter as a Friend', *Edward Carpenter In Appreciation*, edited by Gilbert Beith (London, 1931), pp. 37–8.

9 'Personal Impressions of Edward Carpenter', Beith op. cit., p. 59.

10 Page references in the text are to *Civilisation Its Cause and Cure and Other Essays*, 11th edition (London, 1910) and to *Love's Coming of Age*, 7th edition (London, 1911).

11 Virginia Woolf draws on Coleridge for her ideas on the androgynous nature of the artist in *A Room of One's Own* and explores these ideas in *Orlando*; for G. Wilson Knight and the androgynous, see his *Byron and Shakespeare* (London, 1966).
12 P. J. Keating, *Gissing: New Grubb Street*, Studies in English Literature, 33 (London, 1968), pp. 42–3.
13 Adrian Poole, *Gissing in Context* (London, 1975), p. 135.
14 Introduction to the Penguin edition (Harmondsworth, 1968), p. 20.

Notes to chapter 10

1 All references are to *The Bodley Head Ford Madox Ford* (London, 1962–71).
2 Samuel Hynes, op. cit., pp. 34–53.
3 Forster's relation to the liberal tradition is studied by Lionel Trilling, *E. M. Forster: A Study* (London, 1944) and John Colmer, *E. M. Forster: The Personal Voice* (London, 1975).
4 *Ford Madox Ford: The Critical Heritage*, edited by Frank MacShane (London, 1972), p. 93.
5 In *History and Class Consciousness*, Lukács argues that only the worker, not the middle class, knows the inter-relationship of tools and equipment and therefore he alone will come to see the outside world as a totality in which everything is connected with everything else and not as a collection of unrelated things. Fredric Jameson shows the influence of this idea of *totality* on Lukács's writing on the novel in *Marxism and Form: Twentieth-Century Dialectical Theories of Literature* (Princeton, 1971), pp. 160–205.
6 Graham Greene excludes *Last Post* from the Bodley Head edition on the grounds that *A Man Could Stand Up* forms the natural end of *Parades End* and *Last Post* is a 'disaster' because of a 'carefully arranged happy *finale*'.
7 John Colmer, '*Howards End* Revisited', *A Garland for E. M. Forster*, edited by H. H. A. Gowda (Mysore, 1969), pp. 9–22, and *E. M. Forster: The Personal Voice*, ch. 5.
8 E. D. H. Johnson, 'Victorian Artists and the Urban Milieu', *The Victorian City: Images and Realities*, edited by H. J. Dyos and Michael Woolf, 2 vols (London, 1973), II, 461–2.
9 C. F. G. Masterman, 'The English City', *England: A Nation*, edited by L. R. F. Oldershaw (London, 1904), p. 47.
10 G. R. Hibbard, 'The Country House Poem of the Seventeenth Century'. *Journal of the Warburg and Courtauld Institute*, 19 (1956), pp. 159–74.
11 J. Delbaere-Grant, 'Who Shall Inherit England', *English Studies* (1969).
12 In chapter 8 of *The Condition of England*, C. F. G. Masterman singles Wells out for special praise for picturing the Edwardian period as 'an age in the headlong rush of change', for his determination to understand the present and not yearn for an irrecoverable past.
13 'Everybody's read Chatterley', *Listener*, 8 Jan. 1976, p. 27.

Notes to chapter 11

1 See Robert C. Elliott, *The Shape of Utopia: Studies in a Literary Genre* (Chicago and London, 1970), p. 85. See also Richard Gerber, *Utopian Fantasy* (London, 1955).
2 'Varieties of Literary Utopias', in *Utopias and Utopian Thought*, edited by Frank E. Manuel (London, 1965), pp. 25–30.
3 Despite the fact that historically there never was a contract, 'nevertheless', Coleridge asserts 'it assuredly cannot be denied, that an original (in reality, rather an ever-originating) contract is a very natural and significant mode of expressing the reciprocal duties of subject and sovereign'. *The Friend* edited Barbara E. Rooke, vol 4 of *The Collected Works of Samuel Taylor Coleridge* (Princeton and London), I, 174.
4 Quoted by Northrop Frye, *op. cit.*
5 Introduction, p. 11, of Penguin edition of *We*.
6 J. C. Garrett, *Utopias in Literature since the Romantic Period*, The Macmillan Brown Lectures, 1967 (Canterbury, Christchurch, 1968), p. 14.
7 'From "Know-not-Where" to "Nowhere". The City in Carlyle, Ruskin and Morris', *The Victorian City: Images and Realities*, edited H. J. Dyos and Michael Woolf, 2 vols (London, 1973), II, 514–15.
8 'I like that idea of fantasy, of muddling up the actual and the impossible until the reader isn't sure which is which, and I have sometimes tried to do it when writing myself.' 'A Book that Influenced Me', *Two Cheers for Democracy*, (Harmondsworth, 1965), p. 226.
9 Ibid., p. 225.
10 *The Collected Essays, Journalism and Letters of George Orwell*, edited by Sonia Orwell and Ian Angus (London, 1968), III, 188; hereafter cited as *CEJL*.
11 *The Bodley Head Ford Madox Ford* (London, 1962–71), V, 420.
12 Patrick Parrender, *H. G. Wells* (Edinburgh and London, 1970), pp. 22–3.
13 *CEJL*, IV, 75.

Notes to chapter 12

1 Irving Howe, 'The Fiction of Anti-Utopia', *A World More Attractive*, New York, 1963, p. 222.
2 'The Young Eric', by Jacintha Buddicom, in *The World of George Orwell*, edited Miriam Gross (London, 1971), p. 2.
3 'Wells, Hitler and the World State', *The Collected Essays, Journalism and Letters of George Orwell*, edited Sonia Orwell and Ian Angus (London, 1968), II, 144; hereafter cited as *CEJL*.
4 Orwell's Introduction is printed for the first time, with commentary by Bernard Crick, in the *Times Literary Supplement*, 15 Sept. 1972, pp. 1037–40.
5 *Down and Out in Paris and London* (London, 1933), ch. xxxi, new uniform edition repr. 1966, p. 173.
6 See Raymond Carr, 'Orwell and the Spanish Civil War', in *The World of George Orwell*, pp. 64–73. In his discussion of Orwell's *Homage to Catalonia*, a

vivid and moving account of Orwell's experience in Spain, Raymond Williams emphasises that disillusionment with the left did not lead to right-wing conclusions and that after the experience in Spain, Orwell's position was 'that of a revolutionary socialist', *Orwell*, Fontana Modern Masters (London, 1971), p. 60.

7 Quoted by David Pryce-Jones, 'Orwell's Reputation', *The World of George Orwell*, p. 150.

8 'Politics and the English Language' was first published in *Horizon* No. 76 (April, 1946); it is reprinted in *Selected Essays* (Harmondsworth, 1957) and *Inside the Whale and Other Essays* (Harmondsworth, 1962); also in *CEJL*, IV, 127–40.

9 *Inside the Whale*, p. 153.

10 See 'George Orwell and the *Road to Wigan Pier*' in Richard Hoggart, *Speaking to Each Other*, vol 2, *About Literature* (London, 1970), pp. 111–128; Raymond Williams, *Orwell*, ch. 2.

11 *Times Literary Supplement*, 15 Sept. 1972, p. 1037.

12 Preface to the Ukranian edition, *CEJL*, 111, 405.

13 George Woodcock, *The Crystal Spirit*, (Harmondsworth, 1970) p. 154.

14 See p. 176.

15 According to James Connors, in 'Zamyatin's *We* and the Genesis of *1984*', the most one can say on behalf of Zamyatin 'is that he supplied Orwell partial confirmation for one of his views regarding Totalitarian rulers – the Leader with semi-divine attributes', but 'that *1984* would have emerged exactly as it did had Orwell never read Zamyatin'. *Modern Fiction Studies*, vol 21, no. 1 (Spring, 1975), p. 124.

16 See Keith Alldritt, *The Making of George Orwell: An Essay in Literary History* (London, 1969), to which my account of *Nineteen Eighty-Four* owes something.

17 *Essays on His Own Times*, edited by Sara Coleridge, 3 vols (London, 1850), II, 596.

18 For general discussion of Shirley Hazzard's fiction, see my essay in *Contemporary Novelists*, edited James Vinson (London, 1972), pp. 578–80, and 'Patterns and Preoccupations of Love: The Novels of Shirley Hazzard', *Meanjin*, 29 (Summer 1970), pp. 461–6.

[Extracts from *People in Glass Houses*, by Shirley Hazzard, are used by permission of McIntosh and Otis Inc., as representatives of Shirley Hazzard.]

Notes to chapter 13

1 'Unreal Estates', *Spectrum IV*, edited by Kingsley Amis and Robert Conquest (London, 1965), p. 21. In the discussion, Aldiss remarked that he would much rather write Science Fiction than anything else, because 'the dead weight' was 'so much less than in the field of the ordinary novel' and 'there's a sense in which you're conquering a fresh country'. And Kingsley Amis confessed that as 'a supposedly realistic novelist' he had experienced 'tremendous liberation' through writing bits of science fiction. All agreed that 'Science Fiction' was a hopelessly inadequate label.

2 'The Social Content of Science Fiction', *Science and Society*, 17 (Spring, 1953), pp. 99–118; see also L. W. Michaelson, 'Social Criticism in Science Fiction', *Antioch Review*, 14 (Dec., 1954), pp. 502–8.

Notes to chapter 14

1 'Joseph Heller's *Catch-22*', *Approaches to the Novel*, edited by John Colmer (Edinburgh and London, 1967), pp. 71–2.
2 My account draws on Jan Soloman's 'The Structure of Joseph Heller's *Catch-22*', *Critique*, 9 (1966–7), pp. 46–57.
3 Soloman, p. 52.
4 Carl Oglesby, 'The Deserters: The Contemporary Defeat of Fiction', in *Radical Perspectives in the Arts*, ed. Lee Baxandall (Harmondsworth, 1972), p. 50.

Notes to Conclusion

1 Fredric Jameson, *Marxism and Form: Twentieth-Century Dialectical Theories of Literature* (Princeton, 1971), p. 413.
2 'Remembering Eliot', in *T. S. Eliot: The Man and His Work*, edited by Allen Tate (London, 1967), pp. 55–6.

Name and Title Index

Subject Index